Evolution
and
Creation

With all good wishes for
your investigation of
the evolved & created
world!

Arthur
Peacocke
27-iii-88

Evolution
and
Creation

A European Perspective

*Edited by Svend Andersen
and Arthur Peacocke*

AARHUS UNIVERSITY PRESS

Copyright ©: Aarhus University Press, 1987
Typesetting: Werks Fotosats
Printed in Denmark by Werks Offset, Århus
ISBN 87 7288 114 3

Volume 3 in the *Complementa* series of the
Forum Teologi Naturvidenskab, Aarhus

AARHUS UNIVERSITY PRESS
Aarhus University
DK-8000 Aarhus C
Denmark

The publication of this book has been aided by a grant from the Aarhus
University Research Foundation

Contents

Preface

The relation between the Judeo-Christian doctrine of creation and the biological theory of evolution have for well over a century been popularly regarded as the *locus classicus* of the supposed conflict between "science" and "religion". We say "supposed conflict" because even from the very first publication of Darwin's ideas there were Christian theologians, of many different schools, who thoughtfully began to integrate the new perceptions from biology with their interpretation of the doctrines both of creation and of man. However, the front of the stage, at least in the subsequent mythology about it, was occupied, certainly in the English-speaking world, by vigorous antagonists (which did not actually include Darwin himself) – self-appointed spokesmen for either "science" or "religion".

The recent recrudescence of "creationism" in the USA, and to some extent also in Europe, reminds us that there is much unfinished business for theologians firstly, in fully integrating the biological perceptions with Christian theology and, secondly, in making any new synthesis more widely known, at least to the Christian world. Even churches whose theologians have satisfied themselves that they have been making such a synthesis, are often surprised at the misconceptions of their own laity about the relation of evolution and creation. So it is particularly timely that this first European conference on science and religion should be concerned with the argument about evolution and creation, with the specific aim of refining theological perceptions and concepts. Of course, such an exercise has to take account of the history of this exchange, the actual current state of biology and the philosophical issues that are inevitably raised when two distinct epistemological enterprises are in dialogue.

The papers from this first European conference on Science and Religion, held on 13-16 March, 1986, in the Evangelische Akademie, Loccum, are collected in this volume. It does not, however, simply mirror the course of the conference: some alterations both in respect to content and order have been necessary. For example, Professor Carsten Bresch did not have a manuscript for his original and lively survey of the contemporary status of the theory of evolution and was not in a position to reproduce it afterwards. Fortunately, we were able to persuade him to give us a German paper of very much the same content as his talk, the original title of which was "Was ist Evolution?" (originally printed in *Zufall und Gesetz in der Evolution des lebens* (Herrenalber Texte 9, 1978) As we wished to have in the volume a contribution on the origin of life from the group at Göttingen and neither Professors

Küppers or Eigen were, in the event, able to attend, the former has now contributed a paper which also originally appeared in German (*Molekulare Evolution und der Ursprung des Lebens,* in: Deutschland. Porträt einer Nation. Bertelsmann Lexikothek Verlag).

The aim of the conference was to consider the biological theory of evolution and the Christian doctrine of creation both historically and from a contemporary perspective. For the purposes of presentation in this volume, it has proved natural to group the material presented on that occasion into the four sections: history, biology, philosophy, and theology. These groupings reflect the situation that science and religion/theology cannot always be compared or confronted with each other directly. In order to understand their relations as clearly as possible, it is usually necessary to take into account both the historical background and the basic conceptual frameworks which it is the task of philosophy to elucidate.

The two papers by Viggo Mortensen and Arthur Peacocke under the headings "Retrospect" and "Prospect" serve much the same purpose in the volume as they did in the conference, namely, to sum up the discussion and to survey the broad field in which this work progresses and to raise questions for further investigation. The Epilogue, consisting of an address by Hans May in the context of worship may remind the reader that – at least from a theological point of view – the relationship between science and religion is not just an academic affair.

A few words are appropriate about the origin of the conference itself. Since the early 1950's there have throughout the Western world gradually been forming a number of groupings of scientists and theologians (and scientist-theologians!) who have been concerned with the deep cultural divide between science and religion, a fissure which goes far deeper than that which is the principal concern of this volume. Some of these groups have formalised their existence into continuing bodies with a definite structure; others remain *ad hoc* and more fluid. It so happened that in 1983, one of us (ARP) was present at the annual summer meeting of the American Institute of Religion in an Age of Science (*I.R.A.S.* – one of those early post-war groupings that had become a flourishing organization) on Star Island, off the coast of New Hampshire, USA. He was asked to assist, as a Vice-President both of *I.R.A.S.* and of the British *Science and Religion Forum,* in establishing more liaison between the various groupings. Discussion with Dr Karl Schmitz-Moorman, who was also at the Star Island meeting, led to the proposal that an attempt should be made to bring together the various European groups interested in the relation between science and religion, hoping that, meanwhile, our American friends would link up their dispersed activities so that – one day – a truly international perspective might be engendered.

In response to this suggestion, a two-day consultation was convened during September, 1984 at Clare College, Cambridge (where ARP was then Dean) of 11 people who were acting as the delegates of science-and-religion groups in six different European countries. The need and desire for interchange between the different groups and cross-fertilisation of our cultural perspectives soon became apparent. So the planning of the first European conference on this theme was set in hand by the formation of an organising committee consisting of Dr Svend Andersen (Denmark), as chairman, and Drs J Hübner and K Schmitz-Moorman (Germany), who were later joined by Pastor Hans May, Director of the Evangelische Akademie at Loccum which provided both essential financial support and a splendid and evocative venue for what we hope will be a continuing mutual exploration of this difficult terrain.

We acknowledge gratefulle the work of this organising committee, the role of the Loccum Akademie, especially the personal involvement of Hans May and of Meinfried Striegnitz, and the helpful cooperation of all the contributors to this volume. We thank Dr Paul Wooley, Department of Chemistry, Aarhus University, for his willingness to translate the papers of C Bresch and B Küppers. We are especially indebted to grants from the Deutsche Forschungsgemeinschaft for support of the conference and from the Aarhus University Research Fund towards the costs of publication. Finally, we wish to express our gratitude to the officers of the Aarhus University Press for their helpful cooperation and advice in this enterprise. We hope that this collection will contribute to a wiser understanding of one of the main problems that has emerged within our European tradition: the complicated relationship between religion and science.

Arthur Peacocke   *Svend Andersen*
Ian Ramsey Centre   Aarhus University
St Cross College   Denmark
Oxford
England

9

A Critical-Historical Perspective on the Argument about Evolution and Creation

John Durant

Creation versus Evolution?

Just a few weeks before the convening of the first European Conference on Science and Religion, the University of Oxford's undergraduate debating society, the Oxford Union, saw fit to consider the subject of evolution and religion. Representing religion on this occasion were A. E. Wilder-Smith, a pharmacologist and a consultant based in Geneva; and Edgar Andrews, a Professor of Materials Science in the University of London. These men are prominent spokesmen in the English-speaking world for what has come to be known as "scientific creationism"; and for more than two hours they defended the motion "That the doctrine of creation evolution is more valid than the theory of evolution" against two prominent British evolutionary biologists, Dr. Richard Dawkins, and Professor John Maynard Smith.

There is a great deal of historical irony in this event. For it was in the Oxford University Museum, and as long ago as 1860, that Charles Darwin's young supporter Thomas Henry Huxley clashed with Bishop Samuel Wilberforce over the very same question. On that occasion, less than a year after the publication of the *Origin of Species*, Huxley condemned the Bishop of Oxford for attempting to defeat Darwinism with nothing more than ignorant contempt. 126 years later, Oxford University's undergraduate body finally gave its verdict on the issue. After due consideration, it came down cautiously on Huxley's side: on 14 February 1986, the motion "That the doctrine of creation is more valid than the theory of evolution" was defeated by 198 votes to 115.

At first glance, we may be inclined to suppose that Huxley would have been pleased at this outcome. A master debater himself, he knew the importance of winning crucial public engagements of this kind. On reflection, however, we may wonder instead whether Huxley would not have been both amazed and disappointed at this second Oxford debate: amazed that religiously-motivated anti-evolutionary sentiment is still so strong that it can command the support of no less than 115 undergraduates at one of Europe's foremost universities;

and disappointed that the scientific community still has to spend its time defending ground that was supposedly won for it more than a century ago.

Over the past 10-20 years, religiously-motivated anti-evolutionism has grown to the point where today it constitutes a significant threat to the teaching and practise of evolutionary biology in North America and, to a lesser extent, in Europe as well. For the first time since the early-nineteenth century, significant numbers of Protestant evangelicals are today attempting to develop a non-evolutionary view of origins, a so-called "creation science"; and in pursuit of this aim, they are writing articles, publishing textbooks, founding colleges, and entering into political battles with evolutionary biologists in the media, in local school boards and colleges, and even in the lawcourts (for reviews and analysis see Durant ed. 1985, Godfrey ed. 1983, Kitcher 1982, Montagu ed. 1984, Nelkin 1982).

The single crucial assumption which underlies the so-called creation science movement is that the theological doctrine of creation is fundamentally incompatible with the scientific theory of evolution. The scientific creationists believe that people must choose between creation and evolution; they believe that as the Oxford Union motion put it, the one must be "more valid" than the other. Professor Edgar Andrews, who was one of the Oxford speakers, is President of the British Biblical Creation Society, an organization with several hundred members whose purpose is "to demonstrate the importance of the Biblical teaching on Creation, and its incompatibility with the general theory of organic evolution" (*Biblical Creation* 2, 1980). Though rather different in emphasis, this society shares with the much larger and more explicitly fundamentalist American Creation Research Society the belief that evolution is inherently and profoundly anti-Christian. Indeed, leading American scientific creationists have equated evolution with atheism, materialism, and immorality at a personal level; as well as with anarchism, liberalism and communism at a political level (Morris ed. 1974). For them, Darwinism is not just wrong; it is of the devil.

Extravagant claims such as these are but one, albeit extreme, reflection of what is a long-standing and widespread sense of unease in the Christian community about evolutionary theory. Many even among those who accept that evolution is true do so rather reluctantly, almost as if by making this admission they were giving house-room to an unwelcome guest. Some theologians, for example, who are happy for the most part to take on trust the conclusions of theoretical science, stumble when they are confronted by the Darwinian theory of evolution by natural selection (see, for example, Montefiore 1985); and innumerable ordinary Christian folk, who take no particular interest in science, nonetheless feel obliged to "have a view" on this matter. Far beyond the circles of the scientific creationists, there is a conviction that evolutionary theory presents special problems or difficulties for Christian faith. Indeed, this is surely implied by the fact that "The Argument about Evolution and Creation" was chosen as the topic for the first European Conference on Science and Religion.

The Historical Perspective

Faced with this widespread religious unease about evolution, it can be helpful to look back to the past. History does not, of course, teach us any simple or straightforward lessons; and by itself, it cannot solve any of the great scientific or theological problems in which we may be interested. However, history can give us a better sense of perspective on these problems. In particular, it can help us to shake free from the particular prejudices of our day, both by suggesting new ways of thinking about our problems, and by revealing a wider range of possible solutions to these problems than may have been apparent at first sight.

In reviewing the history of discussions of evolution and creation, however, it is important to bear in mind that the past is another place, in which things were often done differently. For example, from an historical point of view it is not possible to make a clear distinction between scientific and theological discussions of evolution. Throughout the first half of the nineteenth century, which is the period in which modern evolutionary theory first arose, much biology was deeply religious and much religion was profoundly biological. At that time science as a whole was far less insular and far less secular than it is today; and this means that in dealing with our subject we must inevitably move rather freely between science and theology.

Precisely because many early workers failed to make a clear distinction between science and theology, they often argued from the one to the other as if such arguments were free of all philosophical difficulty. Even Charles Darwin, that most cautious of nineteenth century evolutionary biologists, occasionally drew theological conclusions from what were essentially scientific premises. It is a major theme of this chapter that we are to a large extent the unwitting victims of a persistent conflation or confusion between science and theology which has occurred throughout the history of debates about evolution and creation. If today we continue to be worried about the relationship between Darwinism and Christian belief, more often than not it is because we are faced either with science masquerading as theology or with theology masquerading as science. Only history can show us the full extent of the damage that is done by such pretence.

There have been many different ideas and speculations about organic origins; but in the modern period there has been only one really successful scientific theory of organic origins, and that is Charles Darwin's and Alfred Russel Wallace's theory of evolution by natural selection (Darwin and Wallace 1958, Darwin 1859). The great achievement of the Darwin-Wallace theory is to show how in principle new species may arise from ancestor species by a process of descent with modification. The theory is entirely typical of great discoveries in science in that it invokes some relatively familiar features of the living world (the principles of inheritance, genetic variation, and over-reproduction), but draws an entirely unexpected consequence from them: namely, natural selection, or the differential survival and reproduction of favourable over unfavourable variations in the struggle for existence.

Darwin's bold claim was that natural selection has been the principal (though not the sole) agent of organic evolution. This claim has always been controversial, of course; but it is impossible to dispute the fact that natural selection remains to this day the centre-piece of evolutionary biology. Undergirded by modern population genetics, and applied in countless detailed studies of the evolution of both physical and behavioural traits, natural selection is the only half-way adequate theory of evolution that has ever been proposed (Dawkins 1986). For this reason alone, it is to the history of Darwinism and its relations with religious belief that the bulk of this paper is devoted. As a first step in considering the impact of Darwinism on religious belief, however, it is necessary to begin with the earlier view of organic origins that it was intended to replace.

The Theory of Special Creation
Throughout the seventeenth and eighteenth centuries in Europe, the study of life was intimately intertwined with religious, and more particularly with Christian beliefs about the inter-relationships between God, nature, human nature, and human society. In this period, there was fashioned a broad synthesis of natural history and religion which, albeit in many different forms, was every bit as powerful as the synthesis of Aristotelian cosmology and Christian theology in the medieval period. This synthesis is to be found in embryo in the work of the seventeenth century English naturalist John Ray, in vigorous youth in the ideas of the eighteenth century Swedish taxonomist Carolus Linnaeus, in subtle maturity in the writings of the French comparative anatomist Georges Cuvier and the German polymath Johann Wolfgang von Goethe, and in advanced and somewhat decrepit old age in the publications of the Swiss-American palaeontologist Louis Agassiz and the English comparative anatomist Richard Owen (for a competent historical review, see Bowler 1984).

The synthesis which may be discerned in the work of all these and many more naturalists represented the coming together of three great intellectual traditions. In order of age, these were: Greek philosophy, and particularly Plato's idealist doctrine of specific forms and Aristotle's teleological doctrine of final causes; Christian theology, and particularly the doctrine of divine creation; and classical natural history, and more particularly the establishment of a comprehensive natural classification of plants and animals. It will be useful to summarize the contributions of each of these traditions in turn, and then to present a brief description of the resulting synthesis.

From classical Greece the seventeenth and eighteenth centuries took two key notions, among many others. First, there was Plato's doctrine that true reality is not the mundane world of varied and varying sense experience, but rather the transcendent world of pure and immutable forms. On this view, the objects we see around us are the flickering and temporary images of ideal types to which they are at best only crude approximations – in Plato's famous allegory in the *Republic*, they are mere shadows cast by the eternal light on the walls of a cave. There have been many different versions of Platonic idealism, including specifically theological ones in which the pure forms are interpreted as ideas in the mind of God. In one version or another, however, Plato's doctrine of forms has been a recurrent theme in the history of Western philosophy and science.

The same is true of a second Greek idea which is attributable to Plato's pupil Aristotle. Aristotle was a good deal more interested than Plato had been in studying the real world, including the world of life; and in pursuing a combination of philosophical wisdom and empirical ("scientific") knowledge, he modified and added to his master's ideas in many ways. For example, Aristotle took over Plato's doctrine of form, but emphasized the immanence of form within the physical world. Moreover, he complemented Plato's interest in form with a concern for function. According to Aristotle, an essential part of explaining anything consisted in giving an account of the end or purpose for which that thing exists (its "final cause"); and, once again in myriad different ways, this teleological approach shaped centuries of scientific thought to come.

Here, then, in rude outline are two key Greek contributions to seventeenth and eighteenth century ideas about the living world. In contrast, the key Christian contribution was a doctrine concerned primarily not with the explanation of the forms and functions of particular things, but rather with the explanation of why there are any things at all. In the doctrine of creation, Christianity portrayed the universe as the dependent and strictly temporal handiwork of God. This doctrine of creation was quite distinct from (though it was often confused with) Greek notions of origins; for where the one envisaged a free creation *ex nihilo* by a transcendent and omnipotent God, the other envisaged a constrained forming of pre-existent unformed matter by a demiurge. In one form or another, the Christian doctrine of creation has been a major influence on western thought, and more especially on western science.

The third and final ingredient of our synthesis is classical natural history, and particularly classical taxonomy. Taxonomy is the science of classification of living organisms. Aristotle himself had been interested in classification, and he had distinguished many different "natural kinds" of animals within a roughly linear series, the scale of nature or *scala naturae*. The notion of a linear "chain of being" was enormously influential in the 17th and 18th centuries (Lovejoy 1936), particularly as classification moved to centre stage in the study of natural history. The guiding principle in the work of most naturalists at this time was the attempt to construct a systematic and orderly arrangement of species or other natural kinds. Some adopted the principle of the scale of nature, while others went for hierarchical schemes involving nested sets of related groups. Either way, however, the search was on for general principles by which organic species could be classified on the basis of observed structural similarities and differences of form and function.

It is not difficult to see how the three traditions of Greek philosophy, Christian theology and classical natural history may be combined. By identifying the Platonic demiurge with the Christian creator, and giving this creator the task of fashioning out of unformed matter a formal array of exquisitely adapted species, it is possible to arrive at an idealistic synthesis according to which each species (or other chosen natural kind) of plant or animal is the embodiment of a transcendent idea in the mind of the creator; or, with a little more subtlety, perhaps, to arrive at a synthesis in which each species is seen as an individually tailored variation upon a far smaller set of transcendental themes. On this view, the living world is portrayed as a static array of diverse forms, each of which is primitively distinct from all others by virtue of its unique divine origin. For want of a better term, we may refer to this view as the "special creation theory" of organic origins.

It would be wrong to suggest that there was anything like complete agreement among those who supported this way of looking at the living world. For example, and most important of all, there was a persistent tension between the Platonic or idealist and the Aristotelian or teleological elements within the theory. Thus, in early-nineteenth century England two partially separate special-creationist traditions flourished alongside one another, the one concerned primarily with the idealist explanation of organic form in terms of transcendent "Archetypes", and the other concerned primarily with the teleological explanation of organic function in terms of divine design (Bowler 1977, 1984, Ospovat 1978, 1981). The idealist anatomist Richard Owen put his finger on the crucial difference between these two traditions by distinguishing between homologies (cases in which the same basic structure serves different functions) and analogies (cases in which quite different structures serve the same basic function; see Owen 1848). Owen insisted that adequate biological analysis required the investigation of both homologies and analogies; and this claim was part of a campaign to effect a compromise between the idealist and the teleological traditions of special creationism.

From our point of view, these details are of little concern. What really matters is the simple fact that for a very long period of time theoretical explanations of organic origins were dominated by a synthesis in which the Christian doctrine of creation was tied to a very particular set of philosophical and scientific beliefs about the natural world. As we have seen, the philosophical beliefs were overwhelmingly idealist and teleological; and they were used to support the scientific notion that species (or other natural kinds) are primitively distinct. As Owen himself put it in connection with the vertebrate skeleton (quoted in Aulie 1972):

The Divine mind which planned the Archetype also foreknew all its modifications. The archetypal idea was manifested in the flesh, under diverse such manifestations, upon this planet, long prior to the existence of those animal species that actually exemplify it.

From Special Creation to Natural Selection

From as early as the 1830s, when he first began to think seriously about the problem of origins, Charles Darwin firmly rejected the idealist elements within the theory of special creation. However, he did not reject the teleological elements within it anything like so easily. In fact, Darwin was greatly influenced by the Anglican clergyman William Paley, the greatest exponent of teleological special creationism in the early nineteenth century. Paley, of course, had emphasized function at the expense of form, for he had virtually identified the doctrine of creation with the fact of the overwhelming adaptedness of living organisms. In his *Natural Theology* (1802), Paley presented the innumerable contrivances of life as a cumulative argument from design for the existence of God. Paley's God was a craftsman; he was a superlative mechanic who had thrown together not merely cunningly contrived machines but machines so cunningly contrived that they were capable of reproducing themselves indefinitely without external assistance.

Darwin took this view extremely seriously. In fact, for several years he appears entirely to have accepted Paley's version of the argument from design. Throughout his life, Darwin never for an instant questioned Paley's assumption that what required explanation above all else was organic adaptation. For both men it was true that, as Darwin himself once put it, "the whole universe is full of adaptations"; but from about 1837 Darwin added to this conviction the non-Paleyan belief that these adaptations were "only direct consequences of still higher laws" (Gruber and Barrett 1974). Here again, Darwin was following the lead of the special creationists, who had already offered innumerable transcendental laws as putative explanations of organic form and function. The only difference between Darwin and the special creationists was that Darwin would have nothing to do with the esoteric principles of transcendentalism, which he regarded as simply absurd. When he went in search of a "higher law" regulating the production of organic adaptations, what he sought was not a transcendental principle but rather a mundane process capable of simulating intelligent design.

Discovered by Darwin in 1838, the principle of natural selection represented the unexpected fulfilment of the promise of the theory of special creation. It was unexpected, of course, in the sense that it replaced the idea of species as individually crafted products of a Platonic demiurge with the radical idea of species as historical products of the differential survival and reproduction of favourable over unfavourable variant individuals in the struggle for existence; but it was the fulfilment of the promise of the theory of special creation, in the sense that it accounted for the observed pattern of organic form and function with the aid of but a single overarching theoretical principle.

The idea that Darwin's theory of evolution by natural selection represents the fulfilment of the special-creationist tradition is still not widely acknowledged. This is a little surprising, for Darwin himself made it abundantly clear in his own writings. The frontispiece of the first edition of the *Origin of Species*, for example, contained two quotations, one from Francis Bacon on the "two books of divine revelation", and the other from the Reverend William Whewell, an English natural theologian, who had observed that "with regard to the material world...we can perceive that events are brought about not by insulated interpositions of Divine power, exerted in each particular case, but by the establishment of general laws". Together, these passages gave notice to Darwin's readers that his book fell squarely within the conventions of natural theology; and Darwin further underlined this point towards the end of the *Origin* where he stated that, "To my mind, it accords better with what we know of the laws impressed upon matter by the Creator, that the production and extinction of the past inhabitants of the world should have been due to secondary causes, like those determining the birth and death of the individual" (Darwin 1859). Thus, Darwin explicitly invited his readers to see evolution by natural selection as the means adopted by the creator to populate the earth with a diversity of well-adapted species.

Of course, things were not really quite as simple as this. Until well after the publication of the *Origin*, Darwin continued to present his theory in the orthodox language of the doctrine of divine creation; and throughout his life, he insisted that there was nothing either anti-religious or atheistic in his work. Privately, however, he was increasingly troubled and perplexed by these matters. For example in the course of a long and rather inconclusive correspondence about the theological implications of natural selection with his friend, the American botanist Asa Gray, he once wrote: "You say that you are in a haze; I am in thick mud; the orthodox would say in fetid, abominable mud; yet I cannot keep out of the question" (Darwin ed. 1887). To see exactly what the "fetid, abominable mud" was, and why he was stuck fast in it, we must review briefly Darwin's changing views on religion.

Darwin was a "quite orthodox" Christian at the time he travelled aboard *HMS Beagle* in the early 1830s. Indeed, he describes how he was "heartily laughed at by several of the officers...for quoting the Bible as an unanswerable authority on some point of morality" (Barlow ed. 1958). In the late 1830s, however, Darwin gradually abandoned Christianity, first for what may be termed deism (the belief in an impersonal divine author of the universe), and then for a rather uneasy agnosticism. As he himself once put it, "In my most extreme fluctuations I have never been an atheist in the sense of denying the existence of God. I think that generally (and more and more as I grow older), but not always, that an Agnostic would be the more correct description of my state of mind" (Darwin ed. 1887).

In a recent study, the historian John Hedley Brooke has re-examined the causes of Darwin's changing religious views (Brooke 1985). Certainly, he suggests, there were scientific elements in Darwin's abandonment of religious belief: for example, he was greatly impressed by the universality of natural law as an objection to the possibility of miracles; and he appears to have found the arbitrariness, the contingency and the radical purposelessness of evolution by natural selection a real source of difficulty. Yet this was far from being the whole story. For Darwin's loss of faith was also bound up with that moral revolt against Christianity which historians have seen as such a significant part of the decline of orthodox belief in the Victorian period.

Thus in his autobiography, having described his orthodoxy at the time of the Beagle voyage, Darwin moved immediately into a discussion of the causes of his growing unbelief. Significantly, this discussion is not taken up principally with scientific matters. Instead, Darwin records that, "I had gradually come...to see that the Old Testament from its manifestly false history of the world...and from its attributing to God the feelings of a revengeful tyrant, was no more to be trusted than the sacred books of the Hindoos, or the beliefs of any barbarian" (Barlow ed. 1958). Darwin was struck as much by the moral

20

and intellectual parochialism of Christianity as he was by its supposed conflict with the findings of science. He detested the doctrine of eternal damnation, and he found the problem of both animal and human suffering a major objection to religious belief – "I cannot see as plainly as others do, and as I should wish to do, evidence of design and beneficence on all sides of us", he wrote to Asa Gray, "There seems to me too much misery in the world." (Darwin ed. 1887). As Brooke notes, these factors point not so much to Darwin's science as to the resonance between his science and the wider culture as the source of his growing unbelief.

The Divorce of Science from Theology

This brief historical sketch of the emergence of Darwinism, and of Darwin's own views on religion, provides the context for a critical re-assessment of the relationship between evolution and creation. Such a re-assessment undermines all naive notions of any necessary conflict between the two ideas, and in this sense it radically undercuts the position of the so-called "scientific creationists". At the same time, however, it lends support to the idea that the Darwinian revolution did indeed have profound implications for the relationship between science and religious belief. That these implications are not necessarily the ones most commonly associated with the name of Charles Darwin today serves only to reinforce the importance of the historical perspective in contemporary debates about evolution and creation.

We have seen that the theory of evolution by natural selection fulfilled the promise of the special creationist tradition; but it also destroyed that tradition by undermining the particular alliance of philosophy, theology, and natural science upon which it rested. In a Darwinian universe, there was no place for Platonic idealism and no place for Aristotelian teleology; above all, there was no place for special creation. By showing convincingly how in principle new species might arise in nature, Darwin made redundant centuries of philosophizing and theologizing about organic origins. What is vitally important to notice, however, is that neither in aim nor in effect did he undermine the Christian doctrine of creation itself. Rather, by separating that doctrine from its two-centuries-long marriage of convenience with Greek philosophy and classical natural history, Darwin forced the radical re-examination of the relationship between theology and natural science.

Out of this process of re-examination there emerged in the late-nineteenth century a whole array of different "solutions" to the problem of the relationship between science and theology, evolution and creation. To the English biologist, Thomas Huxley, for example, Darwinism was a vindication of an agnostic and liberal scientific world-view that would free humankind altogether from the shackles of theology; to Ernst Haeckel, it was a proof of the truth of "Monism", a secular philosophy in which matter and mind were regarded as but two aspects of the same universal and progressively developing substance; and to Karl Marx, it was the basis in natural history for an atheistic, dialectical, and historically materialist view of human nature and society. Here, then, were a variety of anti-Christian reformulations of the relationship between science and theology in a Darwinian universe.

Yet before we jump to the conclusion that Darwinism was inherently anti-Christian, we shall do well to recall an equally wide range of pro-Christian reformulations of the science-theology relationship which were produced in response to Darwinism in the late-nineteenth century. Thus, to the close friend of Thomas Huxley, the Anglican clergyman, naturalist, and novelist Charles Kingsley, Darwinism entailed a "loftier" view of God's work in creation than that which had been contained in the older, creationist synthesis (Darwin ed. 1887); to the close friend of Darwin, the American Presbyterian Asa Gray, Darwinism afforded "higher and more comprehensive, and perhaps worthier, as well as more consistent, views of design in Nature than heretofore" (quoted in Moore 1979); and to the close friend of the Darwinian biologists E. B. Poulton and G. J. Romanes, the Oxford Anglo-Catholic Aubrey Moore, Darwinism was "infinitely more Christian than the theory of special creation" because it implied "the immanence of God in nature, and the omnipresence of his creative power" (Moore 1889).

Quite clearly, a very great variety of views of the evolution-creation relationship was on offer in the late-nineteenth century. To a very considerable extent, Darwinism appears to have become all things to all men (virtually without exception those involved were, of course, all men); and it was precisely this pluralism that was its greatest influence on debates about science and theology. For any theory of origins that is capable of sustaining an indefinitely large number of different philosophical and religious interpretations is profoundly secularizing in its effects. The greatest tangible result of the Darwinian revolution in the domain of science and theology was not the triumph of any single view within either domain but rather the growing realization that these were indeed two domains, and not (as the theory of special creation had implied) one.

A particularly stark illustration of the dawning of this new realization is provided by an intriguing Victorian institution known as the Metaphysical Society. Founded in 1869 by no less than 62 eminent scientists, theologians, and literary figures, this society met regularly for a period of around 11 years in order to try to find a new foundation for an integrated understanding of the interrelationships between God, nature, humankind, and society. It failed, of course; and this failure has been represented by the historian Robert Young as symptomatic of a profound fragmentation of intellectual culture that took place in the mid-Victorian period. According to William Gladstone, for example, there was a simple lesson to be learnt from the proceedings of the Metaphysical Society: "Let the scientific men stick to their science, and leave philosophy and religion to poets, philosophers, and theologians" (quoted in Young 1985).

The Myth and the Reality of Secular Science
Gladstone's view is the official myth by which we live today. Over the past century science in general and evolutionary biology in particular, have seen themselves as essentially secular endeavours, entirely divorced from the domains of poetry, philosophy, and theology. Officially, at least, contemporary evolutionary biology is precisely what Darwin himself intended it to be: an entirely naturalistic body of knowledge which makes no direct contact of any kind with matters theological. Individual scientists are generally regarded as being free to hold any personal views they like on matters of philosophy and religion; but as soon as they are tempted to claim scientific authority for these views, they are seen as stepping beyond the domain of evolutionary biology and into that larger field that Gladstone wished to leave to the poets, the philosophers, and the theologians.

This, then is the official myth of twentieth century secular science. The unofficial reality, however, is somewhat different. For despite the Darwinian revolution, scientists and others have continued to try to construct coherent world-views embracing philosophy, theology, and evolutionary biology. Among the founders of the modern, so-called "synthetic" theory of evolution by natural selection, for example, Theodosius Dobzhansky, George Gaylord Simpson, and Julian Huxley stand out as men who wished to integrate their science with larger views concerning the nature and significance of life in the universe. That both Dobzhansky and Huxley should have drawn inspiration from the theological writings of the Jesuit palaeontologist Teilhard de Chardin (1959) simply underlines the extent to which the official boundaries between science and theology have remained blurred in the post-Darwinian era (for further discussion of this issue, see Greene 1981).

Despite the complexity of the current scene, however, it remains true that we have come a long way from the days when philosophical, religious and scientific discussions of origins were dominated by the theory of special creation. Today, it is at least possible to distinguish between conventional Darwinian evolutionary biology and that larger evolutionary world-view constructing enterprise that is represented by men like Huxley and Teilhard.

For the plain fact is that those who accept the essentially secular terms of Darwinism are free to select amongst a variety of alternative world-views according to their own particular philosophical or religious preferences. In exercising this freedom, of course, people are not making a *scientific* choice. For Darwinism as such rests upon no distinctive metaphysical or religious propositions; and it offers no distinctive support to any particular world-view, be it pro-Christian, anti-Christian or merely neutral. Rightly conceived, theological questions must be decided on theological grounds, and not upon the territory of the paleontologist or the population geneticist.

Conclusion

I have suggested that much of the argument about evolution and creation arises from the belief that, since these two things are opposed to one another, we must choose between them. This belief is simply false. The theory of evolution by natural selection is not atheistic but rather secular, and there is no necessity for it to be in conflict with, or indeed to make any sort of contact with, the theological doctrine of creation. Historical analysis, however, tells us why the idea that there is conflict between evolution and creation has persisted for so long. For just as in medieval times Christian theology was fused with classical cosmology, so in the 17th and 18th centuries Christian theology was fused with classical philosophy and classical natural history; and just as the Copernican astronomers found themselves confronting the Church, when really they should have been confronting only Aristotle and Ptolemy, so the Darwinists found themselves confronting the representatives of Christianity, when really they should have been confronting only Plato and Paley.

Of course, in one sense to confront Paley *was* to confront Christianity, since Paley was a representative of Christian natural theology; my point is that precisely that was the problem. For Paley and the special creationists attached the credibility of the Christian doctrine of creation to a particular set of philosophical and scientific beliefs about species with which it need never have been directly associated; and Christendom today is still paying the price for this historic association. The so-called scientific creationists of contemporary America portray themselves as defenders of time-honoured Christian orthodoxy. What they are really doing, however, is reviving the old 17th and 18th century theory of special creation, with all of its idealist and classical, as well as Christian, overtones. Thus, for example, in the creationist textbook *Biology, A Search for Order in Complexity* (Moore and Slusher 1970), we find an interpretation of vertebrate homologies that would have delighted Richard Owen:

Creationists believe that when God created the vertebrates, He used a single blueprint for the body plan but varied the plan so that each "kind" would be perfectly equipped to take its place in the wonderful world He created for them.

In connection with this kind of thing, which abounds in creationist writings, those Christians who find themselves troubled by Darwinism may care to ask the following questions: where are the specifically Christian grounds for the notions of "blueprints" and "body plans"? and where are the specifically Christian grounds for supposing that special creation according to a small number of demiurgic archetypes was the divine method of creation? Unless and until they receive adequate replies to these questions, those Christians who are troubled by Darwinism are entitled to conclude that the so-called scientific creationists are not the defenders of time-honoured Christian or Biblical orthodoxy, after all, but rather the hopelessly stranded representatives of the outmoded scientific hypotheses of the past.

This, at an rate, was the view of the matter that was held by that most perceptive of commentators upon the Darwinian scene, the late-Victorian Oxford Anglo-Catholic Aubrey Moore. "The dead hand of an exploded scientific theory", Moore once wrote, "rests upon theology....Christians in all good faith set to work to defend a view which has neither Biblical, nor patristic, nor medieaval authority....If the theory of "special creation" existed in the Bible or in Christian antiquity", he went on, "we might bravely try and do battle for it. But it came to us some two centuries ago from the side of science, with the *imprimatur* of a Puritan poet [the reference is, of course, to Milton]". Thus, Moore concluded, "It is difficult...to see how the question [of evolution *versus* creation], except by a confusion, becomes a religious question at all" (Moore 1889). The confusion that Moore identified almost exactly a century ago is with us still; and it serves the true interests neither of science nor of religion.

Bibliography

Aulie, R. P. (1972), "The Doctrine of Special Creation", *American Biology Teacher* 34, pp. 191-200, 261-268.

Barlow, N. ed. (1958), *The Autobiography of Charles Darwin, 1809-1882,* Collins, London & Glasgow.

Bowler, P. J. (1977), "Darwinism and the Argument from Design: Suggestions for a Reevaluation", *Journal of the History of Biology* 10, pp. 29-43.

Bowler, P. J. (1984), *Evolution. The History of an Idea*, University of California Press, Berkeley & London.

Brooke, J. H. (1985), "The Relations Between Darwin's Science and His Religion", in Durant ed. (1985), pp. 40-75.

Darwin, C. R. (1859), *On the Origin of Species by Means of Natural Selection*, Murray, London.

Darwin, C. R. & A. R. Wallace (1958), *Evolution by Natural Selection*, With a Foreword by Gavin de Beer, Cambridge University Press, Cambridge.

Darwin, F. ed. (1887), *The Life and Letters of Charles Darwin*, 3 vols., Murray, London.

Dawkins, R. (1986), *The Blind Watchmaker*, Longman Burnt Mill, Harlow.

Durant, J. R. ed. (1985), *Darwinism and Divinity. Essays on Evolution and Religious Belief*, Blackwell, Oxford.

Godfrey, L. R. (1983), *Scientists Confront Creationism*, Norton, New York & London.

Greene, J. C. (1981), *Science, Ideology and World View: Essays in the History of Evolutionary Ideas*, University of California Press, Berkeley & London.

Gruber, H. E. & Barrett, P. H. (1974), *Darwin on Man. A Psychological Study of Scientific Creativity...together with Darwin's Early and Unpublished Notebooks*, Wildwood House, London.

Kitcher, P. (1982), *Abusing Science. The Case Against Creationism*, MIT Press, Cambridge Mass. & London.

Lovejoy, A. O. (1936), *The Great Chain of Being: A Study in the History of an Idea*. Reprinted Harper, New York, 1960.

Montagu, A. ed. (1984), *Science and Creationism*, Oxford University Press, Oxford & New York.

Montefiore, H. (1985), *The Probability of God*, SCM Press, London.

Moore, A. L. (1889), *Science and the faith: Essays on Apologetic Subjects*, Kegan, Paul, Trench, Trubner & Co., London.

Moore, J. N. & H. S. Slusher eds. (1970), *Biology: A Search for Order in Complexity*, Zondervan Publishing House, Grand Rapids, Michigan.

Moore, J. R. (1979), *The Post-Darwinian Controversies*, Cambridge University Press, Cambridge & New York.

Morris, H. M. ed. (1974), *Scientific Creationism*, Creation-Life Publishers, San Diego.

Nelkin, D. (1982), *The Creation Controversy. Science or Scripture in the Schools*, Norton, New York & London.

Ospovat, D. (1978), "Perfect Adaptation and Teleological Explanation: Approach to the Problem of the History of Life in the Mid-Nineteenth Century", *Studies in the History of Biology* 2, pp. 33-56.

Ospovat, D. (1981), *The Development of Darwin's Theory: Natural History, Natural Theology and Natural Selection*, 1838-1859, Cambridge University Press, Cambridge & New York.

Owen, R. (1848), *On the Archetypes and Homologies of the Vertebrate Skeleton*, AMS Press, New York.

Teilhard de Chardin, P. (1959), *The Phenomenon of Man*, Introduced by Julian Huxley, Collins, London.

Young, R. M. (1985), *Darwin's Metaphor. Nature's Place in Victorian Culture*, Cambridge University Press, Cambridge & New York.

Theology's Relation to Science

Karl Schmitz-Moormann

The beginnings of Science with the Greek presocratic philosophers, or even earlier in the world of Egypt or Ur and the region between the Euphrates and the Tigris, were certainly not concerned with the question of how to seperate Science from Religion. Rather the very men who were occupied with the religious rituals, the priests, were more often than not those who explored the skies in order to understand the will of the gods. However the world was interpreted in those early times, the order found in the world, the Cosmos, was considered to be something divine – either because of its source, as in the biblical tradition; or because of its origin, as in the Egyptian and near-Eastern tradition; or because its very essence was an expression of an all-governing necessity. The beginnings of astronomy, which are the beginnings of all science, are very clearly linked to the idea that the stars are those powers which guide earthly events, through the movements of the planets. To know those movements and to understand their meaning for man was to understand more about man's destiny. This was inconceivable without reference to the gods who in the Greek world knew about the future of man and of the world though they remained subject to the rules of destiny. To understand the Cosmos would give to man that knowledge about his own destiny which he desired to attain eternal happiness, even though not all interpretations of the Cosmos, as, for example, in the Gilgamesh-Epos or the philosophy of the Stoa, would allow this.

Though Plato did not accept the pre-Socratic interpretations of the Cosmos as valid for mankind, because the causes and the origins they named were not consistent with his experience of the human being as mind(Nous-)guided, he nevertheless remained attached to the principle that we have to understand the Cosmos in order to understand our own destiny.

To Plato it is through the knowledge of the real world – which is a world of shadows as compared with the ideal world – that man will find his way to knowledge of the ideas and, finally, of the idea of the Good. Through this latter all things participate in the realm of the ideas, as explained in the parable of the sun and the parable of the cave in Plato's *Republic*. In this context, it should not astonish us that Aristotle does not reach the question of God in his

Metaphysics, but in the *De Coelo* where God is shown as the unmoved prime mover of the universe.

The natural sciences were not seperated in those days from philosophy or from theology, and there was no reason for theologians to consider the universe to be irrelevant to the reality of human beings and of God. The movement away from concepts of a mythical world, in which matter itself was considered to have divine qualities – for example the water in Thales' vision – towards a world whose matter was regarded as created by the *Nous*, as in Plato's *Timaios*, and, more clearly in the Judaic and Christian tradition, by God, made it possible more and more, to look at the world without violating any taboos. Medieval times thus became an era in which the world and the knowledge about the world were integrated into a theological vision of creation. In spite of the inclination of the age of Enlightenment to denigrate the middle ages as dark and ignorant, there was certainly more scientific knowledge among the clerics of that time than among the philosophers and the specialized scientists of our time. It is worth while remembering that any student of theology before he was even admitted to his studies had to write a thesis on the universe. The Sorbonne registers contain hundreds of titles such as "De universo", "De machina mundi", "De rerum naturae", "De mundo", "De imagine mundi", "De philosphia mundi", "De mundi universitate", "De universitate entium", "Tractatus de luminaribus" etc.[1]

We should not forget that this knowledge was by no means pure book knowledge and Thomas Aquinas, who constantly refers to the *corpora coelestia* as the natural entities to underscore his viewpoint, was taught by Albertus Magnus who was a renowned scientist of his time who used observational proofs for his descriptions of nature. For example, he deduced that the earth is a sphere by pointing out that the Earth's shadow on the moon during an eclipsis can only be thrown by a spherical body. This proof is still sound, and his use of it shows that the astronomical knowledge of that time was quite advanced, even though the geocentric view was held.

This in itself is not very astounding. Keeping track of the planets and the Sun and the Moon enabled the astronomers of the time within the limits of the then possible observations to predict quite accurately the eclipses of the moon and of the sun, as well as the wandering of the planets over the starry sky. Observations and theory fitted together, and the theory enabled them, when the mechanical skills were far enough advanced, to build astronomical clocks which had their place in the great cathedrals and still today show, within the geocentric conception of the universe, the correct positions of the sun, the moon and the planets. Indeed the aberrations from the observed universe are negligible within the limits of correctness of any clock of that time.

28

If the middle ages were so much interested in the natural world, why did theologians and especially the Catholic church have such difficulty in accepting the view of Copernicus? It seems to me there are two reasons: Firstly, the helio-centric viewpoint was far from being shared by the astronomers of the day. Tycho Brahe, certainly the best and most rigorous observer among the astronomers, proposed rather a widely accepted geo- and helio-centered elliptical world structure, in which the earth occupied the centre around which the ellipsis with the other center, the sun, turned itself each day. This theory was welcomed in its time, and successful.[2] Although Kepler helped the Copernician view to be accepted in scientific circles, the new vision was not widely disseminated and the maps of the universe, as published for example in the protestant Netherlands, in the early 18th century still presented the universe as geocentric. The theologians were confronted with a highly controversial theory, not something they had to accept as definitely proven.

So there was uncertainty on the one side. On the other side, theologians were asked to make a theologically not insignificant shift in their vision of the universe. They had integrated the vision of the universe into their theology in a highly competent way. One very material expression of this integration was the already mentioned astronomical clocks in the cathedrals. We admire them today rather as marvellous works of masterly workmanship, but we rarely ask why they have been built inside a church. This question could lead us to see better how closely theology and science were intertwined in the religious visions of medieval times.

To understand correctly the role of the clock-maker's masterpieces we must first realise that scholastic theology, far from being in abstract heigth and relying on biblical revelation only, turned to the universe as God's creation and considered the book of creation as important a revelation as the Bible. The fact that knowledge about the universe was made a condition for admission to theological studies was founded on this recognition of the created universe as an important source for our knowledge of God. Scholastic theology did not invent this importance. Practically all theological traditions – be they transmitted as myths, as articles of faith or as elaborated theologies – link the universe closely to a divine source. The many stories of creation, or cosmogonies, can only be briefly mentioned here. To me it seems highly improbable that man's thought or perception of God could ever separate his world from all kinds of relationship to God without giving up the very notion of God. Furthermore, this relationship is essential inasmuch as the existence of the universe and of ourselves is concerned. The myths as well as the theologies have always tried over the ages to describe the relationship between God and the world in which we concretely live. If God is not to be a pure myth, then he is either the creator of this world or to be identified with it. Between these two extremes we observe in the history of myths a scale of mixed systems which could be read structuralistically or evolutionarily in the direction of a more and more transcendental God-notion. Any creation story to be credible must match the experienced world. This was true for the Creation story of the Bible. It describes the functional world the people of Israel lived in at that time, along with regulations for times to be observed, what food is to be reserved for man and what for animals etc.

The scientific view of the world in the scholastic times did not really correspond exactly to that vision of Genesis. The world of man was no longer governed by laws defining what to eat and what not to eat and knowledge about the different kinds of stars (fixed and wandering) supplemented the narrow picture of heavenly bodies named in the first book of the Bible. In addition, general knowledge about nature and its functioning was enlarged considerably through the influence of Aristotle and of the growing experience of nature. The theologian knew that there are laws of nature and that these are reliable. This reliability had to be explained, and it is understandable that these regularities were not considered to be accidental. Matter itself was considered to be unable to bear the responsibility for the validity of these laws. The very idea of laws had to be linked to a spiritual and powerful being, to an authentic Law-giver.

This vision of a law-governed world penetrated all levels of human and religious life. The middle ages looked upon the universe as God's order which man had to imitate. The planets were not only heavenly bodies that could be looked at, but they were the most perfect representation of the Creator's order in the universe. Man had to look up to this order to find out how to structure his life and his society according to the order he could observe in the skies. When the people of the 13th century prayed: »Thy will be done on earth as it is in heaven", they had only to look up into the skies to see God's will performed in the most perfect way that could be imagined. They did not usually think of the invisible heavens as populated with angels and powers obeying perfectly God's will. The starry sky and its wandering planets were the perfect order for man to imitate.

So we should not be astonished that the number as well, as the ranking of the planets, was of primary importance to the medieval theologians. They were not the first to use this number – seven – but they certainly added to its applications. Thus the number of the days of the week, the days of the creation, the number of branches of the great candelaber in the Temple etc. were all connected by the scholastic scholars. But they also introduced a number of new elements into the perceived order. Man himself was conceived as a microcosm in a very precise way. The planets were ordered into the four lower ones – Moon, Mercury, Venus and Sol – and the three upper ones – Mars, Saturn and Jupiter. A parallel order is to be found in man who is composed out of the four elements, Earth, Water, Air and Fire, which correspond to the four lower planets; and the soul has three abilities, Mind, Memory and Volition, corresponding to the three upper planets. As Thomas Aquinas put it "Quia vero homo habet intellectum et sensum et corporalem virtutem, haec in ipso ad invicem ordinantur secundum divinae providentiae dispositionem ad similitudinem ordinis qui in universo invenitur." (S.c.G. III, 81). Thus the scholastics looked for this basic sevenfold order which they "found" wherever they looked. The number of sacraments is thus in the scholastic tradition seven, and they can be classified in the three essential sacraments of baptism, confirmation and order which could be conferred only once, and the four other sacraments which could be received repeatedly. This number of sacraments is quite astonishing if you look at the quite impressive number of candidates that were available like for example the consecration of the bishops that can claim to have real biblical origins and apostolic tradition for it. The number of seven was not to be exceeded. Thus we have seven 'sacraments' for the priesthood, four lower ones and the three upper ones. The state was ordered as well to the order of the skies: Nobility knew about seven classes from the baronet to the emperor. The moral world was dominated for better and worse by the number of seven. There were seven capital sins and the seven virtues, four cardinal and three theological ones.

Thus the medieval theology moved in a vision of the world order that asked for the representation of God's order inside the cathedrals. The great astronomical clocks were not at all out of place in the house of God. They gave man the possibility of praying knowledgeably and preachers did not hesitate to use the universe as an indicator for right and pious behaviour. Magister Guiardus thus compared the monks to the fixed stars, "which do not move by their own movement but follow the movement of the firmament, and in the same way the cloistered monks are not allowed to move by their own will but are to be moved by the movement of the firmament i.e. of God. ... The star is fixed in one place, and thus the clercs and religious men have to be fixed thus that their places do not change."[3] Thus the known world was not only present in abstract theological speculation, but was part of everyday religious life.

Even though Galileo destroyed the scientific basis of this theological world vision by declaring this world to be heliocentric, only very few people changed their vision of the world and, like Pascal, considered the immensities of space. People continued to pray looking up to the skies and seeing there the glory of the Lord. There is no interruption in the way Christians prayed from the time of St. Francis Hymn of the Sun to that of Beethoven's "The Heavens praise ..." (Die Himmel rühmen des Ewigen Stärke), and we have to look only into the hymnbooks which are in use today to find a great number of hymns making a reference to the skies and the heavenly bodies.

As long as the world vision at the basis of these prayers was considered, true theology could flourish. It was fulfilling its basic task, that is, to think of God as he is revealed through Scripture in the context of the contemporary known world. If theology is successful in this, then religion will not seperate man from the world but will link the world we live in to God. In this the middle ages were highly successful.

The breakdown of the geocentric vision of the universe, initiated by Galileo and completed by the modern multi-galaxial universe of today's astronomers, meant for theology the loss of the hold it had on creation. The theology of creation became a highly abstract affair in which scientific data did not occur in any essential way, though they were occasionally mentioned when they fitted or were believed to fit into the traditional theological view. Theological thinking became thus more and more emptied of any concrete relation with the world we live in. The refusal of theology to consider the new world vision as a contribution to man's understanding of God's creative action is understandable if we take notice of the profound changes it demanded in theology. Thomas Aquinas "argued from the concrete facts of his concrete universe ... and one consequently ruins the argument of Thomas Aquinas, if one tries to reduce it to an apparently purified metaphysics."[4] Actually, theology did follow the Doctor Angelicus for many centuries, but gave up more and more parts of his actual arguments. In a general way, the neo-scholastic theology taught the conclusions of Thomas without any regard for his premises, at least in as much as they were grounded in the concrete universe. Theology, in the Catholic world at least, became thus a highly speculative enterprise which was cut off from most of its roots in the concrete reality which was still, abstractly, proclaimed as creation. Theology turned its back on the created world and considered knowledge about it as threatening and not as a source of information about God's creation. Within the realm of Protestant theology the movement away from the world of God's Creation, away from scientific knowledge took a very similar path though not for the same reasons. We may fairly state that Protestant theology is not deeply influenced by the impact of scientific knowledge. At best it has been used to demythologize, thus giving science a theologically negative cleansing function. More positive approaches have taken place in the Anglican world, referred to by Arthur Peacocke. Time does not allow me to go any further into these different historical aspects.

The relationship of theology to science became more and more difficult as the sciences penetrated further and further into the different aspects of our world. Theologians, whenever they dared to take a closer look at these new insights into reality, became more and more embarrassed with the world. Science, once looked upon as an essential input and help to theology, was now regarded with ever greater suspicion. Many scientists, and especially the vulgarizers of science, like Moleschott and Büchner in the 19th century, considered theologians as obsolete. It would be interesting, though it is beyond my present scope, to inquire into the heritage of science coming from medieval theology. Concepts of nature, natural law and of the eternity of nature might indicate their religious roots. However this may be, it is clear that the relationship of science to theology was no better than its converse. Many scientific institutions just refused to accept Catholics as members, while the theologians mistrusted the sciences profoundly. With the impact of Darwinian ideas things did not become any easier. After the topology of the classical universe of the theologians had been revolutionized to become what we know today as the expanding universe, with the earth far from being the centre of the world but a rather insignificant dot of matter in space, the idea of evolution abolished the notion of a world that started as perfect. Even today fundamentalist theologians feel menaced in their creationist belief by the theory of evolution. Apart from some rare exceptions, the general attitude is to explain the difficulties away by stating that scientific insights are quite compatible with the traditional theological statements or are theologically unimportant. In practice this attitude seems to me quite unacceptable: on the one side it does not take seriously the work of the scientists who certainly do not work as if the world they explore were without relevance to the understanding of man and his place in it. There are certainly many abuses by scientists who generalize their scientific findings in an unwarranted way. That does not make their findings and insights less important, even when they lack comprehensiveness. As far as these findings are warranted, it would be a lack of human and Christian love not to consider them. Far more important, however, is the essentially theological reason that obliges us to reverse the above described negative attitude towards science. As long as the theologian confesses the creed that God is the Creator of the whole universe he will have to take very seriously the concrete reality before his eyes which to him is not only the universe or nature, but God's Creation. Thomas Aquinas knew about this and looked for the best information about the universe he could find in his time, that is, the knowledge of the scientists, in his time the philosophers. Even today scientists obtain a "Ph.D."; the notion of "philosophia ancilla theologiae" must be understood in this way. The servant is no slave, but does

II.
Biology

What is Evolution?

Carsten Bresch

1. Our world is made up of patterns

If we were to describe the fundamental property of the matter of the universe in a single sentence, we would have to say that matter is formed – or created – so as to show continously accelerating growth of patterns. This applies equally to the inanimate, the animate and indeed to the intellectual structures of our world.

The idea of patterns is one of central significance. The concept has existed for more than 2000 years. Thus Aristotle writes in his *Metaphysics* (in the section "The Unity of Substance") "That which is constituted from any separate parts so that the whole forms a unity, not like a disordered heap, but like a syllable (that is obviously more than the sum of its parts)". And later, "Every object derives its properties from the relationships between its component parts." "Every object consists of both matter and form."

Every object consists of matter and pattern. The significance of the pattern for the properties of the object can already be seen in small molecules, for example

$$H - O - N = N - O - H \qquad \text{and} \quad H - \overset{\displaystyle H}{\underset{\displaystyle |}{N}} - \overset{\displaystyle O}{\underset{\displaystyle \|}{N}} = O$$

subnitrous acid and nitramide

Although both consist of the same atoms and have the same empirical formula $N_2O_2H_2$, their properties differ. This difference is due to their difference in "pattern".

A pattern is something that has been assembled. It consists of building-blocks, of elements. A word, for example, consists of sounds or, in written form of letters; a machine, of various component parts. But these elements of a pattern do not just lie in unconnected proximity "like a disordered heap". The elements of a pattern have a relationship one to another. There exist dependences, connections and relationships between its separate units. Their positions and/or functions are not arbitrary, interchangeable, omissible, or extensible at will; they make up a connected whole, which possesses properties that emerge from the number and nature of the constituents *and* the relationships between them.

Everything around us consists of patterns. Matter is patterned, atomically and molecularly. Organisms are enormous patterns of cells, each of which in turn consists of a wealth of biological patterns. The arrangement of the houses in a human settlement is just as much a pattern as are the positions of the pieces of furniture in a room. A song is a time-pattern of sequences of notes; a book is a pattern of letters. We are so used to being surrounded by patterns that we do not give a thought to this fundamental property of our world. But it is matter *and* pattern (structure, form) that determine the properties of an object.

All patterns are the result of a becoming, a development. They have a history. The concept "evolution" should embrace this process of pattern-building in the whole of Nature. The origin of species in the course of the history of the Earth, usually associated with "evolution", is only a part of this – more precisely, it is the second of three distinguishable phases of evolution. Every pattern-formation is the product of the combined effects of co-incidence and restriction. "The fabric of the world consists of chance and necessity" says Goethe. The purpose of this contribution will be to show that this statement is more than an aphorism.

2. Patterns grow in restricted freedom

Human thinking distinguishes between events determined by chance and events determined by natural law. The distinguishing criterion is that of predictability. We have learnt from physics that macroscopic deterministic behaviour – for example, in the gas laws – results from very many microscopic chance events.

However, our everyday causal thinking is less familiar with the principle of stochastic dependence, even though it is precisely this principle that corresponds to the mechanism of the growth of patterns. It is true that patterns grow by random events, but these are not "purely" random, they are "impurely" random. What does this mean?

If we note the results of a game of dice, the following sequence of numbers might be thrown: 4, 1, 3, 2, 4, 5, 5, 2, 6, 4, ... The results of the throws are "purely" random. The sequence of numbers is "chaotic", that is, there is no relation between the individual results.

The Russian mathematician Andrej Markoff (1856-1922) studied processes in which there is no such independence of the individual random results, but in

37

which the random result of previous throws helps to determine the probabilities for the results of future throws. In the simplest case the result of the last throw influences the result of the next.

For example, if the most recent result is not allowed to result from the next throw, then the same number will never appear twice in succession, however long the throws are continued. Each single throw will still be random, but at the same time dependent on a previous result, to which it is related. All throws are then "conditionally random". The deviation from a "purely" stochastic series becomes more clearly discernable as the series of throws becomes longer.

If we generalize the example of the influence of past random results over probabilities, we arrive at "historical processes", that is, at processes in which the existing situation can develop, but the probabilities of future random results are dependent upon existing ones (conditional probability, stochastic coupling).

Every pattern is the product of such a historical process. This means that, throughout the history of the origin of the pattern, development is possible in various directions, but that the pattern already in existence has a restricting effect, in that certain directions of development are more and others less probable, while yet others are impossible. Some examples may make this clear.

Example 1.   The molecular pattern

$$
\begin{array}{c}
H \\
H - C - H \\
H
\end{array}
$$

can be extended or modified in very different ways, for example to give

$$
\begin{array}{ccccc}
H \quad H & & H & & H \\
H - C - C - H & \text{or} \quad H - C - O - H & \text{or} & H - C - Cl \\
H \quad H & & H & & H
\end{array}
$$

However, by no means all extensions or modifications lead to stable molecules. The pattern already present allows certain changes, others it does not.

Example 2. In the base sequence of a gene, certain changes (mutations) are compatible with the organism's ability to survive, and are thus allowed. Other base changes are lethal, that is, not allowed. Again, it is the pattern already present in combination with the global pattern of the environment that decides.

Example 3. The sentence "He is driving the car" can be modified or extended in many ways:

He is driving the car
He is driving the car too fast
He is driving her home in the car

and so forth. But not every modification or extension is allowed, for example:

He is driving throughout these car
He is driving with the car green
He is driving with his daughter the car's

The pattern of the initial sentence is one factor in determining which changes and extensions are linguistically meaningful, that is, allowed.

The essence of all pattern growth is *restricted freedom*. At all stages in the history of a pattern there are many possibilities for alteration or augmentation. What actually happens is determined by chance and is thus indeterminate. But this freedom is subject to constraints that result from the pattern itself and from the patterns surrounding it. That which is new must fit in with that which is already there.

Patterns can degenerate in two ways, viz., when either the freedom or the restriction disappears. The disappearance of freedom means that the restricting rules have become so narrow that the pattern can only be extended in a single way predetermined by the pattern itself – for example, in the chessboard pattern of laying floor tiles. Such cases are dominated by complete "order" and lack of freedom. Everything is laid down by rules, and growth can only be quantitative.

On the other hand, a pattern can degenerate to "chaos", viz., when the constraints disappear and – as in the case of the true dice game – only chance, unaffected by the past, decides over the kind of extension. Here, too, only quantitative growth is possible. Complete chaos and complete order are extreme cases that only exist in the abstractions of human thought. *Nowhere* are these realized in Nature, even if there is a preponderance of order in crystals and of disorder in swarms of dancing mosquitos.

3. Hierarchical integration of patterns

In the first (the material) and the second (the biological) phases of evolution, over and above the formation of patterns in restricted freedom, there occur several kinds of process of pattern integration. That is, several, originally unrelated entities of pattern coalesce and form patterned entities of higher complexity.

This union proceeds by way of several stages of integration, whereby, fundamentally, the entirety of each integration process serves as a component in the pattern of the next step of increasing complexity. All in all, a hierarchical organisation of patterns results, which will now be described briefly.

If we neglect the assembly of the elementary particles from the hypothetical quarks, then most of the matter that existed a short time after the "birth" (big bang) of our universe 10-20 billion years ago, at the outset of physics, consisted of protons and electrons; there were also some alpha particles, which were formed from protons in the course of the big bang. All other particles were very short-lived.

The first "integration" is the union of protons and neutrons (arising from a transformation of the protons) to give atomic nuclei. It takes place in the stars at temperatures of over a million degrees. It releases colossal amounts of energy – a point to which we shall return later. Even in the formation of this initial pattern, restrictions are seen. Only particular combinations of protons and neutrons lead to stable atomic nuclei. After the release of this minimal pattern by stellar pulsation or explosion, Coulombic forces attract and bind an appropriate number of electrons.

The second "integration", which connects atoms so as to give molecules, begins in interstellar space and goes into full spate with the formation of planets from the remains of earlier stars that have exploded. Again, there occur restrictions in the origins of these molecular patterns; again, stability is only possible for certain combinations of atoms and for particular patterns, that is, for particular chemical compounds. (Here, too, energy is released, though it is millions of times less than that released by nuclear reactions.)

In spite of their size and their preponderance, minerals play only a very minor rôle in further evolution. Much more important are the many-faceted molecular patterns of organic chemistry, which are found as single molecules in the water of the primordial ocean and accumulate continuously under the influence of geophysical events on the young planet.

Among the thousands of different molecules in this aqueous solution there are two families of molecules that are capable of further integration. Amino acids can be joined together so as to give polypeptides, and nucleotides to give nucleic acids. In both cases the linking is, interestingly, *one-dimensional*, that is, there arise unbranched chains of molecules.

The restriction on the growth of patterns lies in the fact that only a few, particular molecules, "members of the family", can function as links in the chain. However, there are practically no restraints on the number and sequence of these links. In what order they assemble is thus left to chance.

At this stage there occurs a remarkable "quasi-explosion" of potential multiplicity of pattern. A few elementary particles lead to 92 stable atomic nuclei. From these, thousands of different molecules can form. But with the third integration, a more than astronomical multiplicity is reached. A chain of 100 amino acids (there are 20 different ones) can produce $20^{100} \approx 10^{130}$ different sequences. In the entire universe, which most physicists regard as finite, this multitude can never be realized. There is just not enough matter. Physical measurements show that the detectable universe contains "only" some 10^{79} protons.

The next integration leads us out of the first, material phase of evolution over into the *second phase*, the development of living matter. In the "primeval soup" of the planet, some of these molecular chains came together to form a group – that is a pattern that has already become quite large and that possesses the surprising ability of replicating itself. We shall return to this remarkable event in Section 6.

The first living patterns collect component-molecules from their environment and join them together to make a copy of their own pattern. This copy is then in turn ready to copy the living pattern, and so forth.

It is presumably by way of a further union of such proto-organisms (protobionts) that a macroscopic pattern finally emerges that resembles present-day cells. Through this, or from this, the separate kingdoms of plants and animals develop.

Around one-and-a-half billion years ago, the integration of unicellular organisms to multicellular organisms took place. This must have happened at least twice, for plants and for animals respectively. The multicellular organism is initially a mere agglomerate of single cells that have arisen in division processes and simply remained adhering to one another.

In the course of further evolution different cells take over specialized functions. This differentiation is reiterated in the embryonic development of later multicellular organisms and leads finally to gigantic complexity in the pattern of beings living today.

With many species, yet another integration takes place. Even when individuals do not fuse into a spatially fixed entity, their interrelationship has become so close that the individual becomes a fully dependent member of a more efficient whole. This integration step has been reached by the colony-forming insects and above all by our own species. By division of labour and industrialisation, human society provides for its members an existence of steadily increasing comfort. It is based upon a new kind of relation between its individuals, that of communication by speech, a primitive form of which can also be seen among the colony-forming insects.

There is good reason to believe that the integration process is not yet complete, and that it may come to embrace the entire biological world on our planet. Even today, many plant and animal species, that are useful or enjoyable for mankind, are becoming almost completely dependent upon being tended by humans. It is becoming increasingly clear that the biological phase of evolution is approaching its end with rapid steps. The organisms that survive are not, as once was the case, those that are well adapted to their biological environment, but those that are adapted to humans. A third phase of evolution is becoming evident - a phase of development of thought. This too we shall return to discuss (Section 7).

4. Questions of energy

The two phase-changes of evolution in the universe are both characterised by a sudden increase in the need for energy, leading to rapid consumption of the energy resources available.

At the beginning of biological evolution, a massive supply of chemical energy lies stored in the vast number of molecules present in the aqueous "primeval soup". This supply is the result of many physical and chemical processes in the material phase.

Soon after the formation of the first patterns capable of replication, this picture changes. The need for energy-rich molecules increases exponentially, growing with the number of replicating units. Only these energy-rich molecules can be used for copying patterns or for providing the energy needed for making all the chemical bonds in the copy. Since this rapidly-rising consumption is compensated for only by a very slow, constant supply, energy resources diminish rapidly. Replication comes to a standstill. By growing exponentially, life on this planet has steered itself into an *inevitable* energy crisis.

The surprising way out of this dilemma is produced by patterns, originated by chance, that succeed in carrying out photosynthesis, that is, the synthesis of energy-rich molecules from small molecules by the direct use of absorbed light-energy from the sun. These proto-plants are the evolutionary starting-point of all present-day plants. They provide the ground for the existence of all living organisms, since all animals cover their need for energy and matter by eating plants or other animals. Nothing in this principle has changed up to the present day.

In later biological evolution, this photosynthesis is so successful that huge quantities of dead plant and animal matter lay down a new energy supply in the form of coal, mineral oil and natural gas. Only with the help of these supplies could humans develop modern industry and technology. But also in this transition from the biological to the intellectual phase of evolution, the requirement for energy is increasing so sharply that all supplies will soon be exhausted. Modern mankind is unaware that it consumes 80% of all its mineral oil supplies within one human life-span, and that in the course of at most 500 years it will consume the *entire* coal supply. Before that, completely new ways of producing energy must be found, unless all culture – all evolution – is to come to a halt.

The special rôle of consumers of these stocks of energy, which is played by our generation, obliges us to work scientifically to secure the existence of future generations. It would be tantamount to a crime if, instead of this, we allowed our greed both to exhaust present supplies and, for the first time in history, to mortgage future generations by maintaining our high standard of living at the price of depositing long-lived radioactive waste. All history to come would castigate us as the immoderate – the egotistical – indeed, the criminal generation.

The sun itself, or technically-produced microsuns – for which read fusion reactors – appear to be the only possible sources of the energy needed by mankind.

Naturalistically speaking, we need to realize that both the past evolution of all biological patterns and the possible future evolution of the super-pattern "humanity" has until now been fed by proton fusion, and must continue to be so. The formation of micro-patterns from elementary particles makes possible the preservation and further development of the giant pattern.

Our universe began with an inconceivable wealth of energy, of which up to now only a few per cent has been consumed. This started not with atoms or molecules, but with single elementary particles. The beginning of the arrangement into pattern, the formation of atomic nuclei, releases energy in enormous quantities, of which the largest patterns to date have only been able to use the minutest fraction for their own sustenance and propagation. Almost all the energy goes to waste as radiation in the outer reaches of space. But, twice in the course of evolution, energy reserves have been laid down, on the basis of which new break-throughs have become possible.

5. Information and pattern

The concept of information is of just as much, if not more, importance for evolution as that of energy. However, it can easily lead to misunderstanding. In probability theory and communication technology, "information" is defined as a measure of the dependence of two random quantities. This is related to, but not identical with, its meaning in everyday speech, which corresponds to something like "knowledge" or "message" and is specially associated with the "meaning" of the message. In order to emphasize this distinction, we speak of the "semantic" and the "pragmatic" aspects of information. In biology it has become usual to denote the hereditary matter of an organism as "genetic" information. This is clearly an allusion to the possibility that, just as a statement in a language possesses "meaning", such information can have a concrete effect.

Since patterns, too, can have an effect, when they come into a relationship with other patterns, the concepts of "pattern" and "information" are obviously closely related. At any rate, information is only conceivable as a pattern and can be defined as the specific potential effect this pattern has upon another pattern.

If we consider patterns in the course of evolution, we must – in accordance with its division into phases – also distinguish patterns of three qualities. The patterns of the material phase, alpha particles to molecules, make up the *patterns of the first kind*. Their principal property is the tendency of uniting to give larger patterns.

With the beginning of life, *patterns of the second kind* appear, which show a further property that raises them out of the plethora of other material patterns: the property of self-replication. To a pattern with this ability we would ascribe "life"; in such a pattern resides "genetic information". Concepts such as "life", "self-replication" and "genetic information" are fundamentally nothing other than this new *dynamic force* of certain complicated patterns – patterns of the second kind.

These are assembled from a myriad of molecular part-patterns (all patterns of the first kind), which, however, are selected and integrated to give a new whole, in such a way that this has the capacity of generating new, (nearly) identical patterns. This new possibility is based on the presence of genetic information laid down in the nucleic acids and the simultaneous existence of structures that fit them and that both replicate this information and, by transferring it to protein structures, make it operative.

The biological phase is the history of development of these patterns of the second kind, whose size increases, in the space of four billion years, by some 20

(!) powers of ten. The growth in complexity closely connected with this enables multicellular organisms to develop a brain, which becomes the starting-points for yet another, a third group of patterns.

What are these *patterns of the third kind*, and what criterion – which new ability – distinguishes them from the earlier patterns of the biological phase? As patterns of the third kind I would like to denote those structures in which "intellectual information" is laid down – the biological structures of the memory, in which experience and knowledge are stored. These are the engrams in the giant circuit of the nerve cells of the brain.

Patterns of the third kind thus exist as partial areas in larger biological patterns, which so to speak constitute the raw material from which a pattern of the third kind is built up. (The analogy with biological patterns, built up on the raw material of material patterns, is evident.)

Biological patterns have the tendency to multiply by a mechanism of self-replication. The parent patterns are passed on to the daughter structures and only to these. Patterns of the third kind have likewise the tendency to propagate themselves. For this they employ a new mechanism that sets them apart from the other biological patterns.

These patterns have their first successes in self-propagation with the help of the social and imitatory instincts of higher animals. For example, the experience of where water can be found in times of drought is taken by young animals from their elders, simply by going along with them. The engram "there is water at a certain place" thus arises from their "own" experience and spreads out over more individual brains.

The transfer of patterns of the third kind comes into its own with the start of human language. *Communication* has the same significance for the spreading of "intellectual" patterns as replication has for the spreading of biological ones. However, the method of the new pattern-type is much more effective, since the transfer is not restricted to biological descendants, – and freshly-formed engrams can be passed on at once – with the help of interpreters, even over linguistic boundaries.

Through the medium of language, patterns of the third kind are passed on from person to person and from generation to generation. Just as genetic information in the pattern of the second kind contains structures for its reading, that is, for its effective realization, so the intellectual information in the brain possesses an apparatus for its own reading, its manipulation and finally its conversion into external action. For this – through the nervous network connected with this control center – practically the entire organism is employed.

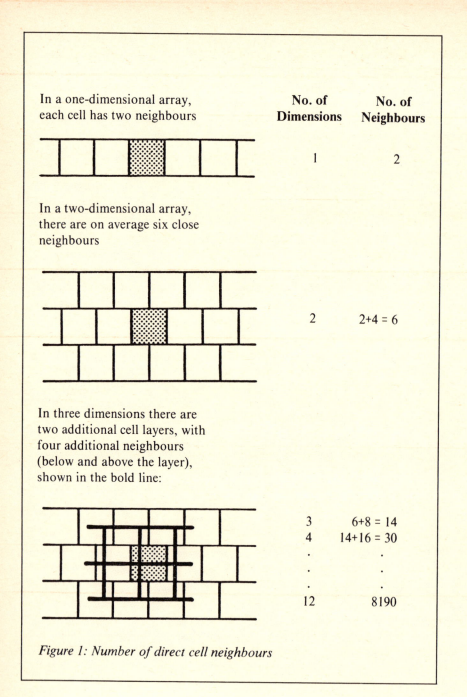

In a one-dimensional array, each cell has two neighbours

In a two-dimensional array, there are on average six close neighbours

In three dimensions there are two additional cell layers, with four additional neighbours (below and above the layer), shown in the bold line:

No. of Dimensions	No. of Neighbours
1	2
2	2+4 = 6
3	6+8 = 14
4	14+16 = 30
.	.
.	.
.	.
12	8190

Figure 1: Number of direct cell neighbours

The achievements of this "information-processing machine" are, however, imcomparably greater than those of genetic information. Their key ability is that of putting intellectual information into other pattern-forms.

The pattern of the third kind – originally an engram in a brain - can be converted into language, that is, into a representation built up in a completely different way, a sequence of sounds in time. This is in turn convertible into writing, again a sequence-pattern of symbols. When this is heard or read, another transformation of patterns takes place. A multitude of nerve connections convey impulses in time and space into the brain, in which finally – although the nerve excitation patterns coming from the eye and from the ear are completely different – they are reconverted into engrams in the brain.

We may assume that the "morphology" of the engrams possess no similarity from brain to brain – yet they *mean the same thing*. (Our knowledge of the brain is not sufficient to allow serious statements about the morphology of engrams.)

If we look for the brain's unique characteristic, it is certainly the multitude of multiply-branched neurone connections. A brain cell is in direct contact with thousands of others, by the branching of its axons. In a certain sense, the brain is thus a structure with 12 spatial dimensions. How is this to be understood?

In a normal three-dimensional tissue, a cell will on average have some 14 direct neighbours, cells with which it is in direct contact and with which it can thus exchange information. If we extend the series of numbers in Figure 1 to the 10,000 "immediate neighbours" of a brain cell, this corresponds to a 12-dimensional space in terms of the normal packing of cells in a tissue.

In spite of our great ignorance about the function of the brain, it is clear what new powers of self-propagation patterns have gained by this method of communication, especially when account is taken of the multitude of secondary patterns of a material nature that are produced by intellectual patterns – houses and machines, books and computers.

6. The first change of phase

In the entire course of evolution, there are two periods of especial importance: the transition from the material to the biological phase, i.e., the origin of life, and later the transition from the biological to the intellectual phase of evolution – a process that began basically with the first linguistic communication and culminates in our own life-time.

Only in the last few decades has "the origin of life" moved over into the area of serious scientific hypotheses, thanks to the achievements of molecular genetics. Three aspects lead into our discussion:

We must not expect that science will in the foreseeable future be in a position to explain by unassailable logical proof the actual events of these historical processes. But it is possible to develop a scientifically-based hypothesis that outlines how such a beginning could be conceived. The refutation of particular ideas is also possible, if these turn out to be in contradiction with physico-chemical data or mathematically unsound.

No explanation can skirt past the need to postulate the occurrence of some seemingly implausible events. The task of science is simply to keep the "miracle" of the origin of life as small as possible, that is, to demonstrate that the obvious improbability of the event is compensated by the large number of possible trials, so that on balance the first appearance of living – that is to say replicative – structures ultimately appears plausible.

Every model of the origin of life must proceed from the realities of present-day biology. Fundamental principles such as the replication of information in the form of nucleic acids, and their translation into polypeptide chains by the use of a code or dictionary, can indeed be simplified down to their basic core, but it is impossible to assume that such basic principles have been altered in the course of evolution. Such an experiment by Nature would collapse in ruins. To give an example: it would be unthinkable that the present-day triplet pattern of the code (three nucleotides of a nucleic acid determine one amino acid of a polypeptide) only arose at a later point in time, before which perhaps merely a doublet pattern was present. However, the assumption that at the beginning only a few (4 or even 2) amino acids could be coded for is both possible and indeed necessary.

So how is the origin of life to be understood, according to modern knowledge? We know that physico-chemical events on our prebiotic planet led to amino acids and nucleotides, and that polypeptides with random sequences of amino acids could form spontaneously. We also know that enzymes exist today that are able to join nucleotides up into chains and even to replicate these chains.[1] It is thus conceivable that, among the huge number of spontaneously-formed polypeptides there were also occasionally ones that possessed a similar (very imperfect) ability to produce and replicate nucleic acids. On account of its easier replicability, for a given stability, ribonucleic acid (RNA) is preferred over deoxyribonucleic acid (DNA) by most experts in this field.[2]

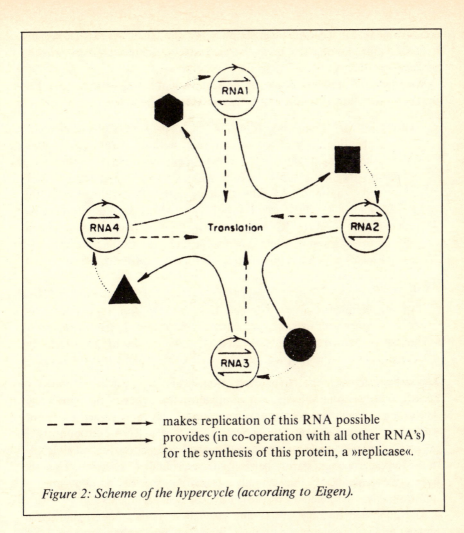

makes replication of this RNA possible

provides (in co-operation with all other RNA's) for the synthesis of this protein, a »replicase«.

Figure 2: Scheme of the hypercycle (according to Eigen).

Already in this period of evolution, still pre-biotic, a "selection" of certain structures takes place. The decisive criterion for the "survival" of a molecular chain is its stability against, for example, spontaneous decomposition or hydrolysis. By this means, chains with secondary structure (folding) are selected. Among RNA chains, GC-rich polymers will prevail, on account of their stronger binding.

The replication of such RNA is quite accurate, even without an enzyme. An incorrect base is incorporated only every 50th to 100th time.[3] It is therefore conceivable that in a certain local region many, similar RNAs exist, especially if in this area, among the many polypeptides present, some promote the replication of RNA.[6]

We thus stand at the threshold, at the beginning of biological evolution. For the events to follow there are two different conceptual models:

> The "classical" model, according to which "packages" of nucleic acids and polpeptides (denoted by various authors [4] as coacervates, microspheres, aggregates, etc.) are formed, and where several such structures are joined randomly to give an assembly that guarantees their continued proximity and thus makes possible the replication of the RNAs and also the formation of new proteins – a co-operative achievement of several RNA chains. Possibly such packages can then be divided up by physical effect. With some luck, two similar packages can arise, each of which has inherited the ability to transfer this "similarity".

> In the "hypercycle" model, suggested by Eigen in 1971 [5], several RNAs become coupled to give not a spatial bundle but a *functional* unit. How this is conceived in detail is clarified in Figure 2. The number of hypercyclic members is not fixed. It can, according to Eigen, be expanded or reduced at will (minimum 2 x 2 complementary RNAs).

The debate between the "hypercycle model" and the "package model" is decided by Eigen and Schuster [6] unambiguously in favour of the hypercycle. According to their argument, the package model inevitably comes to grief on account of internal competition between the different RNAs. Proponents of the package model would reply that the necessary bifunctionality* of all RNAs in the hypercycle could hardly be realized, on grounds of selection. Thus the hypercycle remains an intellectually fascinating speculation, but must – unfortunately – definetely be discarded by genetical arguments[8].

The interested layman will at any rate observe that modern molecular biology no longer regards the origin of life as an "unsearchable miracle", but that there is general agreement, in spite of discrepancy of detail, that the origin of life can be made plausible, or even perhaps shown to be a necessity, on the basis of the admittedly very remarkable properties of complex molecules. The gate to the evolution of living matter is thus flung open. Mutation and selection lead inevitably to the further development of this beginning.

---

* Each RNA must show specificity for "its" replicase and at the same time code for the next replicase.

7. The second change of phase

The transition from material to biological evolution – from patterns of the first to those of the second kind – took place in many, tiny steps over long reaches of time. In this period of overlap, it is a matter of taste which of the small steps of progress is associated with the "actual" origin of life. The physico-chemical properties of the participating patterns of the first kind were, by their gradual integration to give patterns of the second kind, not put out of action, but instead taken into account and incorporated into the programme of events in such a way that at the end of all elementary processes stood the completed replication of the pattern.

The appearance of patterns of the third kind also required a long phase of preparation. Basically, the evolution of animal multicellular organisms is just an evolution of better sensory organs and a more efficient central nervous system. Individual learning from experience begins – as training experiments show – on a very low level. By group formation, memory content can later be transferred from one individual to another. Genetic information provides the basis upon which brains with this capability arise during embryonal development.

The actual breakthrough to the propagative capacity of patterns of the third kind occurs with the beginning of human linguistic communication. This is accelerated greatly by the invention of handwriting and later of printing.

It is important to recognise that both information systems (genetic and intellectual) contain an inevitable inner drive towards their own perfection. In the principle of mutation – i.e. the modification of a pattern of the second kind in a random direction – and in the essence of selection – the competition of all these variants for the most successful, i.e., above all, the fastest replication – there lies clearly and necessarily a development towards an ever-greater quantity of information and to an ever-better handling of this information. Patterns of the second kind must develop to greater and greater achievement levels, in competition with one another.

The properties of patterns of the third kind seem to lead to a similar situation. The perpetual passing-on of intellectual information leads to its steady accumulation. This in turn generates a need for expanded storage capacity, which itself leads to the solution of this task: first, the invention of written records gives the individual an "extra memory", and then printing makes possible the conveying of this stored information to arbitrarily many other individuals. Intellectual information has thus crossed boundaries which were previously imposed by the structure of the brain, as generated by genetic information. With the introduction of writing, the system of intellectual information takes, to a certain extent, its future development into its own hands. To do this, it employs lower-level genetic information, just as this in turn once used patterns of the first kind, yet it no longer allows its potential to be limited by the possibilities of the low level.

This new freedom allows an accelerated growth of information – pure and applied science become possible. Development reaches a pace with which that of the biological phase can no longer be compared. By telegraph and, shortly after, by wireless communication, information can be broadcast over vast distances without loss of time. Experience acquired in electronics very soon leads to the last, missing step in the process of emancipation of intellectual information: 6000 years after the unlimited expansion of the storage capacity of the human brain through writing, the development of computers since 1941 has set a process in motion which allows even the genetically-conditioned limits of human information processing to be exceeded. Our brain, which is the course of several million years of biological evolution developed from that of our animal predecessors, has now begun to expand its own potential for achievement by the construction of "additional brains". Since this is inevitably an escalating process, it is clear that each existing generation of computers assists in the development of the next, more powerful computer-generation; the computer aids both the design and the production of its successor.

If we regard evolution as perpetual reproduction, improved processing and increasing efficiency of information – and that is the most general and most fundamental way of regarding it – then it becomes clear what a painfully unique age of evolutionary break-through we live in. A glance at the successes and problems of our time makes this clear: without computers (robots) our present-day standard of living, in spite of decreasing working hours, would be impossible. But without computers we would not have the problem of unemployment. Without computers, the modern bureaucratization of our existence would be unthinkable; but man would not have stepped onto the moon. And it is also computers that make modern weapon technology so fundamentally threatening for human existence.

Mankind of today is seeking to solve all these problems using the methods of yesterday, because it has not yet understood that it has been sucked up into a tornado of evolution. Solutions can only become possible when this fact is fully recognised and taken account of.

At a first glance, it may appear that we can save ourselves from our present-day problems by destroying all computers – as the iconoclasts once did. But this would be a fatal error. No-one can hold up the progress of evolution. Soon only those peoples or societies would be left that had found out how to co-exist in harmony with the new "supplementary brain".

Have we in this century crossed the threshold to a third phase of evolution?

Ultimately, this is again a question of definition. It is certain that problems of the change of phase have in our lifetime become unprecedentedly acute. But one can hardly claim that we have already attained a harmonious integration of our biological past with the new abilities of patterns of the third kind. It is by no means certain that the human race will be able to steer their space-ship Earth back into calm waters. In my own opinion, we should not speak of having attained the third phase of evolution until Marxists can see the fulfilment of their dream of a classless society, or Christians theirs of a Christendom of true brotherly love.

In the days since the debate over Lamarck's conception of the "inheritance of acquired characteristics", at the beginning of the 19th century, two opinions have clashed repeatedly both in scientific and in political circles. These could be termed the "optimistic" and "pessimistic" viewpoints, or perhaps the "environment" and the "heredity" hypotheses.

One side has represented and continues to represent the belief that a person's character and intelligence are formed through pedagogical and psychological influences in their environment, and thus are alterable in any desired direction.

The other side has emphasized, and still does, the fatalistic determination of human characteristics by the relevant elements of heredity: a biological legacy from millions of years of animal behaviour cannot be eliminated even by the most well-meaning efforts.

It is very probable that, not long from now, the future of the human race will be decided by this alternative. This makes it all the more important to make clear to teachers, psychologists and the political left that genetic information really does exist and that its effect permeate human behaviour down to many of its smallest details. On the other side, biologists and the politically conservative must be convinced that on the intellectual level of human existence a second and increasingly strong information system exerts an influence that, in conjunction with the genetic system, ultimately determines our reactions and our characteristics.

Who ever directs his attention exclusively to one system or to the other will inevitably end up by drawing false conclusions. However, how the balance of genetic plus intellectual information will come to look cannot be decided on the basis of present-day knowledge, because of the complexity of the interactions involved.

8. Insight or global suicide

Never before has the human race stood at the edge of such an abyss as it does today. Will it learn to fly, and rise up to real humanity, or will it plunge into the depths – sweep itself off this planet? We already possess the weapon capacity to do this.

Our present situation was unavoidable. It will, with high probabiblity, also arise on other inhabited planets when these arrive at the transition from biological to intellectual evolution.

Our problem lies simply in the fact that the attitudes and values of yesterday, which we humans developed at the end of biological evolution (and which alone were appropriate to bring us on to our position of today) now collide with the technical possibilities of tomorrow, which characterize a completely new phase of evolution. The thinking of yesterday and the technology of tomorrow cannot be reconciled in a prolonged co-existence.

As was once already the case, at the transition from material to biological evolution, that which yesterday was so useful and stimulating for evolution tomorrow becomes a deadly danger. As a matter of life or death, we must reorient our thinking today. Three detailed examples:

Every biological species reaches by selection a level of fertility that is just right to allow its population to increase slowly. A cow-elephant brings about 4 calves into the world during her life-time, while a she-mouse produces 6-10 progeny every 4 weeks. The greater the threat to a species, the greater is its fertility. Man, too, arose out of a biological world of this kind, with a birth rate of 6-8 children per mother. Accidents, famine and above all infectious diseases allowed an average of about two of these to survive. The species was in biological equilibrium. It had sufficient space for its population to live in.

But then intellectual information grew, from that of the medicine-man to that of the doctor for infectious diseases. Parallel to this, the population of Europe and, a little later, that of the rest of the world, grew rapidly. The present-day population of 5 billion will certainly rise to at least 10 billion (neglecting major catastrophes). Our planet could feed all these, but our energy supplies and raw materials are limited, and everyone wants the standard of living enjoyed by the rich. The problem of over-population is not a direct threat to the existence of the species *Homo sapiens*, but it is a major factor in worsening almost all the other problems of our time. That which formerly was biologically useful, when overlaid with modern knowledge, leads us into a crisis.

Early man was a collector. Whatever he found that could be used, he dragged off to his cave. He needed water supplies, nutrition, skins, wood, and also suitable stones that could be made into scrapers or hand-held axes. He collected plants, in order to extract fibres, or juices, with which he could paint himself for festivals. He wanted to possess everything and to drag it home. And that was good. His supplies helped him through the long winters and the dry summers.

But with his knowledge grew his prosperity, and with it his need – he wanted more and more. And then came technology, production by machines. And we still want everything – more and more humans want more and more.... How much longer can this go on?

Fear was the "Greek gift" of the growing intelligence of mankind. From fear grew aggression, which no longer stopped short of the killing of fellow-humans. But precisely that was necessary. A war against other hordes guaranteed food and living-space. The more intelligent hordes possessed the better weapons – better communication and co-ordination – which gave them the victory. They, the intelligent, the warlike, the fearful survived. So men remained in perpetual preparedness for war and fear of their neighbours, who were of course so aggressive and so cunning. They still think in the same way – on both sides.

But the ABC of mass destruction has kept pace with all other developments. He who shoots first today, dies an hour later – or wastes away, weeks or years later. Large-scale war has become meaningless: no-one now can "defend his home country" – one can merely destroy the enemy's with equal thoroughness. How can we break open the vicious circle of escalation of deterrents? Will we, after two thousand years of deafness, finally listen to Jesus of Nazareth saying: "Put your sword into its sheath. For he who takes the sword shall perish by the sword." Will we learn at last? The time-bomb is ticking. All the computers are programmed.

We have been sucked into a tornado of evolution. None of yesterday's recipes can save humanity.

We are therefore confronted with the question of whether intellectual information will be strong enough to overcome our biologically-implanted fear, our accustomed resort to violence in the face of apparently insoluble contradictions, our intolerance of other interests and opinions. Can mankind be changed quickly and fundamentally enough?

I am hopeful. I build on the connection between the instinct of self-preservation (genetic) and reason (intellectual).

9. Chance and Law

When one stands before the great edifice of the natural sciences, the question forces itself on one: is evolution just the product of coincidences – we have mentioned them often enough – and is evolution open-ended? Or is it a process that continues along a path given by natural laws towards a defined goal? To me this question seems equivalent to another, namely: has this universe, has this evolution – has our human existence any meaning?

With such a question, we move into the area bounding science and religion. We must therefore be especially careful not to fall foul of prejudice. So we start by asking simply: has evolution, growing out of innumerable random events (conditional chance, with restriction by that which already exists) a steady direction? The answer is an unambiguous "yes". In all three phases we see the growth of patterns, of information and the ability of the latter to generate further patterns. Indeed, this growth is faster than exponential.[7]

Everywhere in the universe there arise, in obedience to the laws of physics and chemistry, first atoms and then molecules. On suitable planets – as the example of the Earth demonstrates – patterns of the second kind, that is, living organisms, can develop. No-one knows how probable this is. But that is not so important, if only enough planets and enough time are available.

The capacity of replication – of randomly-determined, inaccurate replication – leads inevitably to a competition between organisms, if nutrient or another important factor is in limited supply. The best-performing organism, usually the one with most genetic information, will inevitably prevail.

As soon as the multicellular animal, organism has developed sensory organs and a nervous system, its performance will affect decisively its survival. Again, the greater storage capacity – now for intellectual information – and its processing machinery is led inevitably on to greater perfection.

In summary, material evolution proceeds spontaneously; in the biological and apparently also in the intellectual phases there arise, from the principles of replication and communication respectively, constraints that automatically – that is, following natural law – lead to the multiplication of information. Once moving, evolution continues to run as on rails, even though there are many sidings and death ends.

The statement that evolution has a direction (towards ever greater complexity of pattern) must not be confused with the idea that evolution is aimed towards the human being. On other planets it may lead to beings quite different from those on the Earth. But I regard it as an inescapable fact that all biological evolution is based on the principle of pattern replication, and that the next phase, that of the communication of information, can only begin on the basis of a highly-developed biological evolution.

Where does the deeper cause of all evolutionary events lie? Science can only give one answer. *Evolution is a consequence of the initial conditions of our universe and of the properties of matter.*

If our universe had "begun differently", for example, with completed atoms instead of elementary particles, then there would be no evolution, because there would be no shining sun, without which life would be inconceivable. If the properties of matter were different, if for example gravity did not exist, then there would be no stars or planets – or if molecules could not be joined up in chains – there would be no evolution. Or – or – or ...

Science could give a long list of phenomena without which evolution would never have taken place – without angular momentum all the matter in a galaxy would collapse to a huge chunk – to a gigantic black hole. Without the remarkable dielectric properties of water (dielectric constant) or without the antiparallel nature of complementary nucleic acid chains – there would be no biological evolution!

The beginning is the ground of everything – the law. Chance is the method of reaching the goal.

To say more would mean to depart from the terrain of the natural sciences. But that is not my task today.

References

1. Sumper, M. and R. Luce (1975), Proc. Natl. Acad. Sci U.S., 72, 162.
2. Crick, F. C. R. et al. (1976), *Origins of Life 7*, 389.
3. Pörschke, D., in Pecht & Rigler edts. (1977), *Chemical Relaxation in Molecular Biology*, Springer, Heidelberg, 191.
4. Fox, S. W., *Nature* 205, 328 (1965).
   Oparin, A. J. (1968), *Genesis and Evolutionary Development of Life*. Academic Press, New York.
5. Eigen, M., *Naturwissenschaft 58*, 465 (1971).
6. Eigen, M. and Schuster, P., *Naturwissenschaft 64*, 541 (1977) *65*, 7 and 341 (1978).
7. Bresch, C. (1978), *Zwischenstufe Leben*. Piper, München, 266ff.
8. Bresch, C. et al. (1980), J. theor. Bid. 85, 399.

Molecular Evolution and the Origin of Life

Bernd-Olaf Küppers

The Origin of Life

The origin of life has many scientific aspects, and these, taken together, build up a mosaic picture of a phenomenon unique in the evolutionary history of the earth. The chemical aspects of this have particular importance, since they allow fundamental attributes of living matter to be seen at a molecular level.

The key materials of biological systems are two classes of biological macromolecule: the nucleic acids and the proteins. The deoxyribonucleic acids (abbreviation, DNA) are long, threadlike molecules that are localised in the cell and that carry the entire hereditary information (the genes) of every organism. This hereditary information is encoded by the particular sequence of the four basic building-blocks of nucleic acid, in a way similar to that in which a written sentence is encoded by its particular sequence of letters. DNA is built up from only four classes of subunit (nucleotide). The nucleotides are the "letters" of genetic writing. They are denoted by the initial letters of their chemical names. The linear sequence of the nucleic acid building-blocks encodes the entire genetic information of an organism. Each code-word consists of three genetic letters and contains the order for one protein building-block. The building-blocks of the proteins are the twenty naturally-occurring amino acids. The blueprint for protein chains is thus laid down in a molecular language that is uniform for all organisms. Under the physico-chemical conditions of its environment in the cell, the protein chain folds into a three-dimensional, biologically functional structure. The proteins control the construction and metabolism of the entire cell, and they also ensure that, in the processes of inheritance, the DNA is copied and passed on to the daughter cells. Since the blueprints for all proteins are contained in their DNA, there is a mutual dependence between DNA and protein, from which, ultimately, all cellular processes result.

Even a simple bacterial cell is extraordinarily complex: bacterial DNA consists of about four million building-blocks and encodes some two to three thousand different protein structures. Since there are four classes of DNA building-blocks, there are around $10^{2.4\text{million}}$ sequences possible for bacterial DNA, of which, however, only a tiny fraction may be presumed to carry biologically meaningful information. The number of possible alternative sequences is a measure of the complexity of the bacterial blueprint, and shows clearly where the issue of the origin of life really lies. The question to be answered is how, in the initial phase of evolution, some specific DNA sequences could have been selected out of an unimaginable number of chemically equivalent molecular variants. Here we presuppose that molecules with the complexity of a nucleic acid could have arisen at all, under the reaction conditions of the prebiotic earth. This is a major issue in prebiotic chemistry, and can be regarded, since the classical experiments of the American biochemist Stanley Miller, as solved in principle.

The central question with regard to the problem of the origin of biological information lies on a higher level: how did the generation of *specific* DNA sequences come about? Generation by chance is excluded, by reason of its extremely low expectation probability. Equally improbable is the existence of hidden natural laws that are specific for life processes and have directed the synthesis of biologically meaningful DNA sequences.

The Principle of Molecular Evolution
In contrast, the approach suggested by Manfred Eigen runs entirely within the boundaries of traditional science. Eigen describes the process of the origin of biological information as a material "learning process", in the course of which the structures and functions of biological macromolecules are optimised step by step. The basic principle of such *molecular evolution* can be explained with the aid of a thought experiment, as follows.

Consider any carrier of biological information. Let this carry the information needed for the construction of a primitive organism, a bacterial cell for example. On the basis of present-day values, at least four million molecular symbols (nucleotides) are needed for this. As already mentioned, a DNA molecule of this capacity has $10^{2.4 \text{ million}}$ alternative sequences. The probability of obtaining a defined sequence by means of a "blind" random synthesis is as low as that of creating a complete textbook of biology by taking a random sequence of letters.

However, we can instead proceed systematically. In this case, we would start from an arbitrary, random sequence and allow the symbol at each of the four million positions to vary (i.e., mutate) until it is occupied in a way optimal for the "target sequence". A "correct" building-block would be fixed, and its position in the sequence excluded from further mutation. With four types of DNA building-blocks, roughly every fourth experiment would be successful, so that even a target sequence with the complexity of a bacterial blueprint could be reached within the realistic compass of some 16 million "trials". Thus the method of selection is vastly superior to the method of pure chance.

The principle behind this procedure of molecular optimisation is the principle of natural selection put forward by Charles Darwin. The first physical foundation for it was given, and applied to the evolution of biological macromolecules, by Manfred Eigen. According to this, the selective reinforcement of particular, *a priori* improbable structures is based on a scale of value that is deducible from the chemical-kinetic properties of these macromolecules. The scale of value defines at the same time a gradient of evolution, along which the system spontaneously optimises itself. Every distribution of information carriers represents a level of value that is defined by the best-adapted information sequence present. All information carriers whose selection value lies below the average of a certain dynamic function of the selection values become excluded from the process of self-organisation. Thus the average level of value becomes higher and higher. The best-adapted information carriers within a distribution are those that can perpetuate themselves optimally by reproduction under the given environmental conditions. Natural selection is thus an extremum principle, deducible from material properties. It begins on the molecular and *a priori* non-living level, and it represents an important pre-requisite for the formation of living structures.

The Hypercycle
The more errors there are that arise in genetic information transfer, the greater is the number of variants that are subjected to evaluation in the selection process and, thus, the greater is the speed of evolutionary progress. However, the accumulation of errors leads to a blurring of the information. Above a certain, critical error rate, the *convergent* process of the generation of information turns into a *divergent* process of uncontrolled error accumulation, and the result is the collapse and dissipation of all the information collected in the progress of evolution.

The error threshold must have had fundamental significance for the origin of life. Exact analysis has shown that without the help of complex copying machines (see below), on average not more than one hundred genetic symbols can be transferred reproducibly under selection pressure. However, we know that the plan for the construction of such a reproduction apparatus would certainly demand well over a hundred genetic symbols; it could therefore only arise in an evolutionary way, and not by chance. The information capacity of individual nucleic acids was thus highly restricted. The barrier between living and non-living systems set up by the natural error threshold, could only have been overcome by co-operative reaction mechanisms between biological macromolecules. A kinetically simple system that possesses such properties is the so-called "hypercycle" (cf. p. XX). This is a special functional unit, made up of nucleic acids and proteins, by means of which a quantity of information exceeding the limit of the information threshold can be passed on reproducibly. The hypercycle arises through the cyclical connection of individual reaction cycles. Each single cycle represents a complementary pair of nucleic acids that reproduces itself by cross-catalysis. The reproduction is promoted by coupling factors, which increase the rate and/or accuracy of reproduction and/or lower the rate of decay of their respective target cycles. The coupling factors are enzymes, that is, catalytically active proteins. Each ensemble of nucleic acids contains the coded information for at least one coupling factor, which influences the next reaction cycle.

The cyclical connection forces the individual cycles, that otherwise would compete, to co-operate with each other. Although the length at the seperate nucleic acids, and thus their individual information content, is limited, the co-existence of all n individual cycles provides for the *reproducible* transmission of n times as much information as that contained in a single cycle. The hypercycle must be seen as a fore-runner of the biosynthetic cycle of the living cell. It bridges the gap between dead and living matter.

At the Threshold of the Living

The principal features of the theory of molecular evolution developed by Manfred Eigen and his colleagues can today be tested experimentally. Evolution experiments have been carried out on bacteriophage Q_β, a virus that attacks only bacteria. The genetic material of this virus consists of a substance that both chemically and biologically is closely related to DNA: it is called ribonucleic acid or, for short, RNA. After the infection of bacteria with Q_β phages, the host cell synthesizes a new protein that is encoded by the viral RNA and that leads to a many-fold replication of this RNA. The protein, known to biochemists as *replicase*, operates by running along the viral RNA and, as it goes, reading the viral nucleotide sequence and constructing a copy from energy-rich nucleotides. For physical reasons, a certain number of erroneous copies (mutants) occurs.

In 1965, the American molecular biologist Sol Spiegelman succeeded in isolating replicase from infected bacteria. This step led to a series of spectacular experiments. For example: In a suitable nutrient solution containing, besides other ingredients, energy-rich RNA building-blocks and the catalytic replicase, viral RNA could be replicated at will and thus could "come to life" outside the host cell. This scientific feat of Sol Spiegelman and his colleagues opened up undreamed-of possibilities for research into evolution, since now the principles of the origin and molecular development of life could be studied in the test-tube.

"Addicted" Molecules

The point of departure for experimental studies, currently being carried out at the Max-Planck-lustitute of Biophysical Chemistry in Göttingen is a finding that has long been known to Q_β-experts. If Q_β replicase is allowed to stand in a nutrient medium for some minutes, a synthesis of RNA is seen, even though the reaction has not been started by inclusion of RNA to be copied. For a long time it was believed that this "blind reaction" was due to the presence of minute traces of "natural" RNA present as a contaminant. All attempts to eliminate this by intensive re-purification of the replicase resulted in failure. Thus the suspicion became strengthened that the blind reaction took place without the participation of natural RNA. This result surprised molecular biologists, among whom it was generally accepted that the construction of new genetic material can only be based upon the structure of existing genetic material.

Analysis of the products of several blind reactions shows that different reaction conditions as a rule lead to different RNA molecule as products, whereas within a particular preparation the products are uniform. This observation can be interpreted in terms of the selection principle. In the initial phase of the blind reaction, the replicase molecules appear to synthesize spontaneously (de novo) a random spectrum of RNA structures. All species that are equipped with the property of self-replication compete for "unoccupied" replicase molecules. It follows, that the winners are those RNA species which under the given reaction conditions have the best growth properties and thus most often bar their competitors from access to the replicase molecules.

The significance of the selection principle for the origin and evolution of biological macromolecules was demonstrated in a series of impressive experiments. We give one example. For a long time, biochemists have been acquainted with substances that are able to block completely the replication of genetic material. Among these are certain dyes. If a de novo reaction is started in the presence of a high concentration of the poisonous dye, self-replicating RNA molecules are still found in the reaction mixture after a few hours' incubation. It can be shown that the RNA molecules that have arisen in their doped environment are not only resistant against the dye – they are even dependent upon it. If they are transferred to a normal (drug-free) nutrition medium, they are found to be incapable of self-replication.

With experiments of this kind, it was shown for the first time that, under certain conditions, natural selection in the Darwinian sense appears on the pre-biological level of macromolecules, and that this leads to precisely the kinds of adaptive behaviour that are postulated by the theory of molecular evolution.

The Evolution of Mechanisms of Evolution

Diether Sperlich

The question how the mechanisms of evolution evolved might be understood as an investigation of whether the mechanisms of our own origin are basically the same as for all the other organisms or whether a mechanism of higher rank and complexity, or even of a new quality, can be found the closer the process of evolution comes to the origin of man. The problem certainly has a general interest in this way which goes beyond the specific discussions of biologists.

It has become common to divide the process of evolution into four periods:

physical evolution	- 17 to 4.5 billions (= 10^9) of years ago
chemical evolution	- 4.5 to 3.0 billions of years ago
organic evolution	- 3.0 billions of years $\rightarrow$ present
cultural or super- organic evolution	- 0.001 billions of years $\rightarrow$ present

It is thought that physical evolution started some 17 billions of years ago with the "big bang". Later, protogalaxies, galaxies, cluster of stars and stars arose by the effects of gravitation. Among these, our sun originated almost simultaneously with the planets including our own planet, the earth. Whether any kind of pre-evolutionary mechanisms were acting at this time remains open. Yet, it is certain that the physical conditions as well as the chemical composition of the earth are the result of this period of evolution.

No distinct mechanism of evolution can be seen in the first part of chemical evolution either. No doubt – very narrow and extremely specific predispositions existed that allowed organic molecules, including nucleic acids, proteins and lipids, to arise by physico-chemical processes. They accumulated to a certain concentration in the ocean of the primitive earth. Whenever these molecules started self-replication is unknown. In any case, the beginning of self-reproduction was also the beginning of evolution in the biological sense. We shall not deal with the problem here whether life originated on our planet by chance or by necessity but can refer to the work of M. Eigen and his colleagues (Eigen et al., 1981). In particular, from their work on the self-organization of matter, it becomes evident that the main principles acting in auto-replicating systems are "stabilization" as well as "destabilization", "cooperation" as well as "competition", and these result in deterministic or stochastic processes. As we shall see later all these forces of early evolution also again become apparent in the organic evolution.

The main purpose of the present discussion is to investigate the mechanisms of organic evolution in the third part of the evolutionary process and to see whether these mechanisms themselves evolved. There are, however, two preliminary points that should be considered. The first is rather simple but might be important to avoid confusion and misunderstanding. It concerns the possibility of finding a development of the mechanisms which reflects no more than the development of our technical abilities and of our increasing knowledge. The new findings of molecular biology especially has brought us to understand evolution now much better than a few years ago. In connection with this a number of new and hitherto unknown mechanisms of evolution became visible. This is certainly very exciting but has nothing to do with our original question.

The second point is more serious and will directly influence our discussion. It comes from the fact that the evolutionary process of higher organisms is composed of several elements and proceeds differently at different levels of complexity. A good example is the realisation that evolutionary changes at the molecular level are mainly governed by stochastic processes, while morphological or functional changes are due to the simultaneous deterministic effects of directional selection. This means that an evolutionary mechanism acting at one level of complexity does not necessarily become visible on another.

Evolution was classically studied by comparing structures or functions of related organisms. It was then found that most, if not all, of the differences are adaptive, i.e. useful to the organisms under the conditions of their specific environment. The mechanism responsible for this adaptive changes was clearly recognized for the first time by Charles Darwin as natural selection acting on the existing genetic variability. The mechanism of directional selection favouring the fittest is most probably the best known principle of evolution. Yet, it is certainly not the only one and should consequently not be considered as a general property of life that also governs, and is intrinsic to, human social systems or economic organizations. The misuse of the concept of selection in the political philosophy of Nazism is a sad but significant example of how dangerous it can be unreflectingly to apply biological principles to other systems or theories.

Natural selection is mainly discussed as a deterministic destabilizing factor in evolution which increases the overall fitness of populations. It can also be a stabilizing element. Yet, quite a number of other mechanisms become visible as soon as we examine other traits. This is not only true if we consider a more complex characteristic like the behavior or the sociobiology of animals, or step down to a lower scale of complexity like biochemical pathways, or to the organization of the genetic information at the molecular level. In particular, the new techniques of DNA-sequencing, cloning and in situ-hybridization have revealed organizational principles of the genetic material of eukaryotic organisms which bring to light a number of evolutionary mechanisms.

There is neither time nor need to discuss here all the various mechanisms of evolution observable in the different lines of organisms at the different levels of complexity. Besides the main principles of evolution – mutation, selection, recombination and chance – other important mechanisms exist such as duplication mechanisms, transposing mechanisms, regulation mechanisms with input-output subprogrammes, interaction mechanisms between cells, individuals and species or information transfer by chemical or physical signals and many others. Without doubt, evolution is a manifold process and follows very different strategies in the different branches of life.

We are here particularly interested in the evolution of man and it might be interesting to list some of the evolutionary mechanisms as they can be found in the phylogenetic line from simple organized cells to man. We certainly will not be able to give a full report but will concentrate on some remarkable innovations within the process:

i) Mechanisms which increase the accuracy of the copying process during the transfer of genetic information: replication enzymes, repair mechanisms, compartment separation for genetic material (nucleus), more than one copy (diploidy), chromosomes, mitosis.

ii) Mechanisms augmenting the quantity of information: insertion elements, transposons, unequal recombination, chromosome and genome mutations.

iii) Mechanisms for recombination: transformation, transduction, conjugation, sexuality, diploidy, meiosis, differentiation of gametes, differentiation of sexes, behavior of sexes.

iv) Interaction mechanisms: cell interaction, multicellular organization, differentiation.

v) Mechanisms making genetic programmes more open: gene-regulation by repression and induction, programmed feedback mechanisms, nervous systems, receptive organs, memories, immune systems, reflexes, chains of reflexes, individual learning, transmission of experience, signals, use of tools, tradition, language, self awareness, culture.

vi) Behavioural mechanisms for increased interaction between individuals: behaviour, social organization, language, political systems, religion, art, science, culture.

This is, of course, only a very incomplete list. Yet, it might help our conclusion. What we can see immediately is that a number of new mechanisms of evolution come into existence when the complexity of organization increases. One very important property of human evolution seems to be the tendency to acquire independence from environmental constraints. However, we must be careful. Our list is not unbiased; we have not chosen randomly the mechanisms, but have selected those that appeared to us important for human evolution. By doing this, the list necessarily shows a teleological quality. Whether or not we use this as a basis for the construction of a biological "Weltanschauung", as Teilhard de Chardin has done, remains a personal decision. One fact is sure, however; evolution is a natural process following in all instancies the laws of physics and chemistry. Natural science cannot prove or disprove the existence of God.

References:

Ayala, F. J., and J.W. Valentine (1979), *Evolving*. Benjamin Publ. Comp.
Eigen M., W. Gardiner, P. Schuster and R. Winkler-Oswatitsch (1981), The Origin of Genetic Information. *Sci. Amer.,* April. (German: *Spektrum d. Wiss.,* Juni 1981).
Dobzhansky, Th. (1962), *Mankind evolving*. Yale Univ. Press. (Deutsch: Dynamik der menschlichen Evolution, S. Fischer, 1965).
Kimura, M. (1983), *The Neutral Theory of Molecular Evolution*. Cambridge Univ. Press. (Deutsches Übers. Parey, 1987).
Siewing, R. (Hersg.) (1987), *Evolution*. G. Fischer (3. Aufl.).
Stebbins, G.L., and F.J. Ayala (1985), "The Evolution of Darwinism". *Sci. Amer.* (German: *Spektrum d. Wiss.,* Sep. 1985).

The Status of the Theory of Evolution in the Philosophy of Science

Gerhard Vollmer

1. Is there a Theory of Evolution?

Although a thorough presentation of evolutionary theory cannot be the task of a short contribution like this, some remarks on what evolutionary theory is *not* might be helpful.

First of all, we have to restrict ourselves to a special section of universal evolution, namely to *organic* evolution. That is, we are *not* talking about cosmic, galactic or stellar evolution, not about chemical or molecular evolution, not even about the origin of life. Nor are we talking about psychosocial or cultural evolution, about the evolution of science or about the evolution of the theory of evolution.

All these evolutionary processes exist, they are fascinating subjects of scientific investigations, ranging from mere speculations to well-tested theories. But there is as yet no comprehensive theory encompassing all these different phases of universal evolution. We do have some tentative lists specifying the traits common to all kinds of evolution. We also have different theories for different stages of evolution. And one of these stages is the evolution of living systems. The theory of organic evolution accepted today by most scientists is the theory of natural selection. As everybody knows this theory is essentially due to Charles Darwin, but we should also be aware that the modern theory of evolution is not Darwin's any longer. Some of his ideas – those on genetic variations, on the mechanisms of inheritance, and on the time scales necessary for evolution, had considerably to be specified. Others – strict gradualism, blending inheritance, heritability of acquired characters – had to be given up completely. Still others – the principles of population genetics, of molecular biology, and of sociobiology – had to be added to make the theory more self-contained and to account adequately for evolutionary facts. Thus, paradoxically enough, Darwin himself cannot be claimed to be a Darwinian in the strict sense of any modern version of Darwinism or neo-Darwinism.

2. The Principles of Organic Evolution

What exactly does such a modern theory of evolution claim? If you ask somebody – even a biologist – to characterize the theory of evolution, the answer will invariably consist of two words. These two words are "mutation" and "selection". This answer is, nevertheless, *defective*. First, a theory cannot be characterized by *concepts*, but only by principles. Second, your interviewee will, as a rule, not even be able to *define* these concepts adequately. Third, the theory of evolution is *not* characterized by the principles of mutation and selection alone. (These principles would be compatible, for instance, with one single dominant species ruling the biosphere, interbreeding and evolving slowly.) In order to give a more adequate impression of the main tenets of our theory, let us list some of its constitutive principles.

Principle of diversity: All organisms, even those within one and the same species, *vary* from each other. And new variations are constantly emerging (both by mutations and by genetic recombination).

Principle of inheritance: These variations are, at least in part, *inherited*, that is, genetically transmitted to the next generation. (The mechanisms of inheritance were not known to Darwin.)

Principle of overproduction: Nearly all organisms produce more offspring than can possibly survive to grow up and in turn to reproduce.

Principle of natural selection: On average, survivors will exhibit those heritable variations which increase their adaptation to local environments (misleadingly called "survival of the fittest", correctly called "differential reproduction").

Principle of evolution: Therefore, species are not immutable. (Darwin: "transmutation" or "descent with modification" as opposed to creationism, for instance.)

Principle of gradualism: Variations occur in relatively small steps as measured by information content or organized complexity. Therefore, phylogenetic processes are gradual and relatively slow. (As opposed to saltationism or to Cuvier's catastrophe theory.)

Principle of discreteness: Inheritance is of a particulate or atomistic nature. (No blending inheritance as Darwin wrongly believed.)

Principle of blindness: Variations are blind, not preferentially directed toward favorable adaptations. Random processes are mutations, recombinations, fluctuations in population size, and an ensuing genetic drift (Sewall Wright, Kimura).

Principle of irreversibility: The course of evolution is, in the long run, irreversible and unrepeatable.

Principle of unpredictability: The path of evolution is not pre-programmed, not goal-directed, not predetermined. It is essentially unpredictable.

Principle of adaptation: Functional traits are outcomes of natural selection, not of some teleological, goal-setting instance. (This counts against the "argument from design" postulating the existence and activity of an extra-natural creator.)

Principle of opportunism: Evolutionary processes are extremely opportunistic: they exclusively act on what there is, not on what there was or might be. Best solutions may not be found if intermediate stages are disadvantageous.

Principles of increasing complexity: Organic evolution has led to more and more complexity. (Whether this increase in complexity should be called *progress*, is a matter of taste. There is no objective measure for progress. Even complexity can and will decrease.)

Principles of evolution strategy: Not only organisms or populations are optimized, but also the mechanisms of evolution: death and birth rates, life-spans, susceptibility to mutations, step-width of mutations, pace of evolution, isolating processes, capturing of ecological niches, etc.

3. Philosophy of Science

Philosophy of science is a typical metadiscipline. It does not investigate the world, but our knowledge about the world and the methods by which we gain such knowledge. It may be viewed as part of epistemology, concentrating, however, not on knowledge in general, but on scientific knowledge as the most advanced form of human knowledge.

Philosophy of science has several aims or functions: it is descriptive as well as explanatory, explicative as well as normative (advisory or prescriptive). As a *descriptive* enterprise, it investigates how science proceeds, how theories are structured and what the relation between experience and scientific knowledge is. As a *normative* discipline, it studies how science *should* proceed, and gives advices about what scientists should do in order to produce "good" science.

Philosophy of science has led to several interesting results which for lack of space cannot be listed here. One of its main results is the insight into the preliminary, hypothetical or *conjectural character of all factual knowledge*, including scientific knowledge. Although since antiquity passionate sceptics have always insisted on such a claim, modern philosophy of science has very effectively *strengthened* this view by exhibiting new and better arguments (though not proofs, of course).

Now, if scientific knowledge were certain, if the truth of scientific theories could somehow be proven, we could very well dispense with other criteria, at least as long as (true) knowledge is kept as one of the aims of science.

If, however, human knowledge is fallible, if even scientific theories, constituting the most impressive part of human knowledge, can never be proven to be true, then we must look for some other criteria of evaluation, for subsidiary traits and properties.

Philosophy of science has, indeed, developed such criteria. Here, we have to distinguish between *necessary* traits on the one side and merely *welcome* features on the other. Necessary traits of a "good" theory of science are

- noncircularity (it must not contain vicious circles of definition, of proof, of explanation, of justification),
- internal consistency (it must not contain or lead to a logical contradiction),
- external consistency (it must not contradict another theory accepted as true),
- explanatory power (it must explain observed facts),
- testability (it must specify empirical instances by which it can be confirmed (if it is true) or refuted (if it is false)),
- test success (it must survive all empirical test).

Other traits such as generality (or even universality), depth, precision, simplicity, visualizability, predictive power, repeatability, fertility, are welcome, but not indispensable. They may help, however, to decide between competing theories that are *empirically equivalent*.

Much could be said about those criteria, about their meaning and scope, their history and application, their mutual connection and possible justification. The only thing we can and will do here is to apply the necessary criteria above to the theory of evolution.

4. Objections and Meta-Objections to the Theory of Evolution

criteria	objections to evolutionary theory	counter-argument defending evolutionary theory
noncir-cularity	The definition of fitness is, in the last analysis, circular, and the principle of natural selection is, therefore, a tautology (»survival of the survivor«). Thus, the central principle of evolutionary theory is analytic. It doesn't say or explain anything. (Waddington, Popper)	It is perfectly possible to define fitness *without* resorting to *long-term survival*. (Ruse) Eigen's »selective value« (»Wertfunktion«) even gives a *quantitative* measure for fitness: $W = A \cdot Q - D$, where »amplification« A, »quality« Q and »decay« D are defined independently of long-term survival, but nevertheless allow to predict it. (Eigen)
internal consistency	Evolution is said to lead to *new* properties, *new* structures, *new* systems. But »to e-volve« means »to un-roll, to un-wind, to un-fold«. Now, we can unroll only things which are already there. Thus, evolution can never lead to something new. (Locker)	The meaning of a word is not given by etymology, but rather by its definition, by its use, by its context. The word »evolution« means what we make it to mean, either by an explicit definition or by the use we make of it. And if we use it as allowing for the emergence of new traits, there is no contradiction.
external consistency	There are several contradictions between physics and evolutionary theory. a) The law of gravitation: Rocks fall down, birds fly. b) The age of the sun: According to Lord Kelvin's theory of solar heat (gravitational	The law of gravitation is universal, but birds have more degrees of freedom which allow them to use the laws of aerodynamics. This seeming contradiction was resolved by the discovery of a new source of energy, undreamed of by 19th century science: nuclear

criteria	objections to evolutionary theory	counter-argument defending evolutionary theory
	shrinking), there could have been steady solar radiation only for some millions of years. According to Darwin's theory of evolution, it took life much longer to evolve. (Darwin himself rated this as one of the most serious objections.) c) The law of entropy: According to the law of increasing entropy, *disorder* should always increase. But origin, development and evolution of organisms clearly correspond to an increase of *order*. Thus, life and evolution contradict thermodynamics, hence physics. (Heitler)	fusion. Stars gain energy by merging light atomic nuclei to heavier ones. The sun can draw on its resources for about ten billion years of which about five billions have elapsed. (Bethe, Weizsäcker) α) The entropy law only applies to *closed* systems. Organisms, however, are *open* systems. They lower their entropy at the expense of their environment. (Bertalanffy) β) Entropy is not always a measure for disorder. Under certain conditions (existence of attractive forces and low total energy), states of higher order are also states of higher entropy. (Weizsäcker)
explanatory power	The theory of natural selection might explain *some* features of evolution, for instance microevolution (intraspecific evolution). It is, however, unable to explain *macroevolution*, that is, the emergence of new systematic units (species, genera, classes etc.). Thus, the standard theory of evolution is at least *incomplete*. More	The incompleteness of evolutionary theory must be conceded. Many facts are still unexplained. (How do *new* genes arise? Gene duplication cannot be the whole answer.) It should be clear, however, that evolution is not (and never was) just »mutation« and »selection«. Many principles have already been added (cf. section 2). Whether still more factors

criteria	objections to evolutionary theory	counter-argument defending evolutionary theory
	factors are needed, for instance inheritance of acquired characters (Lamarck, Darwin, Steele), macromutations (T.H. Huxley), »hopeful monsters« (Goldschmidt), cybernetic regulations (Schmidt), group selection (Wynne-Edwards), internal selection (Gutmann).	are needed, must be left open here.
testability	The theory of evolution cannot make predictions. Hence, it cannot be tested, not falsified. It is, therefore, not a theory of empirical science, but rather an (admittedly quite fertile) *metaphysical research program*. Only by adding further concrete hypotheses and theories, testable statements can be derived. (Popper)	α) Evolutionary theory is much richer than this objection would suggest. It makes, in fact, *falsifiable predictions*. (Williams) β) Even if it could not predict anything, it still can make falsifiable *retrodictions*. As to testability, retrodictions are as weighty as predictions. (Ruse) γ) Even if the theory of evolution were not falsifiable, it would still make a *difference* whether out of a hundred existential claims only five claims or rather ninety-five are confirmed. (Scriven) δ) Falsifiability is not all there is to the testability of a scientific theory. To transport this criterion

criteria	objections to evolutionary theory	counter-argument defending evolutionary theory
		from physics to biology is some kind of unjustified imperialism. (Bunge) ε) Popper himself has made a recantation: In 1977, he declared that the theory of natural selection was a *testable* theory after all.
test success	The theory of evolution is empirically false. There are many facts in the organismic world which contradict this theory. (Creationists, fundamentalists; Illies, W. Kuhn, Wilder Smith)	There is no known fact which contradicts the theory of evolution or falsifies it. But there are still many unsolved problems. Most critics fail to distinguish incompleteness and falsity.

The Advance of Biological Categories in Cultural Thought and Modern Social Activities

Wolfgang Lipp

There is a growing tendency to define categories in biological terms in our culture and society. This is evident for example in areas of ecology, of medical care in its various aspects, including genetic manipulation, or in that questioning of mankind's survival presented by the destructive potential of our armament systems.

Biological concerns now affect many different areas of everyday life. This development has deep roots in the history of ideas and societies. In this article I will trace the development of biological categories and elaborate on their definitions. First (I), I will distinguish three dimensions of biological categories: 1) relevant scientific and analytical terms, 2) "biocratical value" – orientations and 3) activities of social and practical life, associated with and reinforcing such orientations. Secondly (II) I will discuss my points in the context of the history of ideas. In the third (III) and fourth (IV) sections I will present the more significant biological ideologies and will try to identify corresponding "biocratic" tendencies. Finally (V) I will consider how far the tendencies described are promoted by the type of society in which we are living.

I.

Now, what do I mean, in a broader sense, by "biological categories"?

1) In natural science, biological categories are developed through research and theory building. Biology is a discipline which is parallel to and partly overlaps neighbouring fields such as medicine, ethology and ecology. Moreover, biology is closely connected with disciplines such as physics, chemistry and cybernetics, through continuous fundamental theory-construction. Biological categories in this sense are obviously systematically well grounded. They are also deeply anchored in the modern natural sciences and are joined with many related desciplines under the common title of "life-sciences". It is clear that this system of biological categories is highly

developed. In view of the fact that, as sociological study of the sciences has shown, biology has become one of the most expanding and also most application-oriented sciences today, it is obvious that the terms, models and technologies which are available through its disciplines – the life sciences – will become more and more important.

2) The second class of categories can be referred to as "bio-categorial values" and relates to groups of ideas about life or, more precisely, about life-values. The designation "bio-categorial" expresses the notion that the ideals in question tie in with the concepts of biology in a conscious and direct manner. They tie in, in other words, with the life *sciences*, not with the *myth*, or a mere myth, of life. Moreover, these values are realizable not only in biotechnical terms but also administratively. This enables them to be transformed, generalized and institutionalized socially.

Biocategorial values are then values of life which de-emphasize other-worldly, metaphysical dimensions of society derived from earlier times, in favour of a "positive" physical dimension, crucial for the modern world. They are organized in our present society under such titles as a) welfare ideals, b) the ideals of health, c) ecological ideals and d) the imperatives of survival.

a) Differentiating further, the *ideals of welfare* can be subdivided into: the opting for economic growth and prosperity, for higher standards of living (including the provisions of life assurance and social security), and finally for a certain "quality of life". It is evident in this context that hedonistic ideals tie in with these orientations, which are based, in theory and practice, on the postulate of some kind of "new sensuality" or ultimately of a new kind of human being. It is noticeable, incidentally, how attractive this postulate of a "new human being" is to young people. This postulate is moreover realistic in the sense that its technical or biotechnical requirements (the use of drugs etc.) can be met by the relevant sciences.

b) It hardly needs saying, that one of the most important and prominent biocategories refers to *ideals of health*, which are very highly valued in our society. These ideals go far beyond the wishes and fantasies of former times, and they can now be achieved by technical means. This is demonstrated repeatedly in diverse techniques and practices of modern medicine, which now make possible organ transplants, the prolonging of life, and the direct eugenic programming of man.

c) *Ecological ideals* were first discussed long ago, but have been advanced more recently by the activities of the Club of Rome (cf. Meadows et al., 1972). It is generally understood that the extension of man's expansion into the environment, which has been possible under the command of industrial, technical and scientific progress, places increasing burdens upon our ecology. Our resources evidently are becoming limited, bringing life processes themselves into severe danger. Thus, the ongoing ecological discussion emphasizes the possibility that the continuing exploitation of our environment by industrial societies is not only limiting growth but is endangering the survival of our system. This is not a local but a global challenge to society.

d) The *imperatives of survival* are related to the fact that man, despite possible ecological catastrophes, still continues to utilize atomic energy. This practice is today being fundamentally questioned. Faced, in a way, with apocalyptic visions, man is realizing – as an endless string not only of intellectual, but political statements suggests – that the most obvious and important goal is "survival". This goal becomes prominent, for instance, when one considers the proliferation of atomic energy in the weapons industry, accompanied by the danger of atomic radiation and its uncontrollable genetic destruction. To counteract this great danger, it may paradoxically become necessary to resort again to the use of biotechnical procedures, in particular highly developed genetic biological methods, which may finally result in state-imposed genetic manipulations, in order to prepare mankind to withstand radiation.

3) The third class of categories I am discussing here comes under the heading "life oriented activities". By this term, I wish to indicate that biocategorical orientations are not only part of the cultural superstructure, unconnected with the facts of social reality, but are anchored in the bases of society itself and carried out in special, life-oriented activities.

The fact that biological categories are becoming increasingly dominant is underlined not only by superficial symbolic indications; it is also revealed by analyses of material, social-structural conditions. Thus the whole set of symbols, values and ideals of life we are speaking of, relates to and is produced by the interests, institutions and functional characteristics of industrial society.

By "life oriented activities", I now mean processes which grow out of structural characteristics, as mentioned, and are oriented towards evolving "biocategorial values". These activities utilize biological and biotechnical means more and more intensively. They transform and generalize these means, we must add, through far-reaching, and thoroughly organized, social mechanisms of administration. Life oriented activities, in other words, are processes existing in societies which have developed a highly productive economic system, have, at the same time, established a tight network of welfare institutions as well as of technical and scientific installations, and have generated accompanying, increasingly precarious ecological conditions. The goals, challenges and problems these societies are facing are, or will be, perceived in terms of welfare values and lastly the imperatives of survival. To summarize, I am looking at the context in question as a series of processes which mediate between structural characteristics defining modern world society on the one hand, and their emerging biocategorial orientation patterns, on the other. The mediation occurs so to speak between a given social basis and its new biocategorical superstructure.

II.

I would like now to refer to the background history of ideas which prepared the way for the formation of biological categories. Categorical developments never occur in isolation. They are linked below the surface with other streams of thought through a common channel. There is a typical intellectual climate in which biological categories become dominant while other, primarily religious, metaphysical and transcendental orientations lose influence. This climate is marked by "positivistic" philosophical positions such as those developed by August Comte, and could be referred to as "reductionist". In this context, it is mainly the so-called "anthropological turn" reported within the history of philosophy, which must be mentioned. Indeed, theories such as those of Nietzsche, Pareto, Freud, Marx and others have emphasized the need for "returning the world of man to man himself"; they have portrayed man as a natural being who stands in direct metabolic exchange with the environment. What follows from this orientation, finally is a development of ethical concepts such as those of Bergson, and global images of a religious nature such as those of Teilhard de Chardin. Both were inclined to develop human morals, or the idea of cosmological salvation, from a biologistic standpoint.

III.

Let us approach another phenomenon significant for the present socio-cultural situation. There is, on the level of cultural ideas and "Weltanschauung", an increasing trend towards developing specifically biological ideologies. Some striking examples of this are the doctrines of Organicism, of Social Darwinism and blatantly racist ideologies such as those propounded by Gobineau, Galton, or Chamberlain. Certain scientific elements which have frequently been drawn from Darwin are reversed and presented here in the form of distorted, in a way manichaeistic, concepts, implicitly designed to engender hatred and aggression. The ideologies in question brought about the notions of what was called 'lebenswertes Leben' – a life worth living – on the one hand and 'lebensunwertes Leben' – a life not worth living – on the other, which culminated in the holocaust.

Biological ideologies, however, exist also in other modern sociocultural orientations. Without being primarily oriented towards destruction, they are nevertheless built upon premises which could be dangerous for society. An example would be radical feminist ideologies which delineate history in a reductionist way based on male/female dichotomies. Other examples would be youth cults, and the current ecological movement, the 'Green Philosophy', both of which incorporate results of modern biological research after altering them from their original function. In each case questions of identity and of the purpose of human existence were raised, and decisive social value judgements are made which are globally generalized and may tend, if they run off the rails of moderate sociocultural control, towards cultural decadence, regression or overt political barbarism.

IV.

Finally I would like to address what I call a "biocratic" system. This term was first introduced by Walter B. Cannon; I myself have used it since 1968. There are also recent scientific articles including a book by Leach in 1970 in which the term occurs. Just as politics, made legitimate by the people's voice and vote is normally called "democratic" so could also politics that refers to areas connected with "biology" – that is people who act in the name of biology – be called "biocratic". These areas are of crucial importance in our society and must be seriously discussed. Biological categories, theories and ideologies, as we have seen, have deeply rooted practical implications; they are integrated into the very functions and working mechanisms of social institutions. Biological categories correspond to concrete life-oriented activities, and thus biocratic tendencies can be observed, for instance, in the workings of genetic biology, genetic manipulation, life extension and also euthanasia. Biocracy is also practised, propagated and enforced by the state, e.g. in area population control, where possible demographic catastrophes are envisaged, or wherever eco-political or eco-dictatorial policies are taken into consideration.

V.

So far I have been concerned with the increasing prominence of what I call biological categories. I have attempted to explain the phenomenon by reference to the history of ideas. But it must also be traced back sociologically, to ascertain the social-evolutionary conditions out of which these categories were generated. From the sociological point of view, biological categories become prominent as society attains a certain level of industrial civilization and prosperity, compared with systems characterized by what has been called a "culture of poverty". These conditions are not only present in modern western societies; they were also relevant, at least in principle, in the early capitalist orders, and influenced if not the social masses, then the upper classes of certain transitional systems such as those of the fascists. Set free from the misery of everyday problems, of the disciplined course of work, with its continuous performance requirements and sublimation demands, man in this new state of existence now returns, to some extent, to the physical basis of his nature and feels exposed to new, and quite different, urges, emotions, and aspirations for gratification. Terms such as "God", the "hereafter", and the "social question", are replaced by terms such as "life", "sensual life", "vitality", and "survival", which become, comparatively, more important for present day man. The process has been a long and very complicated one leading from life-reformist movements between the world wars with their vitalistic, eugenic and racist implications, up to the explosion of aspirations in the present affluent society with its new life-oriented values. In any case, the life values in question aim at the goals of both biocategorically renewed cultural legitimation, and structurally reinforced, life-oriented activities. It is the modern "post-industrial world" which is bringing about – partly through its opportunities, its moral and material permissiveness, partly through its self-induced, expanding ecological dilemmas, man's "falling back on himself", and which leads to the restyling of life in ways and forms which appear to be "biocratic".

References

Caldwell, L. K. (1985), *Biocracy and Democracy: Science, Ethics, and the Law*, in: *Politics and the Life Sciences* 3, S. 137-149.

Leach, G. (1970), *The Biocrats*. London.

Lipp, W. (1968), *Biokratismen*, in: ibid., *Institution und Veranstaltung. Zur Anthropologie der sozialen Dynamik*. Berlin, S. 172-189.

Lipp, W. (1971), *Reduktive Mechanismen. Untersuchungen zum Zivilisationsprozeß*. *Archiv für Rechts- und Sozialphilosophie* 57, S. 357-382.

Lipp, W. (1980), *Biologische Kategorien im Vormarsch? Herausforderung und Aufgabe einer künftigen Soziologie*. Würzburg.

Lipp, W. (1984), *Alltagswissen, Kulturideen und Biologismus. Soziale Grundlagen und soziologische Erkenntnis*, in: *Wie erkennt der Mensch die Welt?* Grundlagen des Erkennens, Fühlens und Handelns. Geistes- und Naturwissenschaftler im Dialog, hg. von M. Lindauer und A. Schöpf. Stuttgart, S. 151-176.

Lipp, W. (1985), *Rassenlehre, Jugendkult und Feminismus – Zur Ideologiekritik biologistischer Orientierungen*, in: *Die Frau zwischen Biologie und Biologismus*, hg. von H. Seidler und A. Soritsch. Schriftenreihe Sozialanthropologie, Bd. 2, Wien, S. 28-45.

Meadows, D., et al. (1972), *The Limits of Growth*. London.

Evolution and Ethics*

Gerrit Manenschijn

0. Introduction

It is possible to distinguish between three positions in relation to this subject.[1]
First, there is the view that in some way ethical awareness is a product of
evolution and, in particular, the view that it is only a little step from animals
with highly developed social instincts to human beings with moral sentiments.
The *second* position represents the contrary, namely, that morality must be
seen as counter to natural instincts and for that reason 'moral man' is exactly
the opposite of 'natural man'. Both views are defended by evolutionists, for
example, the first one by Darwin and the second one by Huxley,[2] so it would be
a mistake to say that the first is typical of evolutionists and the second of moral
philosophers. On the contrary, both of these positions are defended in moral
philosophy as well as in evolutionary theory. The view that morality is in
accordance with the social instincts of man was, for instance, taken by
philosophers of the school of moral sentiments, whereas the opposite view was
defended by philosophers of the school of moral rationalists.[3] But both of them
were moral philosophers! It is widely known that Kant was a moral rationalist
and claimed that morality should be totally separated from the empirical
world. His view dominated the scene of moral philosophy for years, but
gradually the opinion gained ground that Kant was wrong in opposing moral
obligation ('Pflicht') to natural inclination ('Neigung'). This does not detract
from Kant's contribution to moral philosophy, especially with regard to the
theory of universalizing moral judgements.

Both of the views mentioned above have been proven to be untenable (For
details with quotations, see Vogel).[4] The *third* point of view is that there exists

* Only a few weeks before the conference I received the invitation to give a lecture on
the subject of "Evolution of Ethics". It was impossible to consider all the literature,
which is mentioned in the following paper. I am very grateful to the members of the
conference, who informed me a little more about the present-day state of affairs in
evolution. Particularly I mention the names of Christian Vogel and Gerhard Vollmer, who sent me their own recent publications.

85

some sort of reciprocal dependency between evolution and ethics. This is too general and vague and it is my aim to clarify it. I hold with Gerhard Vollmer, that much of the social conduct of human beings can be explained in the same way as the social conduct of animals, without making the false assumption that animals are capable of moral judgements or of behaviour that can be judged morally.[5] This is the core of the relationship between evolution and ethics. Evolution, especially evolutionary biology, is relevant to ethics with respect to the boundaries of the applicability of moral norms and with respect to the role that motivation plays in the reasoning of the moral agent.[6] Vollmer gives an example of the boundaries of the application of moral norms.[7] The example is trivial but clear: A man cannot be supposed to have a baby, for he has no uterus. It follows that there is no sense in the statement that a man is morally obliged to have babies. Women, however, do have a uterus and can have babies, provided other hindrances do not exist. In that case, do women have the moral obligation to have babies for the simple reason that they have a uterus? But the fact that somebody *can* do something, does not imply that he or she ought to do it. The whole question can be combined into two rules of thumb:

(1) 'can' does not imply 'ought'; (2) 'ought' implies 'can'.

The prescription to go from 'can' to 'ought' can only be justified by the method of moral reasoning. Here scientific reasoning has no task. Of course, scientific reasoning can *explain* why some person in given circumstances in fact goes from 'can' to 'ought', but only moral reasoning is competent to *justify* the prescription that somebody ought to do what he is able to. This justification makes use of terms like 'ought' and 'ought not', 'right' or 'wrong', 'obliged' or 'forbidden', 'good' or 'bad', and so on. The typical evaluative language of morals is of no use in a scientific approach of morals.[8] But that does not mean that the scientific approach is of less worth than the moral one. Both of them operate in a different realm, and as such have their own worth (See the author's "Reasoning in Science and Ethics" for more information).[9]

I conclude that there exists no need to make a choice between the scientific approach (evolution) and the moral one (ethics) in the reflecting on morality; neither of them can replace the other.

It is now necessary to analyse some concepts of morality and ethics, especially in relation to the concept of evolution.

1.   Some Linguistic Problems

1.1.   Concepts and Definitions

We must distinguish between morality as an *existing moral code of conduct* and morality as a *critical reflection* on moral codes. Let me introduce the term 'ethics' for the latter. I define *ethics* as the critical reflection on moral codes, either at the level of meta-ethics or of normative ethics.[10] In the case of normative ethics the critical reflection takes place from the viewpoint of moral ideals and principles. What this means will be explained later.

I propose to use the term 'morality' exclusively for moral codes as such and no longer as a synonym for 'ethics'. Tentatively I define *morality* as a complex and pervasive network of duties and prescriptions, saying what people *ought* to do to act *rightly*. Morality includes both the factual moral code and the moral ideal, which means that morality is self-corrective and dynamic.[11]

It is realistic to start with the factual moral code, not with the ideals, for our view on morality should be as empirical as possible, to save us from illusion. The critical reflection of ethics never starts in an empty space, but always finds its object already present: the existing moral code of the group to which one belongs. Existing moral codes can be evaluated critically and also investigated scientifically, in the following way.

Christian Vogel makes a useful distinction between three levels of morality.[12] At the lowest level we find a "*biogenetic potentiality*" or inclinations acquired by biological evolution; at the second level "*tradigenetic potentiality*" is acquired. At the third level, the thin layer of consciously accepted action guidelines, called the "*rational potentiality*".

From this three-level model of morality it is clear how scientific research relates to critical reflection. The first level, of the biogenetic potentiality, is the subject of biological and psychological research; the second level, of the tradigenetic potentiality, is subject of historical and social inquiry, and the third level is subject of ethics as critical reflection. It is even possible to state that evolution plays its part not only in the first level, but also in the second and even in the third (ethics as the fruit of cultural evolution).[13] The point I want to make is that the evolutionary approach to morality is as justified as the ethical one.

However, the evolutionary approach is not competent in one respect: namely, in formulating the *principles* and *ideals* to evaluate existing moral codes. A clear example can be taken from the article of Christian Vogel. He says that from the viewpoint of natural selection the killing of children (infanticide) can contribute to the total fitness of a given population, but that nevertheless this utilitarian type of infanticide must be condemned as totally immoral.[14] For morality has in the first place to deal with individual members of mankind, not with an abstraction like the genetic potentiality of the human species as such.

Further analysis of the reasoning at the third level, that of the *rational potentiality* is needed. The most typical quality of morality is its normative function in guiding conduct.[15] That is precisely what makes morality what it is: a *moral* code. Hence the relevant question is: when is a guide to action to be considered as a morality? Frankena here makes a distinction between formal aspects and substantial ones. The formal dimension of morality can be defined as follows:

"x has a moral action guide (AG) if and only if he has an AG of which such conditions as the following hold:

(a)   x takes it as a prescriptive,
(b)   x universalizes it, wills it to be an universal law,
(c)   x regards it as definitive, final, overriding, or supremely authoritative or supremely important"[16] (x = a human person)

I agree with Frankena here that only *necessary* conditions are formulated, not sufficient ones. The *sufficient* conditions have to do with the content of moral action guides. Of course, that content should be proven to be valid with the help of formal criteria, but nevertheless it is always the content that makes morality what it is in essence. Therefore Frankena suggests the following extensions of the formal definition:

"x has a morality or moral AG only if it includes judgements, rules, principles, ideals etc. which

(d)   concern the relations of one individual (e.g.) x to others,
(e)   involve or call for consideration of the effects of his actions on others (not necessarily all others), not from the point of view of his own interests or aesthetic enjoyments, but from their own point of view"[17]

This concept says the following. *Firstly*, there is no unchangeable, universal moral law. Morality is as provisional as are all human undertakings. Realizing this makes us tolerant towards all those moralities which seem strange and unununderstandable from our own point of view.

Second, the attitude of tolerance should not make us indifferent to moral problems or make us think that the ethical relativism is unavoidable. The sceptical position of the ethical relativist can be overcome, without falling back on an ethical ethno-centrism which holds the idea that our morality is the best one only because it is ours. Avoiding both of these extreme positions, Frankena invites us to take the so-called *moral point of view*. In practice this means the following.

In the *first* place, everybody has his own moral norms, principles and ideals. Be aware of them and try to formulate them exactly! Examine if there is any inconsistency in them, any selfishness or prejudice, any harm for others as a result of your supposed moral acting.

In the *second* place, try to universalize your moral guidelines honestly. This means: imagine yourself to be the person which is the object of your behaviour, and ask whether you would hold your view if you were in his place. If not, your moral action guide is not tenable.

In the *third* place, submit the outcome of your deliberation so far to the judgement of all relevant people. Condition (e) said that there should be a "call for consideration of the effects of your actions on others, not from the point of view of your own interest, but from *their* own point of view". To know what their point of view is, you have to ask them. Listen to others and take care of their opinions.

Obviously this method of moral reasoning has a problem-solving function. The idea is that conflicts of interests are unavoidable, but that a *moral* solution of conflicts implies a minimization of violence, and an optimisation of everybody's good. Taking everybody's good seriously involves a willingness to know all the relevant facts. In considering the good of everybody in a broad sense (animals and the world at large included), it is clear that the facts of evolution are relevant for any morality that goes beyond the narrow bounds of ethnocentricity.

From this point of view some characteristics of Frankena's concept are worthy of critical examination,[18] for instance condition (d): there should be a concern for the relations of one *individual* to *others*. This sounds somewhat individualistic, and in my view groups and even mankind as a whole are as relevant as individuals. More important, however, is the restriction implied by 'others'. There is no doubt that other human individuals are meant. Why not animals, future generations, ecosystems and the world at large as well?

1.2. The Use of Moral Language
On reading articles and books of evolutionists I often wonder that moral language is so often used in a descriptive context. Terms like 'altruistic' or 'selfish behaviour' and 'self-sacrifice' appear frequently. Especially in sociobiology, moral terms are used, but only *per analogiam*, in a strict descriptive sense, as is pretended by the authors. The problem how an

individual specimen of a species can lower its survival prospect for the benefit of its offspring, is, for instance, formulated as the problem how it can behave 'altruistically', given the fact that in the evolutionary process a successful gene is ruthless 'selfishness'. So Richard Dawkins, in his wellknown book *The Selfish Gene*,[19] announces: "My purpose is to examine the biology of selfishness and altruism" (p. 1). However, Dawkins did not intend to write a book on morals. His argument is quite the opposite, namely "that we, and all other animals, are machines, created by our genes" (p. 2). According to this view the most dominant quality to be expected in a successful gene is selfishness. This gene-selfishness will usually give rise to selfishness in individual behaviour, but not always. However, words like 'selfishness' and 'altruism' have nothing to do with intentions and motives, only with the effect of an act, whether it lowers or raises the survival prospects of a given individual. "An entity, such as a baboon, is said to be altruistic if it behaves in such a way as to increase another such entity's welfare at the expense of its own" (p. 5). (Welfare is defined as 'chances of survival'). Again, it is very useful to explain why a given specimen of a species can act in such a way as to lower its own 'welfare' and to better that of its offspring or even its species as a whole. But it is confusing to use the language of morals to describe and explain this phenomenon. For to be altruistic or selfish a minimum of freedom of choice is required, and genes cannot be considered to have freedom of choice. It is a mistake to blame the cat for 'immorality', when she catches a mouse, or to praise the duck, who is defending her ducklings against the attacks of the heron, for her 'altruism'. When Vogel says that this unfortunate confusion of terms cannot be eliminated from the language of sociobiologists, and that it is regrettable, I agree with him. [20] It is the very use of this pseudo-moral language that engenders the frequent misunderstandings between biologists and moral philosophers.

However, it should be admitted that the confusion of descriptive and moral language is also evoked by evolution itself. For the adaptations, necessary to help an organism to survive and to reproduce, *seem* to be end-directed and teleological, although they are not. This 'seeming to be' is inevitably expressed in the vocabulary of evolutionists. Darwin, for instance, called the mechanism of *natural selection* a 'struggle for life' (a term, borrowed from Thomas Robert Malthus), which struggle was fought between individuals.[21] The winners in that struggle were 'the fittest'. The term 'the fittest' easily suggests that they were 'the best', since in common language a winner is seen as the best (of course in a non-moral sense). But in evolution that suggestion is false. Since Darwin explained the outcome of the struggle for survival as an effect of the *mechanism* of natural selection,[22] 'the fittest' cannot have the meaning of 'the best'. Evolution does not mean progression towards a *better* situation, only a survival of whatever counts for survival.

It was Spencer, who wrongly claimed that evolution was progressive. He referred to a 'law of progress' (o.c.p. 37-44), and even got a moral code out of that 'law', saying that we are morally obliged to foster a 'fair competition' in the struggle for life (o.c.p. 73-75). His ideas are long out of date, for modern Darwinism had shown that in evolution there is nothing to support progressionism (o.c.p. 19). What counts is *reproduction*, not progression. Even retrogression is biologically possible (o.c.p. 20). Besides Spencer obviously committed the 'is-ought fallacy', for he inferred wrongly a prescription from a description (I suggest that in fact, he did not, for he already had in mind a prescription in the premise, namely that fair competition is a good thing in itself and therefore ought to be favoured). Modern evolutionists are acquainted with this type of a fallacy, and try to avoid it. Sociobiologists are the most frequent users of the pseudo-moral language in a non-moral context. In their vocabulary the occurrence of terms like 'morality of the genes', 'altruism' and 'egoism' are the order of the day. I refer to the paper of Bert Musschenga, called "Can Sociobiology contribute to Moral Science and Ethics?"[23] and the article of Christian Vogel.

2. The Contribution of Evolution to Ethics

As already stated, morality, conceived as an existing guide to moral action, can be *explained* concerning its functioning and can be *justified* concerning its content. Explaining the functioning not only includes the biogenetic and tradigenetic potentiality, but also the rational potentiality. Ruse in fact does so, when he declares that he is not aiming to deduce morality from facts, but to explain the genesis and functioning of our moral awareness, by means of evolutionary theory.[24] He continues by saying that in order to explain morality you must, so to speak, step outside morality itself. On the level of our rational potentiality two approaches are justified; the first by stepping outside morality, explaining the genesis and functioning of morality; the second by staying inside morality, justifying the content of morality. The first approach takes place in the *context of discovery*, the second in the *context of justification*. The point is not to confuse both of these contexts, and to use for each of them the proper language.

As already mentioned, modern Darwinism says that evolution is not a matter of individuals, but of genes. The natural selection of genes can operate by the mechanisms of 'kin-selection'and 'reciprocal altruism'. *Kin-selection* starts from the fact that evolutionary success lies in improving your own gene ratios. But you do not literally pass on your genes, only replicas of them. A child has a half-set of the genes of the father and a half-set of the mother's. It can be expected that a grandchild has only a quarter-set of the original genes of one of the grandparents, and so on. Now the hypothesis of kin-selection is that giving help to relatives rebounds to the favour of one's own reproductive interests, even if those relatives are not able or willing to pay back. (In this way the compassion and forgiveness of the father, in the parable of the Lost Son, could be explained as invoked 'only' by 'kin-selected' altruism, see Luke 15, 11-32). The 'pay back' is the improving of the gene ratios: you *feel* more obliged to help your relatives, especially your children and grandchildren. That 'feeling to be obliged' is according to the theory of kin-selection, a genetically based disposition.

Kin-selection can be seen as one of the great successes of twentieth-century biology, which enables us to explain a lot of until then unsolved problems, for instance the problem of the 'self-sacrifice' of the females in the family life of social insects like ants, bees and wasps. The females are the workers, who are themselves sterile, spending their whole life in raising the offspring of their fertile mothers.[25] Traditional Darwinism was not able to explain this 'altruistic' behaviour, but the theory of kin-selection does. Because of a special reproductive system, females are more closely related to sisters than to daughters. Therefore they are, biologically, better prepared to raise fertile sisters than fertile daughters. The fact that they are themselves sterile, plays no role in their inclination to work 'altruistically'. Raising the offspring of their fertile mothers they are reproducing their own genes in that offspring.

However, to speak of a 'morality of genes' is out of question. For the very essence of moral action is the *intention* to act as one ought to do, whereas the working of the kin-selective mechanism is blind, without any intention.

In respect of the second mechanism, the so-called *'reciprocal altruism'*, another line of argument is needed. For reciprocal altruism is to some extent already a kind of rational conduct. It is presented in sociobiology as a mechanism of natural selection along with kin-selection, but this is unconvincing. This can be shown by means of presenting the rule of reciprocal altruism: helping others seems to be altruistic, but given the fact that the cost of co-operation is on average less than the hope of return, in reality it is a form of self-interest, a kind of insurance. Darwin already counted this kind of reciprocity as a result of the improvement of the reasoning powers of mankind, and probably it is. That is not the crucial point which is that reasoning according to the insurance model is not something like the workings of a mechanism, but more like the intended action of rational beings, who are able to learn from experience, to consider future possible states of affair, and, to a certain degree, to choose freely between distinctive options. The so-called 'reciprocal altruism' is nothing but the wellknown theory of 'rational self-interest' in a new garb. Either 'reciprocal altruism' is a mechanism and cannot be called altruistic, or it is really altruism, and hence not a mechanism.

That brings me to the real point of the distinction between stepping outside morality (the context of discovery) and staying inside morality (the context of justification). In sociobiology 'altruistic behaviour' is usually explained as disguised 'egoism' (as already Thomas Hobbes did), whereas 'altruism' is conceived as essentially moral. However, that is a serious misunderstanding, notably a confusion of the logic of explaining with that of justifying. To do justice to these logics, we have to make two different distinctions. In the first place between the logic of explaining and the logic of justifying respectively, and next, in the context of justification, between egoism and altruism, or rather between self-interested conduct and moral conduct. The first distinction has to do with the distinction between non-moral and moral phenomena, the second, within the sphere of the moral phenomena, with the distinction between morally acceptable and morally unacceptable (immoral) actions. The two meanings of 'moral', which have to be carefully distinguished, are *descriptive* and *prescriptive* respectively. It is illogical to call a phenomenon like kin-selection, being obviously non-moral, egoistic or altruistic. The point is that stepping outside morality implies stepping *outside the context of moral language*. Only within the context of moral language it is reasonable to speak of egoism or altruism. However, from the logic of moral language it is not at all evident that egoism or altruism should be judged as immoral or moral respectively. Reasons should be given, and to do that you have to formulate a *normative moral point of view*, as I in fact did in 1.1. Only from a normative moral point of view can actions and states of affair be judged as moral or immoral, as right or wrong.[26] Further it is premature to classify all behaviour as being either altruistic or egoistic. There is a lot of behaviour which is neither altruistic nor egoistic, and even which combines altruism with egoism perfectly.[27]

What I have in mind can be illustrated with an example, taken from Ruse.[28] In the course of explaining the Darwinian argument that morality is an adaptation to get us beyond random wishes, desires and fears, and that therefore morality works as if morality is objective, he suddenly says (without any proof or reason) that morality is a *collective illusion*, foisted upon us by our genes. That means, the illusion lies not in the morality itself, but in its sense of objectivity. That is a serious mistake, caused by the confusion of stepping outside morality and staying within it. Of course morality is subjective in the sense that it is not independent of human thinking and acting. In a way morality is always man-made. But what Ruse has in mind, notably that human awareness of morality overrides our wishes and desires and even our self-interest, has little to do with a supposed independency of morality from human thinking and acting, but above all with the very meaning of moral language. Making or accepting seriously moral statements and prescriptions, implies taking them as overriding, definitive and supremely authoritative, even if the agent is fully aware of the fact that morality is subjective in the sense that it is man-made. This awareness cannot be an illusion, because defect in that awareness makes a lot of difference to the actions of the persons involved, especially to the persons who are object of his actions.

For the rest of my paper I will stay within morality itself and raise the question whether we are in need of a new ethics or not, considering that we know how evolution works and what its impact is on the living world.

3. In Search of a New Ethic

The starting-point of this section is the view that in the process of evolution man has got a double position, such as is characterized by Peacocke in the following words: "However, although man's destructive character does not place us outside the natural ecosystems of the world, nevertheless his unique combination of intelligence and social organisation, with its modern fruit of technology, adds a new overwhelming factor to his effect on his own and other ecosystems".[29] On the one side man is a product of evolution, on the other he is the most effective factor in the continuation of that process. As Flew says: "... the future of this entire process – the future of all other living things as well as of mankind – lies largely or wholly in human hands".[30] Man is part of nature, and nevertheless transcends nature. Because of his evolutionary heritage he is a threat to evolution, even to the survival of mankind itself; because of his transcendence he *knows* that he is a threat. That makes his position from the very beginning a moral one. Precisely the principal ambiguity of his options on behalf of future evolution, defines man as basically being moral, whether he wants it or not. Man can choose to act morally or not, but he cannot choose not to be a moral being. By being human, he *is* moral. Vogel speaks of a *new responsibility* that goes far beyond the finest moral sensitivity in relation to fellows only, into the realm of not only mankind as a whole, but even into that of ecosystems, inclusive the whole world as the most comprehensive ecosystem.[31] The only thing that remains for us, Vogel says, is to become a steward and director ("Heger und Lenker") of that global ecosystem, that has lost its balance by the many interventions, posed on it by mankind. Now the point is that the necessary attitudes to fulfil the role of steward cannot come into existence within the framework of natural selection. On the contrary, the new ethics, Vogel argues which is considered as a counterweight to man's threat to evolution, has to get rid of all biogenetically conditioned fitness-compulsion and naturally selected egocentrism, of all group-egoism, ethnocentrism and anthropocentrism. I fully agree with him, and will only try to follow his track a little further, by saying something about a certain interpretation of teleological ethics, especially of the so-called negative utilitarianism, as well as about the extension of the realm of beings worthy of moral consideration to non-human beings.

With respect to the first point we have to go back to the so-called 'is-ought fallacy'. We should realize that there is not only an 'is-ought fallacy', but also 'the fallacy of the is-ought fallacy'. By that fallacy I mean the mistake that it is enough not to infer a prescription from a description, whatever the facts may be. But facts are relevant to moral prescriptives. The fact that babies cannot survive without the care of their parents, is of overwhelming relevance for the moral prescriptive that parents ought to take care of their babies (and children). In some sense you can say that the *telos* of a baby is to become a mature person, corporally, psychologically, mentally and spiritually. In the most comprehensive sense, ethics has to do with that *telos*, notably to further the *well-being* of *others* according to their telos. (This counts only if people are not able to make their own decisions; if they are, they have the right to define their own well-being. This principle is called the principle of autonomy). It is of the very nature of morality to be concerned with the well-being of *others*. (To be concerned for your own well-being, however sophisticated and spiritual it may be, is only a sort of rational self-interest; that makes rational self-interest not immoral, but in a way non-moral). Granted that every being depends for its survival on conditions that determine whether it can prosper or not, it could be said that any living being can come to an optimum state of existence, which could be called the *telos* of that being. That is the approach of Bernard E. Rollin.[32] He pays his attention mainly to animals, and argues that animals can be seen as ends in themselves and that in that sense they can be considered to have a *telos* (o.c.p. 51-64). However, we must not take that telos in the traditional, unchangeable sense, but as a testable concept, compatible with modern biology, and always open to revision. To quote Rollin: "The genetic code of a given species provides us with a clear, scientific, testable, physicalistic locus for *telos* ... To understand the nature of an animal in a way that is relevant to ethics, is not a great or profound epistemological problem; it involves only sympathetic observations of the animal's life and activities" (o.c.p. 54). To answer the question how this concept of telos can be made operative in ethics, it is helpful to consider an analysis by Alisdair MacIntyre, respecting the 'is-ought problem' in a teleological scheme of inference.[33]

MacIntyre points out that the 'is-ought fallacy' can only occur in a non-teleological scheme of reasoning from 'is' to 'ought'. According to him we can take the teleological scheme as follows:

I (teleological)

(1) Human nature as it happens to be;
(2) Human nature as it could be if it realised its telos;
(3) The precepts of rational ethics;

Since (2) is a mixture of descriptive and prescriptive meaning, the naturalistic fallacy cannot occur. In a positivist view of science and ethics, however, (2) is eliminated as having no scientific meaning. Consequently the 'is-ought fallacy' is something like an unbridgeable gap:

II (non-teleological)

(1) Human nature as it happens to be;
(2) ????
(3) The precepts of rational ethics;

This scheme not only shows the logical impossibility of the 'is-ought fallacy', but also the factual impossibility to take account of any fact in moral reasoning. This is unsatisfactory, for the lessons, which can be taken from evolutionary biology, means above all going back to a teleological scheme of moral reasoning. The point is that the concept of *telos* should be given its proper place. From that point of view the scheme would be as follows:

III (teleological/evolutionary)

(1) x's nature as it happens to be;
(2) x's nature as it could be if it realised its telos;
(3) the prescription that everyone's well-being according to its telos ought to be advanced;
(4) the precepts of rational ethics.
(x = any living being)

Something more should be said about the basic principle of negative utilitarianism, which is presupposed in (3), but let me first consider the second question, whether we are in need of an extension of the reach of our moral obligations and if so, how far.

Traditionally the reach of our moral obligations is limited to such extent as is comprehended by the realm of rational persons. (I notice that this already means a transgression of the boundaries of tribal and nationalistic egoism). The traditional view is based on the idea that to be rational is a necessary condition for being a *person*, and that therefore only persons are part of the realm of moral relevant beings. However, from that viewpoint it is easily overlooked, that persons can be regarded both as *agents* and as *patients*. It was Kant, who paid much attention to this aspect of ethics, which in the second version of his well-known categorical imperative is formulated as follows: "So act as to use humanity, both in your own person and in the person of every other, always at the same time as an end, never simply as a means".[34] That imperative is valid within a framework of human relations, as is visualized in figure IV.

IV

The realm of beings worthy of moral consideration
(according to Kant)

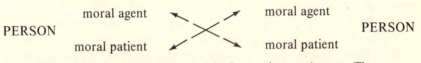

PERSON   moral agent   moral agent   PERSON

moral patient   moral patient

Comment: In this scheme persons are seen both as patients and agents. That means: only human beings can be seen (and treated!) as persons. The relationship between persons ought to be *equal* and *reciprocal* (as a consequence of the categorical imperative). The reciprocity and equality of this relationship is visualised in the arrow ← →.

Essential for a sound understanding of the question at stake, is the insight that non-human living beings cannot be considered to be moral agents. For that reason the relations between human and non-human beings are always asymmetrical, in consciousness as well as in power. That asymmetrical relationship can be visualized as follows:

V

The realm of beings worthy of moral consideration
(non-anthropocentric)

PERSON   NON-HUMAN
                             BEINGS

man as moral agent ——— ——→ moral patients

Comment: With regard to animals and all other living beings on a lower level of existence, man never can be a moral patient, but he necessarily is a moral agent. Conversely, an animal (etc.) never can be a moral agent, but necessarily is – in relationship to man – a moral patient. There cannot be reciprocity and equality, but that is not a sound reason to exclude animals (etc.) from moral consideration. The extension of the range of moral consideration is visualised in the arrow – →

Since agency is a necessary condition for being a moral agent, any type of ethics is in a certain sense always *anthropocentric*, the so-called 'non-anthropocentric ethic' as well. But reading carefully the publications of 'non-anthropocentrics' it becomes clear that they have in mind the patient-position of living beings, not their supposed agency. Their point is that all living beings, either men or animals, should be treated alike.[35] Taking their claims seriously, we are left with two possible approaches, *either* we adapt our ethics to the kind of life of all non-human beings, i.e. to the ruthless struggle for life, as Darwin described it, *or* we extend the range of our moral obligations to non-human beings. The first option is morally unacceptable. For it implies that saving an indoor plant out of a burning house has equal moral worth as saving a baby out of that house, which seems in every sense to be absurd. From an evolutionary point of view the absurdity becomes even greater, since in the process of evolution not the individual life counts, but rather the reproductive chances of the genes. But it is the very essence of morality that individuals count, not genes. For instance, when we are concerned for the future survival of mankind, we do not have in mind the reproductive chances of our genes, but the well-being of future representatives of mankind; and only in consequence of that we are concerned for the reproductive chances of human genes. In ethics the right order of values is of overwhelming importance.

Thus we are left with the second option: the necessary extension of the range of our moral obligations into the domain of non-human beings. Much could be said on this subject, but I confine myself to expose the basic principle, belonging to that second option, namely, the principle of *negative utilitarianism*, or of *non-maleficence*.

4. The Principle of non-Maleficence

As argued above, the care for everybody's telos, can be considered as being an application of the *principle of utility*, which principle should be carefully distinguished from (the theory of) *utilitarianism*. The principle of utility shapes, so to say, the background of utilitarianism, and can be defined as the obligation to maximize the balance of good over evil. Philosophers have argued, for instance William K. Frankena,[36] that this obligation presupposes a more basic one, notably the prima facie obligation to do good and to prevent harm. That principle is called the *principle of benevolence*, which constitutes the very content of morality.

However, the principle works in two different directions: to do good and to prevent harm. In the past utilitarianism was worked out predominantly as a theory of doing good in the sense of increasing good. In order to increase the good, sometimes a little harm had to be done, but as long as the balance was in favour of the good, this seemed acceptable. Doing harm was the unavoidable cost of doing good. In this way utilitarianism became the ideology of capitalism. Gradually the insight grew that increasing good instead of preventing harm, was a sort of injustice to the poor, since the rich got the benefits of utilitarian economic policy, and the poor paid for the costs. Karl Marx especially made us aware of the negative side of utilitarianism. If 'doing good' can be called *positive utilitarianism*, then 'preventing harm' is *negative utilitarianism*. The tendency of the last years, for instance in the writings of Karl Popper, is to prefer negative utilitarianism to positive. That means: 'preventing harm' comes first, 'doing good' later. There are sound reasons for this.

In the first place, preventing harm obviously has the 'evidence of the negative'. Who would deny that saving a child from starvation is far more urgent than making a child happy by showering presents upon him? The slums in the Third World suffice to make one feel ashamed of the wealth, in which European and American children grow up.

In the second place, in practice the good and the harm are seldom equally distributed. Usually we find the good is done to the rich and the harm to the poor. To prefer preventing harm to doing good means rough justice for the poor.

In the third place, the duty to prevent harm is evident, as the duty to do good is not. Consider the following order of reference, as proposed by Frankena:

(1) One ought not to inflict evil or harm;
(2) One ought to prevent evil and harm;
(3) One ought to remove evil;
(4) One ought to do or promote good (in a non-moral sense, of course).

(1) is the most basic in morality, in a way morality itself; (2) is the consequence of (1) and cannot logically be refused, if (1) is accepted; (3) is true if and only if one is able to do so, and (4) can be questioned for different reasons. For instance, why should one have the duty to support a policy that raises the incomes of the average wage-earners in Holland and lower his own, taking it that the incomes in Holland are mostly already equalized. Possibly there are reasons to support such a policy, but to say that there is a *moral duty*, is absurd.

The reason why I prefer (2) to (1) is that in practice 'inflicting no harm' is too passive. We need a more active policy to prevent harm.

The three above reasons for preferring prevention of harm to doing good, apply perfectly to the asymmetrical relations between *men* and non-human beings, let us say *animals*. In the first place, the harm done to animals in our culture, is evident. I point only to the suffering of animals in research, in modern farming, in hunting, in shooting, and even in our houses, where they are cherished as pet animals, far away from their natural environments. Dogs are bred not according to their 'telos', but in order to satisfy human demands for having a dog after the latest fashion. To make men more 'happy', it is taken for granted that animals are treated cruelly.[37] That has to be changed.

Secondly the asymmetrical relations between men and animals involve a tendency toward injustice, since animals are on the powerless side. It is easy to kill seal babies and make fur coats out of their skins, in order to enable a few people to get dressed as they desire. Doing justice always means going the difficult way. But we have to do so, since it is morally and intellectually absurd to tolerate such cruelty to helpless animals, merely to satisfy the degenerated preferences of a small 'elite'.

Thirdly, keeping in mind that animals can suffer, the duty to prevent harm is appropriate to all beings that are capable of suffering. The fact that so many people naturally accept the suffering of animals as unavoidable, is due to the traditional line between men and animals: men are rational, animals not. That is probably true (Hobbes, for instance, denied it!), but not to the point. Therefore the much insulted Jeremy Bentham draws another line: animals can *suffer* as well as men can, and therefore they are beings, worthy of moral consideration.[38]

I conclude that there are reasons to extend the reach of our moral obligations into the realm of all sentient beings. The basic principle of treating them rightly should be the principle of preventing harm. I emphasize that this does not imply the equeal treatment of men and animals, or, within the domain of animals, of animals and animals. The killing of a pig is not equally bad as the killing of a man, as the death of a fly is not comparable with the death of a horse. The principle of preventing harm only compels us to give *reasons* for not preventing harm in a given, concrete situation. In practice we seldom have the chance to choose between doing good and preventing harm, but usually between doing *less* or *more* harm. We have to consider how the greater harm can be prevented. Surplus population is, for instance, a great threat and even a harm, but letting children of the Third World starve because of the necessity to decrease the number of men in order to prevent an ecological catastrophe, would be a greater harm. Such a 'letting-die-policy' runs counter to our moral intuitions.

Is it not arbitrary to draw the line between sentient beings on the one side and all other beings on the other? Why not extend the realm of our moral obligations into the domain of ecosystems? For ecosystems are of great interest to men and animals! That is true, but does not involve the intended extension. Ecosystems, and all non-living environments, are of *instrumental* value to living beings. Taking care of living beings implies concern for ecosystems, but not in the sense that we have a moral duty to do so. Besides, taking care of ecosystems in order to prevent harm to sentient beings, already is a long step towards a new moral consciousness concerning our duties to non-human beings.

5. An Outlook on Theology

Lack of space compels me to present only a few indications of the consequences of my standpoint for theology. In my opinion we are in need of a new understanding of *Creation*. The traditional theology of creation falls short, since it was suspicious of evolution itself and confused social conditions of 'living together' with natural conditions of survival. For instance, regarding marriage as part of the Order of Creation was due to that confusion of social systems with ecosystems. The intended new theology of creation should refer to the ecological conditions of existence as is made explicit by evolutionary biology. The distinction between social conditions of life and the ecological ones should be observed carefully, in order to avoid, for example, the fallacy of inferring any necessary new concept of creation from the current theology of liberation. Liberation should respect the social conditions of life, creation the ecological ones.[39]

Because of the crucial position of man in the process of evolution, attention must be given to the theological meaning of human *stewardship of the creation*, especially concerning the sustainability of the natural environment. Reading the book of Genesis, especially the chapters I-IX, in the light of our responsibility for nature, could be helpful for a new orientation in theology. It is my fixed conviction that for the coming years, theology has more to learn from evolutionary biology than otherwise.

Notes

1. Christian Vogel (1986), *Evolution und Moral*, in Heinz Maier-Leibnitz (ed.), *Zeugen des Wissens*, v. Hase & Koehler Verlag, Mainz, 467-507; Gerhard Vollmer (1986), *Über die Möglichkeit einer evolutionären Ethik* in *Conceptus* 20, 49, 1-21.
2. Vogel o.c., 467-468.
3. L. A. Selby-Bigge (ed.) (1964), *British Moralists*, Bobbs-Merrill Comp., Indianapolis/New York.

4. Vogel o.c., passim; Vollmer o.c., 11-15.
5. Vollmer o.c., passim.
6. Vogel o.c., 494.
7. Vollmer o.c., 16.
8. Vogel o.c., 494 (quoting Kowalski): "Again, biology cannot justify the claim that moral laws ought to conform to human nature".
9. Gerrit Manenschijn (1985), *Reasoning in Science and Ethics*, in Bert Musschenga & David Gosling (eds.), *Science Education and Ethical Values*, WCC Publications/Georgetown University Press, Geneva/Washington D.C., 37-54.
10. G. Wallace & A. D. M. Walker (eds.) (1970), *The Definition of Morality*, Methuen & Comp., London; particularly the Contribution of W. K. Frankena, The Concept of Morality, 146-173.
11. Hector-Neri Castaneda (1974), *The Structure of Morality*, Charles C. Thomas, Springfield Ill., 189: "Since morality as an institution includes both the ideal and a moral code, we can say that morality is *self-corrective*, the idea of progress is central to it... To put it paradoxically, morality remains moral even when it requires overriding itself. This is the peak of the self-correctiveness of morality". That comes near to what evolutionists call 'adaption'.
12. Vogel o.c., 496.
13. Michael Ruse (1986), *Taking Darwin Seriously, A Naturalist Approach to Philosophy*, Basil Blackwell, Oxford, 230: "The claim is that human moral thought has constraints, as manifested through the epigenic rules, and the application of these leads to moral codes, soaring from biology into culture".
14. Vogel o.c., 490.
15. See note 10.
16. Frankena o.c., 155.
17. Frankena o.c., 156.
18. As Frankena himself in fact did in his paper Ethics and the Environment, in K. E. Goodpaster & K. M. Sayre (eds.) (1979) *Ethics and the Problems of 21st Century*, University of Notre Dame Press, Notre Dame/London, 3-20.
19. Richard Dawkins (1976), *The Selfish Gene*, OUP, Oxford.
20. Vogel o.c., 503, note 1.
21. Charles Darwin (1859), *The Origin of Species by Means of Natural Selection*. The reference is taken from A. Flew (1970), *Evolutionary Ethics*, MacMillan, London, 10.
22. Ruse, o.c., 16-18.
23. A. W. Musschenga (1984), *Can Sociobiology Contribute to Moral Science and Ethics?* In *Journal of Human Evolution* 13, 137-147.
24. Ruse o.c., 256-257.
25. Vollmer o.c., 11-18; Ruse o.c., 223-227.
26. Vogel o.c., 494-495.
27. Musschenga o.c., 138.
28. Ruse o.c., 253.
29. A. R. Peacocke (1979), *Creation and the World of Science*, The Bampton Lectures 1978, Clarendon Press, Oxford, 261.
30. Flew o.c., 53-54.
31. Vogel o.c., 500-503.
32. Bernard E. Rollin (1981), *Animal Rights and Human Morality*, Prometheus Books, Buffalo N.Y.

33. Alisdair MacIntyre (1981), *After Virtue, A Study in Moral Theory*, University of Notre Dame Press, Notre Dame, 49-59.
34. H. J. Paton (1967), *The Categorical Imperative, A Study in Kant's Moral Philosophy*, Harper & Row, New York/Evanston, 165.
35. One of my students, Miss Thalien Koopman, recently wrote a Master of Arts thesis, called "Crossing the Boundaries; Non-anthropocentric Ecological Ethics Described and Evaluated". I learned much from her study, which is in Dutch and available only at the Faculty of Theology of the Free University of Amsterdam.
36. W. K. Frankena (1973), *Ethics*, Prentice-Hall, Englewood N.J., 45-48.
37. Rollin o.c., 89-176; Stephen R. L. Clark (1984), *The Moral Status of Animals*, OUP, Oxford/New York, passim.
38. Jeremy Bentham (1982), *An Introduction to the Principles of Morals and Legislation*, edited by J. H. Burns & H. L. A. Hart, Methuen, London/New York, 283: "But a full-grown horse or dog, is beyond comparison a more rational, as well as a more conversible animal, than an infant of a day, or a week, or even a month old. But suppose the case were otherwise, what would it avail? The question is not can they reason? Nor, can they talk? But can they suffer?".
39. Besides the already referred study of A. R. Peacocke the following books could be mentioned: John Passmore (1980), *Man's Responsibility for Nature*, Duckworth, London; Charles Birch & John B. Cobb Jr. (1984), *The Liberation of Life, From the Cell to the Community*, CUP, Cambridge; Jürgen Moltmann, *Gott in der Schöpfung* (1985), Ökologische Schöpfungslehre, Kaiser, München.

Evolution in Different Theological Traditions

Jürgen Hübner

My thesis is that the different traditions of Christianity and their theologies deal with evolution in different ways. In our time the differences and controversies between the great Christian confessions and denominations are beginning to diminish and disappear. Controversial questions today are increasingly being raised in all denominations, and all are confronted by the same problems. But there are specific differences that remain, and I think it would be useful to remember these differences when facing the problem of evolution.

My interest in this question is a more theoretical one. I think the experience of the new spiritual communion between all Christian believers in our generation makes it possible to reflect on the various accents of our various traditions in a new way without attacking each other.

The crucial points of confessional controversy that have characterized the debate have revolved around the doctrine of the Church and its hierarchic structure on the Roman Catholic side, the doctrine of predestination in the Calvinist churches, and Christology in Lutheran life and thinking. To this must be added the doctrinal emphasis of the Orthodox Church, where cosmology is at the centre of Christian belief. Dr. Peacocke will no doubt have more to say about Anglican thought, and excuse me, if I confine myself to the first three I mentioned.

The *Roman Catholic* theory of the Church reflects the structure of the cosmos. In the medieval view of the world there is a hierarchical order, as Dr. Schmitz-Moormann has reminded us. The earth had its location in the centre of the world, but beneath the orbs of the planets and beneath the sky of the fixed stars. Beyond that sphere of the fixed stars there was the throne of God the Creator, the heavenly place of his sovereignty over creation and God reigned there in communion with the angelic choir and the departed who had been received into heaven. You will find an illustration of this vision in the famous Weltchronik of Hermann Schedel in 1493.

The hierarchy of this universe was directed from above to beneath and vice versa. According to the tradition of Stoicism, life on earth was regarded as the image of this heavenly world, the microcosm of the macrocosm of the universe. The spiritual hierarchy of the Church with the Pope up above reflected the order of the cosmos; and the same applied to secular authority with the Emperor above. The forces of divine grace administered by the Church elevated this natural order; they led from earth to and into heaven.

Modern natural sciences have demolished this view of the world. This model of the cosmos has disappeared and the very order of life on earth was thereby threatened. This is the central issue in the controversy between science and religion at the beginning of the modern period.

The problem is a theological one. Classical theology, especially of Western European countries, was linked with the Graeco-Roman view of the world, the Ptolemaic system of the universe. But this system – and the world-view based on it – had diverse components. The scientific aspects were essentially mathematical and physical ones. The differences between them led to the Copernican revolution in astronomy, a change of paradigm as Thomas S. Kuhn describes it. But there were also political and existential aspects in the classical world-view. The breakdown of the cosmological hierarchy – and consequently that of the traditional political order in Church and society – led to the Renaissance and the Enlightenment and eventually to the establishment of modern national states.

The *existential* aspects of the Copernican revolution can be described as a crisis of the human being's habitat, of human life in the realm of the universe. Once the home of humankind in the universe, viz. the earth, was no longer located at the centre of a well-ordered cosmos, the question arose of the meaning and dignity of human life within nature. One could say: it was a question of man's identity in the universe, a question of his orientation. Copernicus and Kepler had answers to this question. According to them, the earth was an exceptional planet, set up in the middle of the orbits of all other planets, most suitable for the best observation of all other parts of the universe.

But then Giordano Bruno had the vision of the boundless universe and an infinite number of world systems; and at *this* point, man lost his old home in the cosmos. As Hans Blumenberg has pointed out, man then had to look around for a new home – he had to construct a new world which matched his intellectual abilities. Human life needs a world-view in order to exist; you must see where you live in order to make sense in your life.

With the end of the old concept of the world as a system, with the earth in the centre and the divine realm beyond its circumference, a new world-view was needed in which the human being could find a new home, his own unique habitat and new meaning for his life. After the dark centuries of the Baroque Age and the Enlightenment, in which the light was artificially created or abstractly constructed and was hardly a living reality for the average person; after this period of doubt and the period in which the human being asserted himself in a world without bounds; and finally, after the period of mechanism, after all these experiences, it was the concept of *evolution* which provided a new perspective also for human life in the world.

The theory of evolution was able to provide the framework for a new vision of the world. The evolutionary process in nature also made it easier to grasp some aspects of human culture and civilization. The process of evolution could even be understood in a mystical sense, as a path leading from individuals to a spiritual community. Jesus Christ himself could be experienced as a sacrament of evolution. I refer to Professor Schmitz-Moorman's contribution to tell us more about this from the perspective of the Roman Catholic tradition.

I myself wish to make some observations about Calvinist and Lutheran traditions of life and thinking with respect to the modern evolutionary world-view. A central and unique aspect of *Calvinist* theology is the doctrine of predestination. In the late version of this doctrine in the early 17th century it was formulated in philosophical terms: God's love wills salvation; and faith in Christ obtains participation in God's grace. In respect to faith, the individual's personal advancement and success in daily life confirms the experience of divine election each day anew.

But not all people believe in Christ; it was already a problem in the Old Testament that the impious and godless person succeeds in life, and the godly suffer. But the participation in the Spirit of Christ in Christian faith gives the certainty of a share in God's love. This faith is of course the condition of coming to be aware of the providence of God.

But the providential ways of God, the Creator, in the world can also be explored in terms of causal analysis, and causal analysis means in terms of scientific research. Science is effective, and scientific thinking operates without theological presuppositions. The real problem of the modern world and its civilization is that it works *better* this way. The result, however, is the crisis of modern civilization. The environmental crisis is bound up with it. The attempt to re-integrate theological truth into *modern* thought, which involves *modern* science, is therefore to develop a *theology of evolution*.

With respect to evolution, the development of human culture within the history of nature on earth and in the universe can be seen as a realization of God's creative will in his creation. But there is a critical moment in this perspective of evolution. The sin of man, the evil of the world does not allow us to propose a purely optimistic view of evolution. There will be the Day of Judgement on this world, for there may be interruptions, catastrophes, and a disastrous end to evolution before the new creation in the kingdom of God is realized. Is the kingdom of God a direct continuation of life on this earth or in another world? No one can penetrate the plans of God. In Calvinist thinking, the best thing to do is to follow the path of evolution and to win the assurance of righteousness in all that is done. But God's decree for life or death is not available to human understanding. However, the life of Christ provides the outlines of God's will and this is the way for man to live his life in accordance with the meaning of creation. The evolution of nature and human civilization is no source of ultimate certainty and peace in private and public life – hope for the future is exclusively grounded in the occurrence of divine grace, in Jesus Christ. Because of human sin, evolution has a very open future – there may be a total destruction of this world, before God establishes his new creation promised according to the tradition of the Bible. The human being is responsible for the outcome of evolution, and through faith in Christ, the human being has the duty to proclaim God's love and justice in this world and to act according to the will of the Creator.

In this manner, evolution as an open process will follow according to God's providence. God's providence is no evolutionary programme for the world, but the gift of life for his creatures down through the ages. This may be described in terms of evolution, but evolution cannot be identified with God. God is not simply the God of evolution or even an evolutor; he is the Creator of evolution and of evolutionary processes. In this sense God is the *critic* of evolution. In so far as the human being is responsible now for the future of evolution on earth, the crucial question facing him is: Who is your God? Whom do you follow in your activities in the process of evolution?

In the *Lutheran* perspective of predestination and providence, the vision of harmony between Creator and creation is essentially lost. The cross of Christ is the sign of disharmony in the world of the human being and of nature. God's love and grace comes to man *sub contrario*, under the contrast of his holy will. In public there can be seen only the cross of Christ, the crucified Christ in isolation. This destiny can be regarded as an expression of God's wrath. But faith recognizes God's love under the sign and symbol of the cross: Christ, the Son of God, took this path to the cross for each human being, for human redemption, for the salvation of all creation.

Therefore the continuing process of evolution does not say anything about God and his grace. Only in the light of the cross and of the resurrection of Christ can the history of life and the process of evolution be seen as a trace of the Creator's activity. The Spirit of Christ reveals the process of nature as a process of creation. Evolution may provide signs, analogies of God's creative activity. But these do not entail any prediction or prognosis of what will happen in the future. The future is open. This radical openness is of the essence of creation and also the essence of evolution as creation. In this sense, in the Catholic tradition, Karl Rahner has spoken of the absolute future. I think there is a parallel here to a biological interpretation of evolution, a parallel, for instance, to the theory of open systems.

From the very beginning, Lutheran theology developed independently of any special world-view. When Lutherans concentrate on the Biblical message, they discover that the work of Jesus Christ and the salvation of humankind and creation through the cross is its central theme. Because of the risen Christ's real presence in his world, in the Lord's Supper as well as in Baptism, there was no need for them to discuss the structure of the universe in theological terms. Christ's presence is real and can be seen and thought of in the context of the old Ptolemaic universe, as much as in Copernican or Darwinian terms. The world can be understood as God's creation in the same way in different systems or paradigms of scientific thinking.

The paradigm of our own time is the model of evolution. The language of traditional theology, however, is based on the old picture of the closed universe of the Middle Ages. So modern theology must discuss the impact of the modern view of the world in its own linguistic terms. The central theme of the Christian message and the real truth of Christian faith must be re-formulated in terms of modern thinking without losing its content; and, on the other hand, modern thinking, especially the language of modern science, must incorporate reflection on the theological roots of science itself.

This is not merely an intellectual problem. It is, I think, a problem of fundamental life-orientation and of life-style for we live in our modern world. In Christian terms, it is in this world that we have the offer of living in fellowship with Christ, and therefore in fellowship with God. This offer comes to us through the tradition of the Bible, delivered by the Christian community. We have to reflect this life of faith in the language of our modern world. And this reflection is once again relevant for the understanding of nature and human life in the present and in the future, and therefore it is relevant for understanding science.

In doing so, I think we must distinguish three ways of discussing evolution: 1. evolution as a biological theory, 2. evolution as a world-view (Weltanschauung) bordering on a religion, and 3. evolution as a phenomenon, as life itself in our modern experience. It is not my task to develop this here. Let me say this much: The theory of evolution is a rational model of thinking, rational in an analytical sense. Scientific theories are in the tradition of medieval Nominalism. Religion, however, includes more than rationality. Therefore analytical thinking can serve only as a linguistic means, as a support for an orientation, not as the orientation itself. Evolutionary thinking as a whole, on the other hand, (and this means "Weltanschauung") is more and something else than merely thinking in terms of an evolutionary *theory*. It is a form of life-style. But evolution, even as a world-view, is not yet life itself. Life itself makes evolution. Life is not only a theory or a world-view. In theological term: evolutionary development is the mandate to live given by the Creator. Human life has an especially great responsibility to live in this world. Science and religion are components of human life. Together they can meet the responsibility of the human being for the evolution of life on earth.

Let me summarize: The roots of modern science and therefore of the modern age of technology are to be found in the Middle Ages. *Catholic* philosophy and theology preserve this tradition of the origins of science in their own traditions. They do so in a more realistic way (in a philosophical sense), whereas science follows the path of nominalistic philosophy, as it is also found in the Darwinian theory of evolution. The Catholic way of thinking is handing down the holistic claim of the medieval world-viewl, now transformed into an evolutionary perspective.

The *Calvinist* tradition refers to the methods of modern science through the discussion of predestination and divine providence. The naturalists of the 17th and 18th century sought to penetrate the mind of God in creation. Science means inquiring into the thoughts of God when he created the world. Inaccuracy therefore is a sin against the Creator (here are the roots of the ideal of accuracy in science). The mechanism of Newton and Darwin is an example of this intention. But at the same time, Calvinist theology and its descendants have a very critical potential: no one is in fact able to penetrate the wisdom of God, least of all his justice and love. Therefore evolution cannot be the last answer to man's quest for God – as certainly as life is evolving.

In the *Lutheran* tradition all is focused on Jesus Christ, through whom comes the redemption and salvation of mankind and nature. Faith in Jesus Christ also enables the believers to be open to evolution, as a scientific theory, as an existential world-view, and as a phenomenon that is life itself.

I think, all three traditions, and to these may be added other Christian and also Jewish and other religious traditions, are guides to the kingdom of God, each of them, however, blind in one eye and limping on one leg. All together can help us to find the right path. This may be a path of evolution, as we are taught by science. Therefore science belongs to the community of all mankind,

Evolution in the English (Anglican) Theological Tradition

Arthur Peacocke

I have been asked to present the particular perspective on evolution that prevails in my own ecclesiastical and, indeed, national tradition, that is, to describe the roots of and responses to evolutionary ideas that can be found within that body which might best be denoted as *Ecclesia Anglicana*. I would like to suggest that there is in fact a particular style and sensitivity to the created order which exists distinctively in that tradition. I leave it to others to say from their own perspectives whether or not it exists as strongly in other ecclesiastical or national traditions. In England, this sensitivity to and awareness of the natural order of creation led to continuing attempts to create a natural theology, sometimes in the quite bizarre forms of 'physico-theology' in the 18th century. It is a continuous strand in the cultural life that I represent.

Had I time and learning enough, we might well peer into the mists of antiquity for there we would, I believe, discern that this strand comes from much deeper roots than those of the Middle Ages. Christianity in Britain was first established by the Celtic Church which of course had its roots in Eastern Orthodox Christendom and the Irish Celtic church kept contact with the East long after it had been lost elsewhere in the West.[1] The Celtic Church stamped a certain understanding and sprirituality on the Christian culture of my own country which, I think, has never quite been lost – a sacramental perception of the whole of the created order as the vehicle of the presence of God and as the revelation of God's purposes. Hence the many legends of the dealings of Celtic saints with animals, birds and fishes.[2]

Incidentally, there is considerable evidence of the influence of Celtic Christianity throughout Europe in general and, in particular, in the area in Italy around Assisi from which St Francis came.[3] It is intriguing to speculate on what these influences on St Francis might have been in his youth and his subsequent re-vitalising of this whole way of thinking in the Western church. With the invasions and fluctuations of population in Britain during the first millenium AD, the Celtic Church with its creation-centred spirituality was driven out to the fringes of the north and the west. Gradually Britain was re-Christianized from those directions by the Celtic Church and this movement eventually encountered the Latin-Roman mission coming from the south-east: the two strands eventually became welded into *Ecclesia Anglicana* of the middle ages.

It appears that that Celtic strand of creation-centred spirituality never quite desappeared from the English scene, even if it often went underground. It comes to the surface in many of the mystical writers of the 14th century, for example, Lady Julian of Norwich. Moreover, there was also at that time a distinct loosening of ties with Rome which eventually, of course, came to the surface under different political circumstances with the Reformation as experienced in England. This was a very conservative kind of reformation in many significant ways and produced that particular kind of reformed Catholicism that characterises the Church of England, and now, the Anglican Communion. This blend of Christian traditions recognized the insights of the Reformation but at the same time maintained its sacramental continuity with the traditional Church. This gave it a certain style which, I think, is particularly manifest in the so-called Caroline Divines, that is, the theologians in the latter part of the 17th century – in the poetry of George Herbert and John Donne and the prose writings of Thomas Trahearne. There is in this literature a deep sense of the presence of God in creation, for the glory of God is to be seen in the world of nature. It is not at all like the *naturphilosophie* of the later German tradition. It is less romantic and more explicitly immanentist and engendered a willingness to read God's book 'written in Nature' as well as that of the Scriptures. This is to be seen in Roger Bacon, the Franciscan scientists, and Grosseteste at Lincoln and subsequently in Francis Bacon in the 16th century. There was a very clear sense of the 'two Books': the books of Nature and of Holy Writ. Both were to be read together but "let men beware ... that they do not unwisely mingle or confound these learnings together", as Francis Bacon said.[4] This background, as is well known, lies behind the efflorescence in the 17th century of the natural philosophy of Newton, Boyle and Ray. Indeed the Royal Society, one of our most distinguished scientific bodies, numbered among its founders a man who became a bishop, John Wilkins. Indeed there was a strong tendency in these founders of the Royal Society to see their scientific work as a work of piety, of devotion, of reading God's thoughts after him, as it were.

Given such a background it is not surprising, coming now to the 20th century, that Karl Barth, did not make much impression on theology in the Church of England. I say "England" advisedly, rather than Britain, because, unlike our more Presbyterian northern compatriots in Scotland, the heirs of

Calvin, English theology never took at all kindly, or indeed very much at all, to Karl Barth's embargo on natural theology and so also on a positive attitude to the created world and to the sciences that unfold its mysteries. Perhaps because of that historical-cultural development which endowed the Church of the English people with a reformed Catholicism – and so with a strong sacramental sense combined with a humanistic outlook; or perhaps because the efflorescence of science in the 17th century occurred at the hands of intellectual giants such as Newton, Boyle and Ray (founders of physics, chemistry and biology) who were committed theists (if not always, in Newton's case, orthodox Christians); or perhaps, because of the influence of our native literature, and poetry of nature – anyway, for one reason or another, England never suffered the blight of the view that the book of Scripture had alone been 'written by God' and that the book of nature was closed or, at least, of too ambiguous an authorship. So I represent a culture more congenial to a rapprochement between science and religion – and, yet, paradoxically one that has seen some of the greatest crises in their inter-relations. Thus even today, in spite of critical and informed religious teaching for at least 50 years, the annual meeting of the British Association for the Advancement of Science still rouses newspaper reporters to remind their readers of how the St George of science (T. H. Huxley) slew the dragon of religious bigotry (Bishop Wilberforce) at its 1860 Oxford meeting; and most adolescents, according to recent surveys, say they give up "religion" because of their increased knowledge of "science!". So complacency is not to be induced by our situation, any more than elsewhere in the Western world.

What I would like to dwell on for a moment now is a major gap in my rough historical account, namely that of the 19th century, which has been called the century of Darwin. There were, in *England* in the mid-19th century, particular cultural and religious features of the scene that are being increasingly better documented and understood by historians of the period – for example, the dominance of the argument from (principally biological) design as the exclusive form of traditional natural theology and the increasingly disturbing analysis, imported from Germany, of the traditional Scriptures by the criteria and methods of historical scholarship. I will not enter into this intriguing history, study of which is revealing a greater complexity in the Christian response to Darwin and a greater flexibility and openness on the part of orthodox Christian theologians than is purveyed by the inherited mythology about this period. All I wish to do here is to pick out one thread in that nineteenth-century and early twentieth-century response to Darwin which seems to me still to be significant for our present assessment – namely that quieter and, in the end, more profound response of those Christian theists who ded the rest of the animal creation, and communicating His vital energy by a spiritual process to subsequent generations of med.[8]

Charles Gore, the editor of that same controversial volume, later in his 1891 Bampton Lectures affirmed that:

...from the Christian point of view, this revelation of God, this unfolding of divine qualities, reaches a climax in Christ. God has expressed in inorganic nature, His immutability, immensity, power, wisdom; in organic nature He has shown also that He is alive; in human nature He has given glimpses of His mind and character. In Christ not one of these earlier revelations is abrogated; nay, they are reaffirmed; but they reach a completion in the fuller exposition of the divine character, the divine personality, the divine love.[9]

One of the most positive Anglican attempts made in the 20th century to integrate evolutionary biology in to Christian theology was that of F. R. Tennant[10] who rejected the traditional pessimism about man, as it had been developed from the Bible by the combination of *Genesis* with the Pauline epistles. Instead, Tennant appealed from the scriptures, understood in the light of tradition to the evidence of the evolutionary process. In the original man, he argued, the moral consciousness awakened only slowly – there was no question of some *catastrophic* change for the worse in his relationship with God, nor was there, at a later stage in man's development, a 'radical bias towards evil' because of the Fall. It was as true to say that God was still making man as to say that God had made him: the origin and meaning of sin had similarly to be sought in the process of becoming. This emphasis on the 'process of becoming' was also a major strand in the philosophy of A. N. Whitehead, son of an Anglican clergyman. William Temple, later Archbishop of Canterbury, and L. S. Thornton were contemporaries of Whitehead and Tennant and were deeply influenced especially by the former and like the latter drew upon that tradition of the interpretation of evolution which went back to *Lux Mundi*.

To read again Willian Temple's *Nature, Man and God*[12] (his Gifford Lectures of 1932-4) reminds us of his percipience in detecting those broad features in the new knowledge of his day – mostly from the sciences – that gave a perspective on the world of a kind that theology could ignore only at peril to its fundamental claims to speak truth and to see it whole. In the manner of the philosophical fashion of his day, Temple continually 'ontologises' Matter, Mind and Spirit, denoting them thus with capital letters, rather than referring to them, as we might, as processes and activities discernible in the world. However, allowing for this, we nevertheless find him taking the measure of the scientific world-view and discerning what it implies – and thereby raising for us here and now similar questions about the world-view of the sciences of our own day. For he perceived very clearly the need first to discriminate, then to relate, the various levels of analysis available in the sciences of his day and this, I would urge, is still a necessary task in any attempt by theologians to take seriously the knowledge afforded by the sciences. It is not my intention to mount a full re-appraisal of *Nature, Man and God* and his other relevant writings, so let me quote a passage typical of those written by Temple on this theme:

Broadly speaking, the modern scientific view affords an apprehension of the world as existing in a series of strata, of such a sort that the lower is necessary to the actuality of the higher but only finds its own fullness of being when thus used by the higher as its means of self-actualisation. Without the mechanical basis in matter, there could be no life of the kind that we know. Without living matter – bodily organisms – mind, as we know it does not arise. Without animal mind (seeking means to an end presented as good) there could be no spirit such as we know (choosing between ends by reference to an ideal standard of Good). Now such a scheme can be regarded from two points of view; but whichever is adopted, care must be taken to avoid obliterating what is evident from the other. We may begin at the lower end of the series, and then there is no doubt about the reality of the material world. But the fact that this is real, and is the necessary basis of the world of life and mind and spirit as known to us, must not lead us to the supposition that there is nothing in these which is not observable in the material world as such. In the last resort it is, no doubt, true that there is only one world, and each department in isolation is an abstraction. We can say, if we like, that there is only one substance, and that the different sciences study not different substances, but different modes of action and reaction on the part of the same substance. But then we must be careful not to say that, because the actions and reactions studies in physics and chemistry are certainly real, therefore those studied in biology, in aesthetics, in ethics, in theology are either unreal or else are only complicated forms of the other group.[13]

This passage expresses *in nuce* Temple's emphasis on the creative work of God within nature and thus on the immanence of the Transcendent; his understanding of man as part of the natural created order and yet as manifesting peculiarly the transcendence of the Immanent; and his insight (in the tradition of J. R. Illingworth) into the Incarnation as the supreme revelation of God who is the Transcendent who is immanent, and whose Immanence is, must be, transcendent.

The last sentence of Temple, just quoted, with its warning against attributing reality only to the simpler levels analysed by the atomic and molecular sciences is echoed in other passages in his work:

...Science, in following its method of using the "lowest" category applicable, is not entitled to deny the applicability of "higher" categories but is only seeing how far it can go without them. Even if it can cover all the facts and hold them together by means of "lower", as for instance mechanical categories, it does not necessarily follow that the "higher" categories, such as purpose, have no rightful application at all. ....the positive work of Science, in giving an account of observable facts by its own method, never justifies Science in proceeding to negative inferences concerning other methods of interpretation, provided that these in their turn do not exclude the method of Science.[14]

This cautionary word seems to me to be as necessary today as it was when Temple first wrote it and indeed to be even more pertinent when we come to reflect on the implications of contemporary biological science for any system of thought that is believable today concerning nature, man and God. For Temple, more explicitly than any other theologian that I know, was concerned to stress the 'materialism' of Christianity in its understanding of 'matter' as a real existent entity and as a necessary vehicle of Spirit. And so the scientific account of matter and of living matter must always be incorporated in to the total theological understanding.

As is well known (at least on our side of the Channel!), Temple in his penultimate Gifford Lecture (XIX) focussed on the Christian understanding of sacraments – as material instruments of God's actions in effecting his purposes and as symbols of God's self-expression and thus as a mode of his revelation – in order to draw these various threads together into his concept of the universe as 'sacramental'. It is not my purpose to develop this penetrating insight further here, but to stress that that insight itself stems from Temple's own understanding of the hierarchy of levels that exist in the world and his recognition that there has been a development in time, with new levels appearing, dependent on and yet genuinely emergent from, the preceding, simpler levels.

The last name I want to mention in this specifically Church of England tradition of interpretation of evolution is that of Charles Raven, formerly Regius Professor of Divinity in the University of Cambridge, and one whom his biographer, F. W. Dillistone, dubbed as 'naturalist, historian, theologian'.[15] His whole life was concerned to integrate the evolutionary perspective of biology with his own Christian understanding, for he embraced wholeheartedly the evolutionary interpretation of biology and believed that it could serve also as the conceptual framework for religious expression.[16] He strove to enhance the place of the life sciences in man's understanding of the universe, then largely dominated by physics, and he pioneered in emphasising the need for ecological policies. The living world was for him the many splendoured sacrament of the activities of the living God. His last words from the pulpit, which I was privileged to hear, expressed in his characteristic eloquence a vision of the unity of Christian insight and aspiration with a perspective on the cosmos that was deeply informed by the natural sciences and above all by that of evolution. This vision pervades this strand of development of Christian theology in Britain. So it was that the impact of Teilhard de Chardin and of process theology was less significant for an

119

indigenous tradition that was already integrating, without the benefit of metaphysics, these two perspectives of science and religion on the nature and meaning of the cosmic process.

To summarise, these perceptions arising from a certain rapport with the natural order, which come through in our general culture and have been frequently expressed explicitly in our natural theology over many centuries are resilient enough, it seems to me, to incorporate positively our new knowledge of the evolutionary process and to see it as not only consistent with but as enhancing our understanding of the immanent presence of God as Creator in the created order, a presence continuously celebrated in the sacramental life of the Church. These perspectives are, perhaps, the distinctive ones, to which I would like to draw your attention as the tradition of *Ecclesia Anglicana*.

References

1. J. W. C. Wand (1937), *A History of the Early Church to A D 500*, Methuen, London, p. 198; H. Mayr-Harting (1972), *The Coming of Christianity to Anglo-Saxon England*, London.
2. L. Hardinge (1972), *The Celtic Church in Britain*, S. P. C. K., London.
3. E. A. Armstrong (1973), *Saint Francis: Nature Mystic*, University of California Press, Berkeley.
4. Francis Bacon (1975), *The Advancement of Learning*, The First Book i. 3., ed. W. A. Armstrong, Athlone Press, London, p. 55, *11* 30-8.
5. A. L. Moore (1889), *Science and Faith*, Kegan Paul, Trench & Co, London, p. 184.
6. A. L. Moore, 'The Christian Doctrine of God', in C. Gore (ed.) *Lux Mundi* (Murray, London, 1891), p. 73 (12th edit.).
7. J. R. Illingworth, 'The Incarnation in Relation to Development', *ibid.* p. 132.
8. *ibid.*, p. 151-2.
9. C. Gore (1891), *The Incarnation of the Son of God*, Bampton Lectures, Murray, London, pp. 32-3.
10. F. R. Tennant (1902), *The Origin & Propagation of Sin*, Hulsean Lectures, Cambridge University Press, Cambridge.
11. L. S. Thornton (1928), *The Incarnate Lord*, Longman, Green & Co, London, New York & Toronto.
12. W. Temple (1934), *Nature, Man and God*, Macmillan, London, (repr. 1964).
13. *ibid.*, p. 474-5.
14. *ibid.*, p. 52-3.
15. F. W. Dillistone (1975), *Charles Raven: Naturalist, Historian & Theologian*, Hodder & Stoughton, London.
16. C. E. Raven (1928), *The Creator Spirit*, London. *Natural Religion and Christian Theology* Gifford Lectures. *I* Science & Religion. *II*, Experience & Interpretation. (Cambridge University Press, Cambridge, 1953).

without any counterpart in concrete reality; or to quote facts which are selected as weapons against adversaries, without being parts of a coherent world-view.

As R. Lay has pointed out, after Galileo the Catholic theologians withdrew from the world as known through science. Certainly, the theologians did not give up their territory in the concrete world without fighting, but they tried to defend a world-view they held on account of tradition rather than from knowledge. There was a clear tendency to disregard more and more the concrete world which was formally still held to be God's Creation.

Over the centuries, Catholic theologians often tried to maintain certain lines of defence. Thus in the 18th century Dom Augustin Calmet defended vigorously the idea of the universality of the flood against the ideas of Vossius. In the 19th century, the *Dictionnaire Apologétique* (1863) treated the subject in over twenty pages, referring to meteorological data about heavy rainfalls as proofs that the universal flood was quite possible. In 1930 the *Dictionnaire de théologie catholique* forgot to mention the subject, and the *Lexikon für Theologie und Kirche* in 1964 explained with reference to the many other flood-myths that we cannot know anything about the historicity of the great flood and that in any case the factuality of the Flood is unimportant, at least as far as the content of Christian faith is concerned. Thus theology withdraw from the known facts into a realm of spirituality which Science could no more disturb. This has been good for theology, and for science, but for one thing: both still pretended to speak essentially about the same world. Theology, at least in the Catholic tradition, was just not able to leave the world to the scientists. The Book of Nature contains essential information about creation, and Catholic theology was always concerned when new knowledge questioned the vision of the world as it was exposed to the faithful. But theology only rarely tried to fight Science on its own ground – as it had done with Galileo. Books were put on the Index of forbidden books, but there were no public arguments about the ideas. There was no Catholic Bishop Wilberforce to fight against Darwin in public. Condemnations were only directed against insiders, theologians or Catholic laity, who dared to accept the ideas of Darwin.

Actually, we might state that the Catholic attitude towards science – which was reluctant to be hostile – was not without reason: It was a defensive attitude. Science – at least as it was seen by the larger public – did not wait for Darwin and the one or the other theories of descent – to start its general attack against religion and especially against the Catholic church. Up to the middle of the 19th century most scientists held the view of Linnaeus, that all living beings were classified by him as they had come forth from the hand of the Creator on the day of creation. But the attacks against Catholic thinking, in the name of science started in the age of enlightenment, not only in France, but also in

Prussia, most vividly in the *Berlinische Monatsschrift*, years before the French Revolution. Everybody knows about the arrogant statement by Laplace that his universe did not need the hypothesis of a creator God. Popular science writers of their time – such as Jakob Moleschott (*Lehre der Nahrungsmittel. Für das Volk,* Erlangen 1850)[2]; Ludwig Büchner (*Kraft und Stoff,* 1855); as well as Karl Vogt with Robert Chambers *Vestiges of Creation* (1844, translated by Vogt as *Natürliche Schöpfungsgeschichte*) – fought vigorously in the name of Science for a materialistic worldview. Darwinism came into this later and the *Origin of Species* was a welcome new argument in a fight already going on against religion in general, and Catholicism, in particular.

Today we may all agree that these men did not really speak in the name of science, they were not really liked by scientists, but, rather, were proclaimers of a new faith. It suffices to read a statement by Büchner such as the following: "With the most absolute truth and with the greatest scientific accuracy we can say at this day: there is nothing miraculous in this world".[3]

Science as it was proclaimed by its vulgarisers of the 19th century appeared as the sober search for facts and natural laws as it likes to see itself. But as an ideology, it was constantly attacking the theological world perception. Throughout the 19th century science was used as a weapon against the Catholic faith. (It might be remembered that many scientific faculties flatly refused to allow Catholic scientists as members (as the Ruhrknappschaft refused Catholic doctors as fully appointed physicians on their payroll up to the thirties of this century!)).

Under these circumstances it was extremely difficult for the Catholic theologian to discuss the findings of Science with an open mind. His own church would treat him as a less reliable man, if not an outright heretic, who must be separated from the flock of good Christians, while the scientific world would either ignore him or consider him as a subversive power that must not be trusted.

Under these circumstances, the appearance of the idea of evolution certainly did not produce an enthusiastic response from Catholic theologians. Even in its earlier manifestations, as it was formulated by Charles Darwin's grandfather Erasmus or by F. Lamarck, it did not stimulate any important Catholic controversy. Condemnations actually concerned materialism and pantheism, both of which used the idea of evolution for their own purposes. The evolution of species did not concern the Catholic faith in any essential point as long as the question of the origin of man was not raised. Even in this domaine some theologians hoped to be able to draw an insuperable barrier by admitting that only the body might have been evolved, while the soul is created immediately by God (v.i.).

123

Such positions were unacceptable to the prophets of monistic materialism like E. Haeckel, who expounded his view in the *Natural History of Creation (Natürliche Schöpfungsgeschichte* 1868). He propagated by every possible means the idea of evolution as serving the goal of his scientific materialism; in his *Riddle of the Universe (Welträtsel* 1899) 19th century materialism reached its apogee, and it is thanks to him and to Thomas H. Huxley that the name of Darwin became regarded as an adversary of Christian faith. A deep gap between the evolutionary world and the created world of the Catholic theologians became more and more evident. Even though Haeckel never created the kind of church over which he wanted to preside – his Monistenbund never reached more than 6.000 members, and did not survive for any length of time – Haeckel and Huxley created a kind of general belief that was perhaps best expressed by a 14 years old Harrow schoolboy who in the late 19th century condensed his knowledge of Darwin in the sentence: "Darwin disproved the Bible".

The arguments exchanged were not really of high quality. Certainly some theologians showed quite a high level of stupidity when arguing with facts. The most outstanding example is perhaps a theology professor in the Catholic faculty of Münster University who was nicknamed the Höllenbautz for the rest of his life when he had once argued that the volcanoes are visible proofs for the existence of hell. All the world laughed at him. On the other hand Haeckel could make nonsense statements like: "We now know that the soul is a sum of plasma-movements in the ganglion-cells", without anybody laughing.

In this world of hostility, of Science versus Catholic theology, it is rather surprising that some people had the courage to try to think in such evolutionary terms as were available at that time. One of the most prominent theologians to speak for the compatibility of evolution with the Catholic faith was J. H. Newman[3a] who stated: "There is as much want of simplicity in the idea of distinct species as in that of the creation of trees in full growth, or rocks with fossils in them. I mean that it is as strange that monkeys should be so like men, with no *historical* connection between them, as that there should be no course of facts by which fossil bones go into rocks. The one idea stands to the other as fluxions to differentials – I will either go the whole hog with Darwin, or, dispensing with time and history altogether, hold, not only the theory of distinct species but that also of the creation of fossil-bearing rocks".

The most prominent among those who dared to speak on evolution in a theological context was St. George Jackson Mivart, the English biologist who early in his life became a Catholic. He was a lecturer in comparative anatomy at St. Mary's Hospital medical school – after having been barred from attending Oxford because of his Catholicism – and published in 1871 *The*

Genesis of Species. He accepted the concept of evolution, but he argued against the Darwinian notion of natural selection postulating an innate plastic power of 'individuation' explaining the production of new Species. In one point – and in this he was to be followed by practically all Catholic evolutionists – he made a definite cut in the process of evolution: To him there was no commonality between human and animal mental faculties. Evolution might have brought forth a human body, but the human soul was created by God. Neither Darwin nor Huxley liked his ideas, and while Mivart was struggling to mediate between religion and science, the scientists kept him at a distance and the Catholic church looked with increasing disfavour on his articles, placing them on the Index (1892/93). Some magazine articles published in January 1900 resulted in his excommunication by Cardinal Herbert Vaughan. His ideas were taken up by the Dominican Leroy[3b] and Father Zahm[3c] of the Holy Cross Congregation and even the Bishop of Cremona, Geremia Bonomelli. But none of them had chance to teach their views on evolution to a larger public and none escaped the sanctions of the Holy Office.

The modernist crisis certainly did not help to improve the situation. Any evolutionary thinking within the Catholic church was relegated to the closed studyrooms where alone reliable friends could speak openly. Any texts published were presented as hypothetical ideas based on hypothetical theories of evolution. Even these hypothetical ideas were strictly limited to the possibility of the evolution of the human body. A classical description of this hypothesis can be found in the article "Homme" of the *Dictionnaire apologétique de la Foi Catholique*, ed. by the P. A. d'Alès, and more especially in the section IV, which treats the human being as seen in the teaching of the Church and by the spiritualist Philosophy, a section written in 1910 by Teilhard de Chardin (pp. 501-514). In a first step – which follows the classical way of theological arguing of the time – we are told what we have to believe about man. There are especially two points:

1. God has created directly the soul of the first man, and most probably rearranged completely the matter destined to form his body,
2. The human race descends entirely from one only couple (monogenism which is made necessary all by itself by the doctrine of Original Sin).

Any form of evolution that does not allow for these conditions is to be rejected (512). On the other hand, if these conditions are allowed for, the "evolutionist conception ... may be accorded a large part of its postulates" (512). It is very clear in these statements, that a new line of defence has been built up against an 'evolution', that can be defined by the above-mentioned two conditions. Roughly speaking, the evolution of animals and plants, and to a certain degree of the human body can be accepted by Catholic faith. A few books conforming to such limits were published over the years. In 1921 the Belgian canon Henri de Dordodot[4] published a book on Darwinism from the point of view of Catholic orthodoxy, which had a certain success, but which did not violate the above-mentioned conditions. More important theological manuals regularily mentioned the evolutionary concept, which they limited strictly to the evolution of the human body, leaving the question open. In this context it must be remembered that the evolutionary concept has always been contended by a certain number of more or less marginal scientists; these were most happily quoted by the theologians such as Bartmann[5], Schmaus[6], Premm[7] etc. After having demonstrated their theological indifference to the question of the bodily origins of man, they all seem to be eager to show that they still have good reasons not to accept the idea of the evolution of the human body. In this two points are remarkable: on the one hand we no longer find quotations of that kind in more recent theological manuals, on the other hand we must state – as Teilhard pointed out to his theological friends in the twenties – that very often there was a profound misunderstanding on the side of the theologians. They did not realise that different evolutionary theories were constantly opposed to one another, and while all proponents – or nearly all proponents quoted by the theologians – admitted evolution as the only concept able to explain the facts, they developed different theories to explain the path of evolution. Very often arguments against a special evolutionary theory were erroneously considered as arguments against evolution as such.

While in discussions of dogma there was thus at least a certain openness towards the idea of Evolution – with the restrictions mentioned – the official Roman position was much more opposed to the idea. In 1936 Father Frey, the Secretary of the Bible Commission, judged in a semi-official letter very negatively on the thesis "Theology and Evolution", which M. Messenger defended successfully in the faculty of Theology in Leuwen, referring to the earlier condemnations of Leroy, Mivart, and Zahm, which demonstrated clearly, "that Rome was at no time favourable towards the transformiste thesis ... and that there is no probability that it will ever become so."[8] And in 1948 Cardinal E. Ruffini wrote a book aiming to demonstrate that "evolution applied to the living species, as it is supported by the materialists, has no scientific basis; and especially that human transformation, even that restricted to the body alone, is not acceptable."[9]

No wonder that in such an atmosphere a real discussion of evolution as a feature of the universe as God's creation never really took place within the

Catholic church. Even when in 1950 the encyclical *Humani Generis* allowed the discussion of the evolution of the human body – still as a hypothesis that is to be considered at best as a probability – this was not a fundamental change. In spite of multiple fossil finds and more refined evolutionary theories, Rome stuck with its old tactics of drawing a new line of defence, which had already been swept away in the real world of Science. The effects of the encyclical on theological thought were not as negative as the text intended. The reason for this could be, at least to a certain degree, the publication of the writings of Teilhard de Chardin who died in 1955, and who during his life-time was never allowed to publish his ideas on theology in relation to an evolutionary world.

There is certainly not enough time to expound the Teilhardian system in detail, and I am not at all sure that the effect he actually had on theological thinking was intended by him. But if I may be allowed to reduce the Teilhardian enterprise to one formula, then it might be stated as the theological attempt to understand the evolving universe as God's creation, i.e., the question is not one of compatibility between a traditional notion of creation – that is mostly said to be given to man by revelation – and the notion of Evolution, but the meaning of Evolution as the most general description of the universe for our understanding of creation, for our possibility of thinking about creation, about God's relation to this world as his creation.

It appears that the notion of evolution in Teilhard's language has a much broader meaning than in any other evolutionary school, such as Neo-Darwinism. In Teilhardian thought – which has not in this respect been contradicted by scientific discoveries since his death – evolution has become a universal category describing the whole of our experimental reality. No wonder that this meant an enormous challenge to scientists, philosophers and theologians - and the unending flood of publications on Teilhard testifies on the fact that many brains were stimulated by him. The interventions of Rome to stop the Teilhardian ideas did not work. Even in the Vatican II Council his ideas were hailed in the bishop's sessions – and naturally fought as well. In some points his concepts marked even the very wording of the Pastoral Constitution *Gaudium et Spes*.[10]

It cannot be said that Teilhard's thinking has actually been integrated into theological thought. But it most certainly had an effect on the way theologians approach today the notion of evolution when they speak about creation. The old fearful way of circumventing the problem has given place to an open discussion, at least among most Catholic theologians.

The first steps in this direction in Germany were made by K. Rahner and P. Overhage, who though using a Teilhardian terminology – e.g. the term "hominisation" – never quote the name of Teilhard. But the texts were published some years after the Teilhardian ones, and it would be barely thinkable that they would have happened without the Teilhardian precedent. While the scientific part of these texts, as well as later publications by Overhage, still show a tendency to over-emphasize the gap between man and animals, the contribution by Rahner introduces a new vision – very cautiously and trying to show these new concepts to be quite classically Thomistic – by using the term of "Selbstüberbietung", which allows us to understand the process of becoming as "Self-Transcendence". This new terminology has never been contradicted officially and therefore a door in theology has been opened through which the evolutionary world-view can start to penetrate theological thinking. Of course, alongside the Teilhardian approach, this is only a small opening, but it is a genuine one. The basic change in attitude is significant: evolution is no more conceived of as something one has to defend oneself against, but as an important fact that changes philosophical and theological concepts.

Some influences towards an evolutionary comprehension of Creation have also come in Catholic theology from the process philosophers, but the main stream of process theology flows in Protestant territory. This interesting approach to evolutionary reality is certainly as radical as the Teilhardian one, going in some points even further than he would, e.g. process theology rejects the notion of a creation out of absolute nothingness, a *Creatio ex Nihilo*.[11] Process thought as well as the Teilhardian world-view, are both penetrated by the all-encompassing notion that we live in a world of becoming and the comparative studies on Teilhard and Whitehead, which began quite promisingly in the 1960s,[12] could prove quite helpful in clarifying the notions of both forms of evolutionary thinking.

The more widespread influence of Teilhard's thinking can be found in multiple publications – I do not include here the strictly Teilhardian literature with its more than 10.000 titles – which integrate more or less overtly Teilhardian concepts in their theologies of creation. Among others we find that Joseph Ratzinger integrates the notion of growing complexity as the parameter of evolution and uses it for a Christian understanding of creation that continues in human evolution towards mankind as a whole.[13] This happens more in a Christological context, and this seems quite characteristic of the time in which Barthian influences in Catholic theology are predominant. The Christocentric Teilhardian position is as well regarded by Scheffczyk[14] who sees the world created in Christ as Alpha and Omega, the world thus being in process on its way to the final Omega. Scheffczyk accepts even the Trinitarian speculations of Teilhard, which are based on the metaphysics of union he developed very early out of his speculations on evolution. The

Munich dogmatics professor speaks without hesitation of a cosmic Christ and a Christocentric cosmology, a world in which evolution helps us to understand the meaning of creation. These new ways of thinking in a Catholic dogmatics textbook are obviously an encouraging sign which could indicate a renovation of theological thinking. But a closer look at Scheffczyk's thesis reveals that he can follow the Teilhardian ways only at an abstract level. When confronted with concrete consequences of an evolving universe, he has to withdraw into his philosophical fortress which refuses entry to any idea that does not clearly accept the notion that everything created in the beginning is to be qualified as good though he accepts the idea that they may aquire new qualities of being. This somewhat strange mixture of old metaphysics and new concepts is certainly disturbing for the outsider who is not subject to the traditional constraints of thinking of Catholic theology, but we should no more expect the latter to make jumps than any other species – at least not suddenly. But if we look back over the last fifty years we can say that even rather conservative theologians have advanced into new territories.

In a more radical way the Dutch theologians Schoonenberg and Hulsbosch[15] not only accepted some of Teilhard's notions but made his methodological axioms their own. Thus Hulsbosch postulates that, instead of trying to reduce the traditional formulas in a way that makes them acceptable without violating the fact of evolution and conserving the essential points of the theological formula, it would be much better to find out which elements of this wording must be inserted into the static world-view. (35). It is quite clear for Hulsbosch that this change in world-view from static to evolving brings about a change in our concept of creation. "The essential difference between the creation-notion, which functions in a static world-view, and the creation-notion which functions in an evolutionary world-view is this, that in the static world-view God creates *in the beginning*, eventually with virtual implications of everything that is to be developed in the course of time out of the cosmic reality, while in the dynamic world-view the attention is directed *towards the end* (...). The intention of God's creational activity is directed towards the end, while creation is realised along the path of cosmic evolution. This is the all-dominating starting point of a *theology* of evolution." (36).

There are certainly many other ways for theologians to come to grips with the challenge of the evolving world, and we could quote many examples from around the world. As in any field that has only recently become open to theological thought (or any other field of thinking) many ideas are pullulating.

All this might create the impression that in Catholic theology the notion of evolution is today generally accepted as a positive input. But this would be an exaggeration. There are still quite a number of integristic theologians around who fight the notion of evolution as a kind of atheistic materialism – Catholics are no better than Protestants who have their creationist fundamentalists. They cannot all be placed into the same camp. Even thinkers who believe themselves to be on the frontiers of theological thinking, as for example J. B. Metz who has developed a highly irrational idiosyncratic position opposed to evolution. Metz introduces the notion of "Logics of Evolution" which he unfortunately does not relate to any statement by any evolutionist.[16] I do not see where he could have found the kind of "Logics of Evolution" he presents. He has built – quite in the style of the ancient apologists writing against the gnostics - a kind of bogey which he fights violently. Unfortunately for him, this kind of non-argument does not do away with the fact that we live in an evolving universe, in an evolving creation.

We will have to continue to live for a time with anti-evolutionist theologians, and therefore there will be for a certain time at least as well anti-theological scientists, who feel menaced by this form of reactionary thinking found in quite important Catholic theologians. But I am sure, at least as far as evolution is concerned, it will be the conceptual tool that will allow us to understand the universe as scientists and as theologians. In the meantime we should not forget that old theologies not less than old philosophies or scientific theories are eliminated by arguments. Arguments are necessary to make the new vision acceptable, and this means there must be people who – mostly not without some kind of suffering – will develop the arguments and profess them. We should be aware, as Whitehead told us, that outdated theories, philosophies and theologies die away only with those who profess them. Only if more and more people will hold up the notion of an evolutionary Creation will it finally become the accepted world-view in the Catholic church, as elsewhere.

References

1. Cyrill von Jerusalem (*9.Catechesis for the catechumens*, nr. 2, Bibliothek der Kirchenväter 136).
2. Cf. the review of the book by L. Feuerbach in *Blätter für Literarische Unterhaltung* (9. nov. 1850), p. 1082 where he remarks that according to Moleschott "Der Mensch ist, was er isst" (Man is what he eats).
3. L. Büchner, *Force and Matter*, 4th ed., English Translation, p. 95.
3a. J. H. Newman, *Sundries* p. 83.
3b. M. D. Leroy (1891), L'évolution restreinte aux espèces organiques, Paris.
3c. P. Zahm (1899), *Dogma and Evolution*.
4. H. de Dordodot (1921), *Le darwinisme au point de vue de l'orthodoxie catholique* t. I. L'origine des espèces, (Coll. Lovanium), Brüssel-Paris.
5. B. Bartmann (1923), *Grundriss der Dogmatik*, Freiburg.
6. M. Schmaus (1941), *Katholische Dogmatik*, Bd. II, Schöpfung und Erlösung, München.

7. M. Premm (1951), *Katholische Glaubenskunde*, Wien.
8. Letter quoted by R. d'Quince (1970), *Un prophète en Procès: Teilhard de Chardin dans l'Eglise de son temps*, Paris, pp. 92-93.
9. E. Ruffini (1948), *La Teoria dell'evoluzione secondo la scienza e la fide*, Rome, p. 1.
10. Cf. the commentary by J. Ratzinger (1968) on the Pastoralconstitution in LTHK, *Das zweite vatikanische Konzil*, Freiburg t. III, 313-353.
11. Cf. John B. Cobb Jr., David Ray Griffin (1976), *Process Theology*, Westminster Philadelphia.
12. Cf. E. H. Cousins ed. (1971), *Process Theology*, Newman Press, New York.
13. J. Ratzinger (1968), *Einführung in das Christentum*, Kösel München, 190-198.
14. Leo Scheffczyk (1975), *Einfürung in die Schöpfungslehre*, Darmstadt.
15. A. Hulsbosch (1963), *De Schepping Gods*, Roermond; P. Schoonenberg (1963), *Gottes werdende Welt*, Limburg; idem (1970), *Ein Gott der Menschen*, Einsiedeln; idem (1970) *Bund und Schöpfung*, Einsiedeln.
16. J. B. Metz (1978), *Glaube in Geschichte und Gesellschaft*, Mainz, pp. 149-158.

The Concept of Life in Theology

Per Lønning

Is 'life' an important issue in Christianity? It may look as if it is not, because it has left little imprint on the conceptual framework of theology. "Creation" – yes, and "Nature" – yes, and in the other end of the Creed: "regeneration" and "resurrection", maybe also 'eternal life'. – At the same time, 'life' is a concept which occurs frequently in the Bible as well as in common theological discourse. There is a striking contrast between the high frequency of the term and its low level of conceptual clarification. This discrepancy may partly be due to some inbuilt resistance of the term "life" – designating the most living "thing" of all – to conceptual analysis and definition; and partly to the obvious ambiguity which is there in the Bible, above all in the Johannine writings in the NT, between an unreflected biological and an extremely reflected theological use of the term. Other strains of biblical language are preferred in theological theory-building, because they seem to promise a simpler access to the determinant 'reality behind'.

For reasons which will probably become apparent in the following, I think that the traditional theological 'zoo-phobia' is largely overdone and that it may have had unintended and unconscious repercussions in terms of pulling apart what should rightfully be kept together. In the following, I shall focus attention on (1) the vision of 'life' in the biblical tradition, and after (2) a few hasty glances at important cross-sections in Christian thought, on two typical contemporary sources, namely (3) the 1983 Assembly of the World Council of Churches with its main theme "Jesus Christ, the Life of the World", and (4) a particularly interesting book from 1980, written jointly by a biologist and a theologian, namely *The Liberation of Life* by Charles *Birch* and John *Cobb* Jr.

1.

The Hebrew Scriptures, in their dealing with 'life', are, as always, concrete and event-centred and are not concerned with definitions and conceptualized theories. "The Lord God formed man of dust from the ground, and breathed into his nostrils the breath of life, and man became a living being" (Gen 2,7) – this is how the oldest of the two creation accounts in Genesis introduces the term "life". We could say that life is here conceived of as breath. This is characteristic. "When thou takest away their breath, they die and return to their dust – When thou sendest forth thy Spirit, they are created", states the big creation hymn Psalm 104 (v. 29f). This applies to "God's creatures" in general with no exclusive reference to humans. The Spirit of God as agent of creation is mentioned in the second verse of the Bible, and there is an obvious connection between Spirit and breath, between the Creator Spiritus and life as dynamic. Spirit means "wind", means "breath", means "life" as a principle of incessant movement, change, growth, over against the still-standing stagnation of death.

The vision of God as life-giver is basic. "With thee is the fountain of life; in thy light do we see light." Here, in Psalm 36 (v. 9) "life" and "light" occur as synonymous, a manner of speaking which is later on confirmed by the Johannine writings in the NT: "In him was life, and the life was the light of men" (John 1,4). Light, thus referred to, is a symbol of openness, confidence, unrestricted fellowship with God as the genuine source of being. And "life" becomes an expression of similar qualities: undisturbed contact with "the fountain of life", with the Creator. "As the Father has life in himself, so he has granted the Son also to have life in himself", Jesus is quoted to say in the Gospel of John (5,26), thus indicating that all others have life not "in themselves", but only through a constant receptive contact with their Creator.

The ambiguity which we distinguish already here, between "life" in what we would call an ordinary everyday meaning and "life" as a fundamentally religious term can be traced back to the Jahvistic creation narrative to which we have already referred. Adam and his wife "Eve" (which – by the way – means "life") are instructed that the day they eat of the tree of knowledge of good and evil, they will certainly die. Eating of this tree is the original sin, namely as expression of the desire 'to become like God, knowing good and evil' – that means: of becoming self-controlling self-sufficient, no more in need of divine instruction. Adam and Eve, as an immediate result of their insurgence do not die physically. What they lose is their confidential communion with God, including: their organic fellowship with a friendly earth. Life persists as a physical event, but has come under a constant threat through the faltering relationship of human being to human being and through the disturbed relationship of the human to nature. Life is lost, even if it continues. Divine orders and regulations have become necessary in order to secure a maximum protection of life and an urgent minimum restriction of death.

The understanding of life as uninterrupted contact with a universal source, the "Giver of Life", means in the OT no turning away from the world of biological life and of physical matter. On the contrary, it means a sanction and a sanctification of this world, confirming both the unity of all entities and the foundation of this unity in a universal, all-comprehending design. All living creatures share, according to their designation and order, in the universal event of life. When the human species, created to reflect the Creator's own image and thus to make conscious and verbalize the universal hymn of praise in which all of creation shares, refuses to respond to this glorious vocation, this causes disturbance to the whole balance of the eco-system.

This vision is taken over by the NT, where Christ, as the visible representative of the Creator, appears on earth in order to restore 'life'. "I come that they may have life, and have it abundantly" (John 10,10), Christ speaks, again according to John. And: "I am the resurrection and the life; he who believes in me; though he die, he yet shall live, and whoever lives and believes in me shall never die" (11,25f). A more definite duality of language can hardly be demonstrated. But seen in the full biblical perspective, there is nothing inconsistent about it: a certain connection with the fountain of life exists even where the reply of conscious adoration is being denied. All expressions of life, however, aim at their final integration in the one glorifying celebration of life in its all-embracing fullness. The tree of life, the river of life, the book of life – those are the final symbols that characterize the biblical vision of the future. At the same time as they point beyond life as a merely biological function, they confirm it and give to our 'common' human experience of life the transfiguration of an unsurpassable finality.

2.

The big problem in the history of Christian thought has, of course, been to keep the two dimensions together: life as empirical event on a biological (and, one should add, social) level and life as transcendental, all-unifying event. A more than widespread tendency has been to extoll "eternal life" to the exclusion, and sometimes to the renunciation, of "temporal" life. This tendency has generally been supported by a Platonic distinction between spirit and matter, ideal vision and phenomenal realisation, from the promotion of which the great Church Father *Augustine* cannot be completely acquitted. In a Platonic perspective, "life" in its dynamics does not offer itself as an obvious concept, the basic distinction being that between unchangeable ideas and transitory manifestions. A powerful resurgence of Platonic dualism took place more than 300 years ago in the Cartesian promotion of Galilean physics: the material universe with all its manifestations being envisaged in the life-denying image of a gigantic machinery, supra-mechanical qualities being attributed to the human mind only. The communication of human beings with their Creator becomes exclusively a mind-to-mind event and the world of non-intellectual events is seen as unconditionally subordinate and subject to that of intellectual activity. The doors thus stand wide open for the unrestricted triumph of technology. Christian thinking to a large extent embraced this vision as a triumph over sceptical (or over pantheist) trends of thought and as a confirmation of human uniqueness as the only creature shaped in the Creator's image.

A more balanced contribution was that of the Aristotelian tradition, integrated with Christian theology by Thomas Aquinas in the Middle Ages and celebrated not at least by the so-called Physico-theology of 18th century Enlightenment. Even if the unifying concept here is not that of "life" but that of "being", reality is thought of as basically one, and "life" in its way becomes a prominent criterion: as the realm of minerals is surpassed by that of vegetables, this in its turn is surpassed by that of animals, which is surpassed by that of humans, but always so that the next step includes the essential assets of the former. By analogy, this, in itself unfinished, pyramid is continued upward in a supranatural and supersensual "space" to comprehend the reality of the angels and, finally, of God as the organising principle of the whole. The essence of the phenomena is conceived in terms of their teleology, i.e. their intrinsic constant movement towards a universally integrated aim. Neo-thomism, the last great branch of this tradition, was still flourishing around the middle of our century. Then, in the course of very few years, it was generally abandoned by Roman Catholic theology. Evidently, for good reasons, since in its systematic perfection it had become very much of an intellectual strait-jacket. But perhaps its integrative approach to life, nature, culture, meaning, universality was a little too swiftly swept aside.

I do not think the existentialist trend in modern, especially Protestant, thinking deserves a particular review in our context. In many ways Jean Paul Sartre's slogan "L'existence précède l'essence" (the basic motif of his "L'existentialisme est un humanisme", 1946) is exemplary of an anthropocentrism and an individualism which really leave no attention to "life" in its givenness, i.e. as a source of laws or principles directive of human choice and behaviour, but leaves the horizon of human self-determination perfectly open. There is no such thing as "life", there is only a basically unlimited freedom of choice – which makes it perfectly possible for Galileo-Cartesian technocracy to go on. A similar observation applies to the "existential" theology of, say, Rudolf Bultmann. Indeed, his appeal for a "demythologisation" of Christianity also involves a disintegration of any idea of "life" as a self-reasserting reality prior to human choice.

In the opposite direction, 20th century Christianity has also been exposed to the influence of vitalist philosophical currents, which in several regards have been able to reactivate biblical suggestions of "life" as the comprehensive frame of human orientation. Even if these currents to a large extent can be

136

traced back to Darwinism (in its wide, 'geistesgeschichtliche' meaning) with whom the Church had a complex and not altogether happy confrontation; and to Friedrich Nietzsche (by the way, son of a German Lutheran pastor) whose hymn to "life" developed into a dark denunciation of Christianity as the principle of absolute life-betrayal (symbolized by "the Crucified"), certain trends of theology shew an amazing capacity to integrate even these impulses. Through the French thinker Henri Bergson, spokesman of a candid religious humanism, concepts such as "life" and "creative evolution" (*évolution créatrice*) were turned as arms against the petrified rational categories of established philosophical and scientific positivsm. The famous Jesuit paleontologist Pierre Teilhard de Chardin developed an evolutionary theory aiming at an all-embracing synthesis, where the entire universe is being conceived of as a living organism. A similar description partly applies to the influential contemporary process theology, which today seems to be rapidly spreading from North America to the other continents, and to which I shall return towards the end of this introduction.

These historical snapshots have been presented mainly to give a quick idea of the complexity of the Christian attempt to handle the unity and duplicity of the biblical term of "life". To communicate and to reinforce that vision in face of ever changing historical circumstances has been, and is, a stimulating challenge, but by no means simple.

3.

An illustrative example – and a thought-provoking actualisation too – is provided by the last Assembly of the World Council of Churches, in Vancouver, B. C., July 1983. The Assembly had as its main theme "Jesus Christ – the Life of the World", and its most spectacular feature was, beyond doubt, the endeavour to unite the universal and the every-day aspects of that theme. Deep biblical meditation on the spiritual meaning of Christ, representing the presence of the Creator in the midst of his creation, intermingled with concerned discussions of the palpable threats to life in our contemporary world and the responsibility of Christians to confront them. Even if a conceptual clarification of the term of "life" in its linguistic ambiguity was not achieved, and there was a certain tendency for the term of "life" (obviously as a tribute to the main formulated theme) to arise in contexts where a different vocabulary might have been more appropriate – even so, I think, as one of the delegates and as a member of the preparatory committee, that there was a major achievement in the field of conceptual integration. What did not immediately take place on the conceptual level, was more or less fulfilled on a level which, after all, may be much more important – the liturgical

– and in the subsequent reflection on the liturgical event. Let me explain what I mean.

Much has been said by Vancouver participants of the unique impact of worship and of eucharist on the entire work of the Assembly, and I think that that dimension has been of basic importance not only for the Assembly as a social event, but for its whole style of theological thinking. As never before in the history of ecumenism, worship proved to be of cognitive importance – "life" was explored, not primarily through an analytical approach, but through shared living, living as receptive and thanksgiving communication. But, of course, also this kind of cognition is bound to find some verbal expressions, as in the "Message" of the Assembly:

Our world – God's world – has to choose between "life and death, blessing and curse". This critical choice compels us to proclaim anew that life is God's gift. Life in all its fullness reflects the loving communion of God, Father, Son and Holy Spirit. This is the pattern for our life, a gift filled with wonder and glory, priceless, fragile and irreplaceable ... Constantly, in public and private, fellowship is broken, life is mutilated and we live alone. In the life of Jesus we meet the very life of God, face to face. He shared food with the hungry, love with the rejected, healing with the sick, forgiveness with the penitent. He lived in solidarity with the poor and oppressed and at the end gave his life for others. In the mystery of the Eucharist the resurrected Lord empowers us to live this way of giving and receiving. (*Gathered for Life,* WCC Geneva 1983, p. 2)

This unifying perspective is more explicitly spelt out in the report of the group particularly occupied with Christian Unity (Issue Group II). Here the whole orientation of the Vancouver Assembly is summed up under the concept of a *"eucharistic vision"*:

Christ – the life of the world – unites heaven and earth, God and world, spiritual and secular. His body and blood, given us in the elements of bread and wine, integrate liturgy and diaconate, proclamation and acts of healing (*ibid.* p. 44)

So the focal motif of Christianity – the incarnation, God present in a physical human person, a presence furthermore expressed in the sacramental function of terrestrial elements, symbols of organic life and growth – underscores and visualizes the comprehensiveness of the Christian vision of life. Jesus' saying "I am the life" conforms an indissoluble unity once established between life in its infinity of observable manifestations and "life" as the universal, all-creating reality: "With you is the fountain of life, in your light we see light."

4.

I come to my final set of observations, those on the book of Charles Birch and John Cobb Jr.: *The Liberation of Life.* Even if it appeared three years before the Vancouver Assembly and was not particularly geared to the Assembly theme as such, it is appropriate to see it in fairly close connection with the Assembly, both through the influential cooperation of the Australian biologist Charles Birch in the WCC over several years, and through the active role played by both the authors in the World Conference for Church and Society in Cambridge, Mass. July 1979 on "The Contribution of Faith, Science and Technology for a Just, Sustainable and Participatory Society" – a conference which could rightly be characterized as an ecumenical explosion of the theme of ecology. It is remarkable, and maybe an interesting sign of the times, that a biologist and a theologian here cooperate and produce a unified presentation of biological and theological observations, where the hand of the one author is hardly to be distinguished from that of the other. This has got to do, at least to some extent, with the fact that both the writers already, before their cooperation, were firm supporters of A. N. Whitehead's process philosophy and its use as a foundation of theology. For that and some other reasons their book may also be seen as a fairly representative presentation of the position today taken by the expanding school of process theology on the issue of "life".

What the two authors undertake to do, is: by means of a scientific exploration of the issue "What is life?" – (1) to provide the basis for an "ethic of life", (2) to develop "faith in life" as an all-comprehensive vision of what reality is about, and (3) to sketch perspectives for the future of "life" which materialise into viable ethical options. As their research turns out, the vision very soon takes the shape of an "ecological" model of life. Everything interrelates, everything and everybody have their value and their rights confirmed and limited by their interaction with others. And this ecological model, again, has to be seen not only in the synchronical perspective of topography, but in the diachronical perspective of events and of process so determinant for their entire perspective of reality. Ethically, this orientation does away with the two opposite, extreme attitudes of, on the one side, a rigid absolutism which tends to identify "right" with prescriptions that are valid independently of time and place and circumstances; on the other side, with a myopic individualism or situationalism ready to exclude the ecological context from decision-making deliberations. The basic characteristic and the basic requirements of "life" is that of universal integration: this necessarily, on the level of practical deliberation, means an integration as wide as possible. In notable conflicts, like those of abortion or of euthanasia, this means on the one hand that no pre-established standards should prescribe unconditional answers, but nor should the individual be allowed to take a decision alone. Voices from the family concerned and from the wider society involved should have their say, in order to secure the decision as an ecologically responsible one.

"Trusting life" is defined as the authentic human attitude in face of reality,

Can a Theology of Nature be Coherent with Scientific Cosmology?

Philip Hefner

The basic considerations that attend the question that forms the title of this piece were stated will by Ernst Troeltsch in a 1906 essay entitled, "Religion and the Science of Religion" (Troeltsch 1977):

The idea of God is admittedly not directly accessible in any other way than by religious belief. Yet it asserts a substantial content which must stand in harmony with the other forms of scientific knowledge and also be in some way indicated by these. (p. 117).

James Gustafson (1981) has provided a helpful commentary on Troeltsch's comment in his *Ethics from a Theocentric Perspective* (p. 271). Religion provides a unique means of access to its subject, God, but what it asserts about God must be in *harmony* with scientific knowledge and also *indicated* by that knowledge. Transposed to our specific topic, the Troeltschian question is, "Can our fundamental theological understanding of nature be harmonious with scientific knowledge and indicated, in some way at least, by that knowledge?"

In these comments, I will not provide any fundamental answer to the question, but do propose to reflect upon the necessary conditions for answering the question. If these conditions are not dealt with satisfactorily, then a theological understanding of nature cannot be coherent with scientific cosmology. If they are dealt with, we can proceed further. I discuss these considerations under the following rubrics: (1) Defining "nature"; (2) Placing the human; (3) Setting theology's mandate.

1. Defining "Nature"

It is not a simple matter to define "nature". Indeed, there is so much variation possible in the usage of this term that we most likely will simply have to decide to use it in a single way or in a few ways, so as to enable coherent conversation with one another. In the Critique of Pure Reason (A216, A684), Immanuel Kant spoke of nature as the multitude of our sensible intuitions and also as a regulative idea which includes the unity of all sensible intuition (Norman

Kemp Smith 1958, pp. 237, 558f.). Kant distinguished these as "corporeal" and "thinking" nature. When we speak of the theological understanding of "nature", we refer to both. We seek to integrate our sensible intuitions with our knowledge of God, and we also attempt to relate our unifying ideas of nature (which is what we mean by "world" in the Kantian scheme) to God.

R. G. Collingwood (Collingwood 1945) has called our attention to "nature" (translating the Greek *physis*) as the "things which go to make up the world" (p. 44) as well as "something within, or intimately belonging to, a thing, which is the source of its behaviour" (p. 44). This distinction is not so simple as it may at first appear, but both components of it are relevant to our topic. We might agree that uranium, for example, is part of nature, because it is part of what makes up the physical world. Is a description of that uranium's atomic and subatomic composition a description of things that make up the world, or of the source of its behavior? Or both? To speak of *Homo sapiens* may be to note something that makes up the world. Is a description of evolutionary processes an addition to this list of what makes up the world, or is it a description of the source of that creature's behavior? Or do the two blend into one another?

Is "nature" the easily discernible environment in which human beings live, or does it include the microcosmic and macrocosmic ambience in which the easily discernible exists? That is to say, the realm of the subatomic and the realm of immeasurably vast cosmos?

The popular genre of theology that commonly goes under the term "theology of nature" has arisen largely in response to the current ecological crisis. Consequently, it tends to speak of "nature" as equivalent to our earthly environment, to earth. Paul Santmire's *The Travail of Nature* (1985) cites "dozens" of definitions of nature (p. 11), but chooses "earth" as the most relevant. George Hendry (1980) analyzes theological reflection upon nature as falling into three basic definition – nature in the *cosmological* view (the sum total of the reality that surrounds us); the *psychological* (what is accessible to our experience); the *political or historical* (this earthly world and its history). Despite his broader analysis, Hendry's view of nature approximates Santmire's.

Is Nature on a Human Scale or Macro/Micro?
The motives for defining nature on a human scale, on the scale of Earth, are clear. Earth as our home corresponds most nearly (although not fully) to our common sense experience. Further, the earth-scale is most congenial to our attempts to frame meaning and meaningfulness. For many earth-viewers, the realm of nature is our home, our charge, for which we must care, or even our

Mother. The same can hardly be said for the subatomic realm of nature, or for the vastness of the universe.

Nature-as-Earth is *relevant*. It is possible to trace a good deal of the history of the planet, and to recognize ourselves as part of it. The trajectory of the planet, at least in its recent past and not-too-distant future, is easier for us to identify ourselves with. Further, our involvements with and commitment to Earth are a vivid reality for us. It makes sense to think about our basic responsibility on the planet and toward the planet, just as it is satisfying to map strategies that can implement that responsibility.

The motives for defining nature so as to include the microscopic dimension and the macroscopic vastness of the universe are ambiguous. On the one hand, it is plainly not adequate to restrict our understanding of nature to the common-sense experienced Earth, because the Earth that we experience is also known by us, through our scientific experience, to be but a portion of larger processes that are microscopic and macroscopic. Without a knowledge of the microscopic, we could not map ecosystems and their processes, nor comprehend the effect of much of our action upon them. We know that we and our Earth would not be in existence today, apart from macroscopic processes in the universe, processes that have formed us. It is highly artificial to separate Earth from its macro-micro ambience.

On the other hand, the vastly small and the vastly large realms of nature seem irrelevant. We give thanks for weather and crops. We work to minimize hunger, to avert erosion of the landscape, to protect the planet from nuclear war – and these are realities that are accessible to our gross experience, to our common-sense. It seems an esoteric thing to bring in cosmology and particle physics. For the person of religious faith, it seems clear that the divine revelations and injunctions pertain to the palpable sphere of experience, not to the esoteric.

These three considerations – that the planet cannot be understood apart from the micro/macro processes, that the Earth is the most relevant natural realm for most persons, and that to most persons the micro/macro world is an esoteric one – all three of these considerations are worthy of respect; none can be dismissed. Our theological understanding of nature must reckon with all three.

A Preliminary Concept of Nature

Our concept of nature aims at integrating all three realms that we have considered – Earth as experienced by common-sense, the realm of the microscopic, and the realm of the vastness of the universe. The arguments we have surveyed above demonstrate that our concept of nature is inadequate if it omits any of these three. That set of arguments also suggests the difficulties that confront our attempts to integrate.

There are a number of basic elements that emerge for our theology of nature when we take the micro/macro dimensions seriously. Here we will only mention them, leaving them for fuller discussion later. (1) The almost unimaginable size of the universe. Awe at the magnitude of the heavens is an ancient response. Today's cosmological knowledge goes beyond sheer magnitude to the point of incredulity. 100 billion billion stars. Incredibly large processes located in the galaxies and clusters of galaxies, which have produced the stars and the earth-forming processes. These considerations are seldom taken into account by our theology, but they must be. (2) The immense time span of the cosmic processes. 15-20 billion years since our universe's beginning, and at least an equally far distant future. Any conceptuality of God and world must take the significance of this time span into account. (3) The complexity and strangeness of the microscopic world, which includes quantum physics, is an essential aspect of nature, and thus of theology's reflection.

(4) The universe is a process, an evolution which moves from microscopic reality to the vastness of the universe as we now know it. The process of cosmic evolution constitutes the reality of the universe. If we ask, "What is the cosmos?" The reasonable answer is that it is a process. This process calls all the constituents of the cosmos into being; the process makes them and unmakes them. Wherever the process is, including its workings on planet Earth and in the human sphere, it seems to follow the strategy of producing a manifold of forms which, in "a powerful process of trial and error look for increasingly adequate structures of adaptation" (Theissen 1984, p. 171. Prigogine & Stengers, 1984).

These four elements must be taken into account by any theological understanding of nature that claims to meet Troeltsch's criteria of harmony with scientific knowledge and of being also indicated by that knowledge.

One methodological characteristic must also be integrated into our theological understanding: the familiar dictum that the map is not the territory. The quantity of data which we possess from our quest for knowledge about nature in its various reaches is staggering. Even this data itself is not synonymous with the "territory" which is nature. Even less can the theories which have been propounded to order these data claim to be anything but the "map". Our theological attempts to understand nature will also be attempts at map-making.

This is our preliminary concept of nature: It refers to the world of our common-sense experience, to the microscopic realm, and to the macroscopic.

Nature is viewed as incomprehensibly vast in size, as well as incredibly small and complex, occurring over an immense span of time; nature is fundamentally a cosmic process. Finally, our concept of nature may grow out of involvement with the territory that is nature, but it rests upon the map-making activity of others, and it is itself a map.

2. Placing the Human

(1) Traditional dogmatic theology has insisted that the doctrine of the human being be considered an integral part of the doctrine of creation. It is *not* for this reason that I am introducing the human phenomenon into a discussion of cosmology, just as it is not for the interest of an anthropocentric emphasis that I do so. Rather, human being must be considered within the context of cosmology, because the cosmos has come to this, namely, to enter the phase of the human. It is from within the matrix of the cosmic process itself that Homo sapiens has emerged. This fact cannot be avoided, and thus placing anthropology within cosmology is also unavoidable. This *unavoidability* of the human is the *first* basic consideration that we must deal with in our attempt to place the human. Frequently, biology, anthropology, and culture are considered out of place in cosmological schemes, since pride of place is given physics and astronomy. We do well to recall the insight of astrophysicist Eric Chaisson, who, when reflecting on the fact of life emerging from a material matrix, writes: "This is a transition of *astronomical* significance, the dawn of a whole new reign of cosmic development". (Chaisson 1981, p. 298, emphasis added).

(2) When we place the human phenomenon within the cosmic process itself, we must understand that the human is thereby perceived to be one form of the process' own strategy of adaptation. We reiterate the description of the cosmic process that appeared in the previous section: a process that produces a manifold of forms from which some few are selected through a powerful process of trial and error. This process apparently operates by way of what Donald Campbell calls "blind variation and systematic selective retention" (Campbell 1976, p. 169). What we know as human being, human genotype and phenotype, as well as human culture, has emerged on this loom of variation/selection/retention on which all the rest of the process has also been woven. Since, however, we must finally say that the cosmos *is* the process (or, which means the same thing, that it is the process itself that is in process), human being is an adaptation of the process itself.

(3) The actuality of its emergence from within the cosmic process is itself ground for asserting the cosmological significance of human being, but it is not the only ground of this significance. It is also the case that it is human being

that undertakes the enterprise of cosmology. The decisive trait of human being is grounded in its self-awareness, and that self-awareness is the basis for the human being who not only receives the sensible intuitions that comprise Kant's "corporeal" nature, but who also fashions the regulative idea of nature ("thinking" nature, for Kant). The human being not only traverses the territory that is its segment of the cosmic process, but it conceives of maps and does indeed provide the mapping that moves from territory of the cosmos to the rationality that is cosmology. And further, it is the human being who fears that we may not be able to survive the anthropocentricity that is embedded within our mapping activity.

If we relate this reflection to the previous point, we must conclude that the activity of mapping, cosmology, is also to be viewed as an aspect of the process of adapting. Cosmology itself, then, both in its very existence and its shape, is an adaptation of the process of variation/selection/retention. This line of thinking is a variation on the arguments of Ralph Burhoe (1981) and Stephen Toulmin (1972). Cosmology is dependent upon human beings, particularly their culture. Hence, we may use a term of Ralph Burhoe's (1981) to conclude that cosmology is rooted in the human culturetype (Burhoe 1981, pp. 97-8).

(4) This human phenomenon has emerged from the cosmic process itself, and its entire being, including its rational activity (even that of cosmology) is fully an aspect of the evolving cosmos. When we reflect more deeply on this fact, several important facets of meaning are highlighted. As is the case with all of nature, evolution in the human zone of the cosmos is concrete. The scope of the universe in space and time is almost beyond imagination, and it has been such for billions of years. Nevertheless, the process happens in the concrete, and even when we do speak of the universe as a totality, the concreteness of its constituent processes cannot be overlooked. Further, even its larger components, as for example, the clusters of galaxies, are small when compared with the whole.

With concreteness comes the fact that we have emerged and continue to develop in a local environment. In our locale, we have evolved in co-adaptation with other components in our neighborhood. This means that our powers of observation, perception, and capacity to gain knowledge are also thus co-adapted – to the locale in which they have been conceived and nurtured, or perhaps more accurately, to the locale in which they have been spun out as variations, selected, and in certain ways retained.

In the human being, however, we have the remarkable activity of the locally co-adapted entity reaching out to know and map the trans-local realms of the universe. Beyond this, however (no pun intended!), the human being is quite possibly attempting to extend the neighborhood of its evolution and thus adapt itself to new locales. Whether this behavior of the human being is a "first" in cosmic history, we do not know.

The human's co-adaptation to local environment has left its mark; the creature is not endowed "naturally" with the systems of perception that enable genuine knowledge of other neighborhoods in the universe or of the trans-local cosmos itself. The systems of perceiving and gaining knowledge that have co-adapted to a local setting have developed the technological assistance themselves that make the larger knowledge possible. The human is in the process of adapting to a large locale in which it has not originally evolved, a realm of which it was only vaguely and inadequately aware.

This remarkable reaching out by *Homo sapiens* has been undertaken in response to packets of information that co-exist in the human being at several levels – in the genes, in the central nervous system, and in human culture, for example (Burhoe 1981, pp. 73-112). Each of these packets is blind in relation to the outcome of our developing their information and acting upon it. The motivations which impel us to develop the information and extend it are also blind in the same way. The human being has no other recourse but to follow the lead of the blind motivators and the blind packets of information in whatever ways seem best to humans.

The human being is aware of all that we have reflected upon in these last paragraphs. The creature knows that what we are now engaged in is still an aspect of the single evolving cosmos, the cosmos adapting. The human creature knows as well that what we are now engaged in is part of the variation/selection/retention process of evolution, which in some respects may fail and be selected against, which may prove successful for adaptation, and which surely in one way or another will be retained in future packets of information.

(5) *Summary*. What have we said about placing the human? That the human is an aspect of that cosmic process itself adapting. That self-awareness, the ability to fashion maps of the cosmos, is a leading characteristic of the human. That cosmology is an aspect of the human and also an aspect of the cosmos' adapting. Finally, that the human being, acting on the basis of packets of blind information and blind motivation, which have been coadapted to the local environment in which they evolved, is reaching out to adapt itself to the translocal universe.

Within the perspective of cosmic evolution, the chief questions concern (a) the nature of this remarkable adaptive strategy that is manifest in the human and (b) the outcome of this strategy, whether it will prove adaptive or not, and in what ways it will be retained in the ongoing information pool of cosmic evolution. These questions are basically the theological questions about redemption and consummation. I have cast them in a way that is different from, but in a similar spirit to that of Gustafson (1981, p. 266).

3. Setting Theology's Mandate

This section will set forth no final manifesto for theology to follow as mandate. It will suggest several fundamental considerations that apply to any theology which seeks to take seriously contemporary scientific/philosophical reflection on "nature". These considerations may throw light on the title-question, whether a theology of nature can be coherent with scientific cosmology.

(1) *Religious symbols and reflection on the cosmos.* We have spoken of the blind character of the information that is available to humans as they launch their attempts to gain knowledge of the cosmos, and also the blindness of the motivations that drive that quest for knowledge. Within the rich matrix of various levels of information packets (genetic, central nervous system, cultural, etc.), there exists the information that is rooted in religious traditions, specifically in religious symbols. This information presents itself as direct discourse from the cosmos and its source. Humans have discerned, however, that this information, too, is a map, not the territory, even though it often hugs the terrain of the territory. That is to say, humans have learned that the symbols *are* symbols.

How ought we relate to symbols and the myths that are comprised of symbols? How can we believe in symbols and myths, once we know that they are just that? Paul Ricoeur suggests that we drop our first naivete when we gain knowledge of symbols, and through philosophy we must fashion a second naivete. This is done by turning the symbol into a *wager*. "I wager that I shall have a better understanding. . . if I follow the *indication* of symbolic thought. That wager then becomes the task of *verifying* my wager and saturating it, so to speak, with intelligibility. In return, the task transforms my wager: in betting *on* the significance of the symbolic world, I bet at the same time *that* my wager will be restored to me in power of reflection, in the element of coherent discourse." (Ricoeur 1967, p. 355). This is not dissimilar from our opening quotation from Troeltsch – the religious traditions contain information that can be gained nowhere else, the knowledge of God, but that knowledge must be in harmony with and indicated by scientific knowledge. The notion of wager in theological thought was not foreign to Troeltsch's outlook.

The theologian, therefore, may be described as one who *begins* from religious traditions, winnowed in whatever way the individual theologian decides, and trusts those traditions enough to turn them into a wager. The theologian pursues a strange mode of thought, it might seem (or is the theologian simply following a path that all persons must follow who think

148

about ultimate questions?). The theologian accepts the information contained in tradition and seeks energetically to place it in its context of wider knowledge, specifically scientific knowledge, thereby permeating it with intelligibility. Wagering turns the tradition into a hypothesis to be tested. If the test is positive, knowledge has been deepened. If not, the theologian is faced with the question of honesty.

The information of the religious tradition is also blind. As Donald Campbell writes, the wisdom of tradition is "wisdom about past worlds". (Campbell 1976, p. 169). If tradition is to be extended in its validity, it must be illuminated by new knowledge about new situations. I would wish to place this insight in the context of St. Thomas' understanding of theology as the enterprise that is distinctive in that it relates all things to God. That act of relating is in actuality the conversation between the tradition of the past and the things of current existence.

(2) *The relation of God and cosmos.* Gustafson has argued, cogently, that current scientific knowledge certainly suggests that humans and all components of the cosmos are "part of nature, and dependent upon the processes of nature". (Gustafson 1981, p. 260). He considers this to be a non-religious way of affirming the basic religious belief in God. We must ask, however, what concept of the relation between God and the cosmos can sustain the claim that we are *part* of nature and *dependent* upon it. Gustafson himself insists that in light of the temporal and spatial scope of the cosmos, we cannot rightly conceive of the God-world relation in a way that would require an unreflective anthropocentrism, the notion that the cosmos exists for the sake of *Homo sapiens.* I would argue that even though the thought moves might be philosophically simplistic, the very size and character of what we perceive the cosmos to be rules out a concept of God and the world being externally related. There simply is no viable concept of externality available to us today.

Further, it seems that there can be no really persuasive concept of meaning found in the vast cosmic process unless its meaning is that it is itself an aspect of God being (or becoming fully) God. Contemporary scientific cosmological thinking urges us to reconceive nature as grace and grace as nature. Such a paradigm shift enables rich understandings of the classical doctrines of *creation out of nothing* and *continuing creation.* It also points us toward understanding that God's transcendence is most authentically understood in terms of the cosmos' own capacity for self-transcendence.

(3) *Theology done in the light of a scientific understanding of religion.* Ricoeur's first and second naivetes may be understood as responses to the awareness of the scientific understanding of the cosmos. How can I believe in

God and in my status as child created in the image of God now that I know about the temporal and spatial structure of the cosmos? How can I affirm religion and religious faith now that I know the roles of religion in cosmic and human evolution? For the most part, we have considered scientific understandings of religion to be the diminishing of religion (= glue of society, Marx; = a prime means of assuring mental health, Freud). Ralph Burhoe, Donald Campbell, Solomon Katz and others have argued scientifically for viewing religion as an essential agency in the evolution of human beings. Religion in a very literal way has conveyed the information that enabled human being to evolve. For Burhoe, the core of this information is self-giving love ("trans-kin altruism"), whereas for Campbell it has to do with the traditions of self-discipline and for Katz it is associated with peacefulness and cooperation between peoples. Gerd Theissen, a New Testament scholar, has recently suggested that the core of religious information enables persons to engage in life that is transcending genetic selection, thereby reaching a new level of life, in response to the central reality that is God (Theissen, 1984).

If theology is essentially rooted in the religious community (as most theologians believe, even if they do define the community in a variety of ways), then theology can hardly be unaffected by the theologian's (and/or the community's) awareness of the constructive and essential function of the community, as that function is explained by solid scientific thinking. I do not mean that scientific thinking about religion is the last word, or that it goes unchallenged. I do mean that when solid scientific theory suggests a way of interpreting the nature and role of religion in a way that is not diminishing of religion, members of the religious community, including theologians, will be significantly influenced by it. There is a good chance that theology will want to subject the scientific understanding to intense critique, and also the chance that if the scientific view withstands critique, theologians will seek to undergird and advance religion's authentic role in their theology. They will engage in both critique and undergirding because they believe it to be God's will. Troeltsch is correct, that the idea of God is not directly accessible except through religious belief. May we suggest, however, that science may usefully attain the goal of accurately explaining the constructive role of religion in a way that does not diminish its integrity and in a way that the religious community itself acknowledges and which is allowed to shape theology? If this does happen, then we will witness one of the most important grounds for the coherence between theology of nature and scientific knowledge about the cosmos.

References

Burhoe, Ralph W. (1981), *Toward a Scientific Theology*. Belfast: Christian Journals Ltd.

Campbell, Donald T. (1976), "On the Conflicts between Biological and Social Evolution and between Psychology and Moral Tradition". *Zygon: Journal of Religion and Science* 11 (September): 167-208.

Chaisson, Eric (1981), *Cosmic Dawn: The Origins of Matter and Life*. Boston: Little, Brown and Co.

Collingwood, R. G. (1945), *The Idea of Nature*. Oxford: Clarendon Press.

Gustafson, James (1981), *Ethics from a Theocentric Perspective*. Chicago: Univ. of Chicago Press.

Hendry, George (1980), *Theology of Nature*. Philadelphia: The Westminster Press.

Prigogine, Ilya and Isabelle Stengers (1984), *Order Out of Chaos*. New York: Bantam Books.

Ricoeur, Paul (1967), *The Symbolism of Evil*. New York: Harper and Row.

Santmire, Paul (1985), *The Travail of Nature*. Philadelphia: Fortress Press.

Smith, Norman Kemp (1958), *Immanuel Kant's Critique of Pure Reason*. London: Macmillan and Co.

Theissen, Gerd (1984), *Biblical Faith: An Evolutionary Approach*. Philadelphia: Fortress Press.

Toulmin, Stephen (1961), *Foresight and Understanding*. Bloomington, Ind.: Indiana Univ. Press.

Troeltsch, Ernst, *Glaubenslehre*. Cited in Gustafson 1981.

Putting an End to Selection and Completing Evolution: Jesus Christ in the Light of Evolution

Sigurd Daecke

The phrase "Jesus Christ and Evolution" is not one that comes most readily to mind when the relation between evolutionary theory and Christian faith is under scrutiny. "Evolution and *Creation*", "Evolution *or* Creation" have far wider currency and are important. Now, we consider not the first article of the Creed, not the belief in the creation, but rather the second, the belief in Jesus Christ.

Compared with the subject of "Evolution and Creation" few people seem to have mustered the courage to tackle this second subject. Yet, for Christians, this ought to be the decisive question: how does the very foundation and object of their faith, the very centre of Christianity, relate to the evolutionary concept of reality? If we believe that Jesus Christ is the centre of our world and life, while, at the same time believing that this world of ours is a product of evolution, then we cannot but wonder what, in terms of evolution, the meaning of our belief in Jesus Christ amounts to. Is he, too, a feature of evolution? Or – put it differently – can evolution be understood in christological terms?

The possibility of such a relation – in fact of any relation between Christ and evolution – is denied in any dualistic model of the relation between science and religion. In that sense doctrines of science and doctrines of Christian belief are regarded as operating on two distinct levels, occupying as it were different rooms. This rules out even contradictions between them. They are strictly independent of each other. Statements in either field differ categorically from statements in the other. Figuratively speaking, it is the model of the "double key". This is an allusion to an anecdote according to which Faraday (or whoever it is attributed to) used to lock his laboratory securely after him, when entering the other room of his house (i.e. his existence). Many scientists lead quite comfortable lives, shuttling between their two "rooms". They see no problem in studying a purely profane nature, while at the same time believing in a transcendent God. They prefer a clear distinction between believing and knowing, between theology and science, between a transcendent God and a secular "creation". It is such a concept that is probably most widely held by scientists today.

Teilhard de Chardin, however, called this mode of thinking "schizophrenia" and "leading a double-life". For is not the scientist (Teilhard asks) riven apart in his soul by such dualism? Will not every communication between science and theology about the nature of creation (and creation as nature) be stopped, if a godless world faces a worldless God, a secular nature a transcendent creator, a positivist science an "Offenbarungspositivismus"? – if there is in fact nothing to bridge the gulf between objects of reason and objects of faith? Will belief not be completely isolated and become unintelligible in a world dominated by scientific thought, if the ties between nature and God are cut? So there is another kind of scientist determined to look for a unitary, holistic conception of reality, for coherence between the reality of God and the reality of the world. They look for a God who, as creator, has a hand in the evolution that is central to our modern conception of the world. For them nature is not only an object of knowledge but also one of belief, an object as much of reverent wonder as of objectifying research. This implies, however, that the doctrines of science and religion relate to one another.

If we leave aside the Darwinian interpretation of evolution for a moment and ask what the relation between the belief in Jesus Christ and the more general idea of development is, then we note that already the Early Fathers of the Church saw Christ in the light of a history of development. For Irenaeus mankind has, through the appearance of Christ, undergone a comprehensive process of spiritualization. The same is true for Origen to whom Christ is the force leading mankind in a growth process to the height of spiritualization and deification. Gregory of Nyssa interpreted redemption as a process of spiritualization and deification of mankind, as the coming-about of the perfection of mankind in the fulness of time (connecting the spiritual process of man's redemption with the development of the universe).

Other names from the history of theology and philosophy come to mind; but we may go straight into the second third of our century, to Teilhard de Chardin who brought Christ and evolution close together, almost identifying the two. "Cosmogenesis" and "Biogenesis" for him culminate in "Christogenesis". He even talks of the "identification of cosmogenesis with Christogenesis", thus – in his own words – "expanding Christ-Redemptor into a 'Christ-Evolutor'". For redemption, in Teilhard's view, aims at fulfilment of evolution, at a world come to completion. Redemption is the endeavour to raise the world up: "Christ carries the burden of the world in a state of evolution" – a new version of the ancient soteriological understanding of development by the Early Fathers of the Church. Evolution for Teilhard is the hermeneutic principle for both christology and soteriology. It is his attempt to understand afresh Christ and his works in an evolutionary world, giving him his place in it. "If the moving universe has in fact its pivot in Christ-Omega, then, conversely, Christ-Omega gains from its concrete seed, the Man of Nazareth, all his consistency for our experience", i.e. a "universal physical function". More pointedly: "Evolution saves Christ", i.e. gives him meaning, gives him a task of the evolving world. On the other hand, Christ saves evolution: is its mover, animator, pilot, collector and unifier. In short, Christian belief gives meaning to evolution, and the concept of evolution interprets what it is that we believe.[1]

For Teilhard, evolution is the hermeneutic principle through which to translate the belief in Christ into today's language and way of thinking. His evolutionary christology and his christological evolutionism are meant to make Christ intelligible in an evolutionary world, in fact points up his indispensability for evolution.

In Teilhard's opinion the belief in Christ has become unintelligible and unsatisfactory for our time. He sets out to translate it from the obsolete concept of a static universe into a concept of cosmogenesis, of an evolutionary process of becoming. For the Christian God is a God of cosmogenesis, and consequently Christ must become "Christ Evolutor".

This Christ is universal, is the Christ of Resurrection, the Christ by whom and for whom (*vide* Colossians 1) all things have been created and by whom they consist (1,16 f.).

While theologically this model is based on cosmic christology as represented by Teilhard, it implies a synthetic understanding of science and religion. This synthetic model of the relation between the two underlies also the approach chosen by Gerd Theissen of Heidelberg in his *Biblical Belief in Evolutionary Perspective*.[2] But while close to Teilhard methodologically, Theissen differs fundamentally from him in terms of theology. Not Teilhard's resurrected, cosmic Christ, but the earthly, historical Jesus is here placed in an evolutionary context – something nobody had dared to do before him. Theissen attempts not only general doctrines of the Christian faith like Teilhard, but the actual gospel in the light of evolutionary theory. Here "biblical belief is turned into an object of the theory of evolution – the theory of evolution is placed in a fresh light of biblical belief" (p. 67). His evolutionary interpretation of (1) biblical monotheism, (2) the man Jesus of Nazareth, and (3) the experience of the Holy Spirit introduces a radically new hermeneutic approach to the gospel – all recent evolutionary theology notwithstanding.

In principle, of course, nobody denies the need to translate the Christian message into the language and thought of our times. The question, however, is how far this adaptation is to be carried – also: what exactly the language and thought of our times is (The language of evolutionary thinking could surely claim to be the most widely accepted candidate). It was Hoimar von Ditfurth who suggested the "introduction of a new language", the "transplantation of the gospel into a language of images carrying a force as topical and a range of meanings as immediate as the ancient texts did for their time. No need", he goes on, "to invent this new language. It exists. It is...the language in which the science of today describes the universe".[3] Which of course is the language of the theory of evolution. For that language is the only one that by almost universal consent describes the reality of our life and world. By the same token Theissen says: "Perhaps the 'modern' images and similes of evolutionary theory show us a way to overcome the hermeneutic conflict between New Testament christology and the modern mind" (p. 115).

Theissen patterns his evolutionary hermeneutics on the trinitarian concept. Biblical monotheism, New Testament christology and belief in the Holy Spirit receive an evolutionary interpretation through three hermeneutic categories: "mutation", "selection", and "adaptation to the central reality".

Firstly monotheism. It is, strictly speaking, not a product of evolution, but the result of a religious revolution. But for one thing, this revolution can be understood as a "mutation" of our religious life, and secondly an attempt to approach the ultimate reality in a manner better suited to it than through the belief in a variety of divine powers. Thirdly – this revolution can be understood as a "protest against the selection principle": "Biblical monotheism implies the imperative offer of a fundamental behavioural change. Suspense of selectional pressures in exchange for a change of behaviour, Conversion instead of Death – that is monotheism's central maxim" (p. 99). The Old Testament prophets revealed the opportunity (and the conditions) of survival: "Without acceptance of the need to radically change our behaviour, collective doom is imminent. By such radical change, on the other hand, the laws of selection can be suspended" (p. 96). Thus monotheism plays an important part in the transition from biological to cultural evolution, because it expresses most acutely the resistance against the principle of selection, a resistance so characteristic of "culture". So much for evolutionary hermeneutics in the light of the First Article of the Creed.

In Jesus now – under the Second Article of the Creed – Theissen finds a possible object of evolution realized: the perfect adaptation to God's reality.

Again the categories of "mutation", "selection", and "adaptation" are brought into play.

Jesus is seen – firstly – as a "mutation" of human existence, as a "jump in the development, beyond anything in existence" (p. 114). For, according to St. Paul, he is the "new Man" into whose likeness we are to be transmuted, a new form of life. Secondly, says Theissen, in the teachings of Jesus of Nazareth the principle of solidarity replaced the selection principle. A tendency to minimize selection is inherent in all cultural evolution. In the teachings of the prophets this was sharpened into a protest against the cruelty of the principle; in Jesus this opposition comes to its completion.The message Jesus preaches reduces the pressures of society. Those who would be cast aside under the selection principle are given a chance to live: the weak, the meek, the peacemakers, those loving their neighbour as well as their enemies instead of forcing their will upon them.

Anti-selectionist protest culminates in the belief in the resurrection of the man on the cross. And thirdly: Jesus is seen as evidence of the possibility of successful adaptation to the central reality, as a possible objective of evolution. For solidarity, replacing the pressures of selection, is an equivalent of that central reality. Jesus' proclaiming God as father, and his message of the Kingdom-to-come is a successful adaptation to the ultimate reality. The emotional security expressed in this way signifies that fear of selectional pressure has been overcome. That fear ends where the central reality reveals itself as love.

The Holy Spirit finally – with whom Theissen proceeds to the Third Article of the Creed – stands for an inner transformation, a "mutation" of the human race as a whole. This transformation, this unplannable mutation in the soul of the faithful, Christian tradition has called: being overwhelmed by the Holy Spirit. Theissen is aware that religion may at times be nothing better than a survival strategy in one human group at the expense of others. Yet the prophets raised their voices against such an un-holy phantom of selection-orientated behaviour, and with Jesus' commandment to love your enemies an "anti-selectionist revolt" took place. It is true that only with a lot of compromising this "anti-selectionist motivation", i.e. the Holy Spirit, can find its place in the Church. And yet, says Theissen, the protest of the spirit is a necessary ingredient of the Church. Thus, after the categories of "mutation" and "selection", the third of the hermeneutic categories: "adaptation to the central and ultimate reality", is again used as an interpretative key – this time with regard to the Third Article of the Creed. In Jesus the adaptation to the ultimate reality had already been accomplished: "an altogether unlikely evolutionary hit. But what was possible in him, cannot, as a possibility, disappear, it may happen again" (p. 208). Thus Theissen understands the Holy Spirit as "Anticipation of what may come to pass some day" (p. 209). Man can transform himself into the (till then) unknown possibilities that made their first appearance in Jesus. The Holy Spirit is man's adaptation to the Ultimate Reality, the accord with God, participation in the eternal: an aim inherent in the evolutionary process.

So much for Theissen's impressive conception, impressive for its consistency no less than its unwonted boldness. The relation Theissen establishes between the three objects of the trinitarian creed: God, Christ, the Holy Spirit on the one hand, and the idea of evolution on the other is very different from Teilhard de Chardin's. It is true that both men are determined to re-interpret the gospel with (Theissen) "modern images and similes of evolutionary theory" in order to "resolve the hermeneutic conflict between New Testament christology and the modern mind" (p. 115). Thus both turn to new models of thinking that may supplement the ancient ecclesiastical and theological tradition and even replace it.

We must, however, not allow ourselves to be misled by Theissen's trinitarian schema. Not God, Christ and the Holy Spirit, but the religious ideas and the social behaviour of human beings are here treated as evolutionary. Theissen never moves beyond the anthropological and sociological horizon we have come to expect of his theology. Like his sociological and psychological exegesis of the gospel and St. Paul's epistles, [4] his evolutionary hermeneutics is anthropological. He is not interested in God so much as in the idea of God as formed by the prophets and Jesus. He is concerned with the changing of human behaviour, with the freedom from "social pressure" and from the "selection principle". In the same manner religion and church are seen only in their social context. Evolutionary epistomology points the way. His evolutionary interpretation is restricted to the *perception* of God and the *behaviour* of Man.

The fundamental difference between Theissen's and Teilhard's concept is that the one is informed by anthropology and sociology, the other by mysticism. Theissen thinks of religious ideas and social behaviour of people, Teilhard is concerned with the cosmic Christ of faith, who for him is almost identical with God. In a world shaped by scientific thinking, both set out to make the Christian faith not only credible but also thinkable. But the two approaches are hardly compatible. They lack a common denominator. True, both use the theory of evolution for their interpretations of religious doctrines. But even the choice of evolutionary categories each of them makes are completely different. Juxtaposing and comparing them can only serve to show how wide the spectrum of possible relations between Christ and evolution is, covering as it does evolutionary interpretations of the contents of Christian belief as well as religio-sociological ways of thinking and behaving.

To wind up I should like to present a third kind of evolutionary interpretation of christology and christological understanding of evolution. This third model I think will not only benefit communication between scientists and theologians but also serve towards the establishment of an ecological theology and ethics. Its position is nearer to Teilhard's than Theissen's, but is by no means identical with the former.

If, in the words of Col 1,16f., it is our faith that all things are created by Christ and for Christ and consist by him; and if it is in Jesus Christ that God has entered the world which we understand in evolutionary terms, then Jesus Christ and his works must be describable in evolutionary terms, as Teilhard and Theissen have done in their different ways. Similarly to Teilhard and in a line with A. R. Peacocke and H. Montefiore, one can interpret the incarnation of God in Jesus as "the completion of the cosmic process of evolution". The empirical evolutionary process of Man's emergence on earth would seem to have been crowned by Christ becoming Man. To put it another way (and somewhat nearer to Theissen): Jesus Christ would seem to have anticipated the aim and completion of evolution beyond Man. But although the incarnation of God in Jesus Christ is the completion of the evolving humanization of humans, the self-organisation of matter and the autonomy of the evolutionary process need not be rejected by Christian believers; on the contrary, they can be unreservedly accepted.

For Christ is by no means an inner-worldly, if immaterial, causal or finalistic factor, competing with other factors of the same kind. Such a view would again make for division and opposition between natural and divine, material and spiritual, factors and bring about the traditional conflict between them – or dualistic indifference. But God works his ways in Christ with nature – *in* and *through* nature.

In the light of evolution, incarnation then is no abstract dogma, applicable only to an historic Man, i.e. the Jesus of the gospel. It is in fact the promise of something better than evolution as understood in terms of the mechanistic dependence on inexorable selection, an egotistical struggle for existence, allowing only the strongest, "the selfish gene", to survive. God has accepted evolution, taken it up and carried it to perfection. For in Christ God has not only become man but has also entered developing matter, entered nature in the process of evolution. What J. Moltmann in his pneumatologically orientated book on creation[5] says about God's "immanent presence in the world" by virtue of the Holy Spirit can, under the aspect of incarnation, be said of the sacramental presence of God in the natural world. In Christ, too, God is found to be "present in material structures", if, sacramentally speaking, incarnation means that God in Christ has entered matter. Here, too, applies what Moltmann says with a pneumatological emphasis: that "in view of the contingencies of the evolution of universe and life dynamic pantheism" (more precisely: "differentiated" and "differentiating" pan*en*theism) has become rather more acceptable, "according to which God, having once created the world, now inhabits it, and the world he created exists in him" (pp. 109, 115, 219).

The idea of God's immanence in nature is necessary if we want to stress that nature is not god-less and that God is not un-natural; that God is the God of the whole of our natural world. By this we take evolution seriously, not so much as an isolated scientific fact or doctrine, but as the structure of reality and, consequently, a principle guiding also theological thought. We must understand God's immanence in the world not only in terms of creation, but also christologically and pneumatologically, thereby steering clear of all the traditional misunderstandings of pantheism, which simply equate God and Nature, or God and evolution – as demonstrated in the words of E. Jantsch who (*qua* scientist) said: "God *is* Evolution".[6] Even some of the statements of process theology may be understood pantheistically.

Where, however, God's evolutionary immanence is made precise, christologically and pneumatically, the danger of identifying Him and evolution is ruled out. That danger lurks in the fact that the equation may well be reversed, reading: "Evolution is God". But Christ and the Holy Spirit are more than evolution, they are its foundation and completion. G. Ebeling and J. Moltmann express this panentheistically. They set up, as it were, a panentheistic safeguard: "Not that everything is God, but that God is in everything and everything in God".[7] The same precaution against mere pantheism is provided by a christological understanding of God's immanence in the evolving world.

References

1. Teilhard de Chardin, P. (1969), *Oeuvres t. 10*, Paris, p. 184, 191, 211.
2. Theissen, Gerd (1984), *Biblischer Glaube in evolutionärer Sicht*, München.
3. von Ditfurth, Hoimar (1981), *Wir sind nicht nur von dieser Welt. Naturwissenschaft, Religion und die Zukunft des Menschen*, Hamburg, p. 299.
4. Theissen, Gerd (1981), *Soziologie der Jesusbewegung*, München; Theissen, Gerd (1983), *Psychologische Aspekte paulinischer Theologie*, Göttingen.
5. Moltmann, J. (1985), *Gott in der Schöpfung*, München.
6. Jantsch, E. (1979), *Die Selbstorganisation des Universums*, München.
7. Ebeling, G. (1979), *Dogmatik des christlichen Glaubens, I*, Tübingen, p. 292.

Teilhard de Chardin's View on Evolution

Karl Schmitz-Moormann

When Teilhard died in his New York Exile in 1955 the theory of Evolution as it was formulated by George G. Simpson[1] as the 'synthetic theory' of evolution – which has been dubbed "Neo-Darwinism" ever since – was widely accepted as the definitive theory of evolution, and this theory was largely identified with the notion of evolution in the public mind. Only outsiders dared to think in other ways, and the publication of Teilhard's texts, especially of *The Phenomenon of Man* did not need to cause a fundamental change in the scientific world as to the acceptance of the idea of evolution. The difference between Teilhard and his friend Simpson concerned only the interpretation of evolution – the fact was no longer seriously contended.

The situation was quite different when Teilhard started his scientific career. In the late twenties the public, even the scientific world had not really accepted the idea of evolution as the factual description of the origin of living species.[2] Teilhard had at this time not only expounded the idea of evolution but fought vigorously against those who contended against it, such as the anatomist M. Vialleton.

The idea that evolution is not only a local phenomenon in biology was expressed very early by Teilhard. In 1917 he noted: "No other postulate seems to me to be established on more extended grounds of experience and critical judgement (and therefore more assured of surviving in tomorrow's Science and Philosophy) than that of Evolution" (ETG 176). The whole world, the universe is a product of this process. "It is evident," he wrote in 1920, "that the world in its present state is the *result of a movement* ... in every being a past is concentrated – nothing can be understood without its history. 'Nature' is equivalent to 'to become', to make oneself: to this point of view we are irresistibly urged by experience. ... There is nothing up to the most elevated psyche known to us, the human soul, which is not subjected to this common law. The soul as well occupies a perfectly defined place in the gradual ascent of living beings towards consciousness; consequently the soul must also have (in one way or another) made its appearance thanks to the general mobility of things. This progressive genesis of the universe is perceived by all those, who face Reality, with such clarity that any hesitation is impossible." (V, 24-25).

Thus from the very beginning, evolution was to Teilhard a universal phenomenon. This universality, in his time perhaps still more a conviction than a generally accepted theory, has been confirmed with time. The borderline between living and dead matter has, since then, if not vanished at least become very blurred, as has the line between chemistry and physics and between energy and matter. They all find their place in the history of the universe. For us today "scientific evolution is not only a hypothesis to be used by zoologists but a key to be used by everybody to penetrate any compartment of the past – the key to the universal Reality" (1926 – III, 178). Or as a palaeontologist puts it in 1974: "The evolution is like a general property (quality) of all matter, from the initial moments of cosmogenesis on, and with variable rythmical manifestations, in consort with the material on which it acts."[3] The universality of the notion of evolution in Teilhardian thought makes it practically impossible to agree with any restricted form of evolutionary theory. Neither Lamarckism nor Darwinism really fit with the totality of the universal evolution postulated by Teilhard. Both are restricted in the explanatory power by their philosophical background, which is characterised by a form of materialism and a strong faith in the efficacy of Occam's razor for exploring nature. Teilhard was open to the value of Darwinian and Lamarckian partial explanations, but he could see that neither the one nor the other could explain the evolutionary process in a satisfactory manner.

Today there are a number of modern scientists who agree about this with Teilhard. But some try to prove the non-existence of evolution on the grounds of certain difficulties. The Viallettons of Teilhard's time are still around. To them Teilhard would answer as to Vialleton, that historical movements can never be followed to their very beginnings. Teilhard has even formulated a law of the suppression of origins: Under the conditions of the Universe we cannot have a complete experimental picture of the process of evolution (cf. III, 113) – e.g., on the earth the conditions of fossilisation make it highly improbable that the first members of a new species become fossilised; and if they were, it would be highly improbable that we would recognize a new species in those fossils. The anti-evolutionist arguments are based on ignorance of this restriction on our possible knowledge about the history of the universe. There are similar difficulties in other aspects of the evolution of the universe. According to modern computer-simulations of the evolution of a blue giant-star into a super-nova – a condition absolutely necessary for the existence of the elements needed for life, and thus for the existence of planets – a super nova could not happen. If they had not seen them astro-physicists would have concluded they did not exist. The "Transformist Paradoxon" is thus no proof against evolution for that is needed to make sense of our observations in paleontology, astrophysics, biochemistry etc.

But this is not to say that we can put aside all difficulties. They are real enough and we can instance the ideas of Sheldrake to show that Teilhard is not the only one to have sensed the insufficiency of the neo-Darwinist theory of evolution.

The essential points Teilhard insisted on for his interpretation of evolution, can be listed under two principal headings:

1. Evolution follows the basic way of union.
2. Evolution must be read, to be understood, not from its beginnings, but from its ending. In other words, becoming becomes meaningful not at its starting point, but in the fully realised being.

1. Evolution is a Process of Union

The idea that the process of evolution can be described most comprehensively as a process of union was expressed very early by Teilhard in a text entitled "The creative union" (ETG, 169-97). The basic idea was that out of a process of union new things arise, are created or become. To become is equal to uniting in a new unity.

This line of thinking could lead to the fundamental misunderstanding of union as a process of composition. But the process of evolution is not a process of assembling prepared parts which have been prepared according to a preconceived idea of the end product. This would be the way humans would build a machine, a process in which the only really evolving part is the human idea of the machine not the machine itself.

To get a clearer picture of the process of evolution, it is best not to look first at a highly complex level, where we are accustomed to use magic words like 'mutation', or 'chance' or both, to express more or less cryptically that change in the DNA chains took place. This is only a signal of the change that took place at the level of information: evolution and so the becoming of new beings, takes place only if the signalled information is integrated into the living whole which thereby acquires new possibilities to act and to survive. The process of union is highly complicated at this level, and it is much easier to see evolution happening at a level where atoms emerge out of the union of protons, neutrons and electrons. These early elements of evolution – they date from the first second of the universe – *unite* (the details of the process are here presupposed to be known[4]), and out of these unions of elements (which are quite consistent in themselves and which give no sign of having been conceived primarily to be elements of an ongoing process of union) all the 92 or more elements arose, opening up new future possibilities that did not previously exist. Atoms are quite consistent in themselves; they have not been conceived as building-blocks like the wheels of a clock or the pistons of an engine. But it is most significant for evolution, that atoms in their turn became elements in unions which produced what we call molecules which could, in analogy to the realm of living beings, be classified according to their binding or unification behaviour. The number of new species of molecules, the new mode of existence of the molecular level, is so large that the whole matter of the universe, appropriately transformed into useable atoms, would not be sufficient to create all the molecules that are theoretically possible.

Naturally, the union of atoms into one molecule is not the end of the process of union. Small molecules can become units in more complex molecules, as amino acids are formed into protein chains. In a more general way, we can state that everything coming out of the process of evolution, emerging as a higher level of being, will itself become a possible element of some higher stage of union.

By 'union' or 'unification', in this context, must be understood a highly abstract notion, describing not a univocally defined phenomenon, but rather an analogically defined one. The way by which the union of the different kinds of elements may be reached is diverse and could even be ordered in an hierarchical order from purely energetical links, in protons, to personal links like among humans.

We should never forget that the continuing process of union is far from being linear. Only a very small part of one elementary level will reach the next one and there will be a prolific branching of new beings, of new species of atoms, molecules, living beings on the new level giving no immediate indication what elements will survive to a higher level or what the mainstream orientation of evolution will be.

Union must be distinguished from agglomeration and unifying fusion. While agglomerations of all kind are changeable in quantity without changing the structure or the quality of the agglomeration – crystal remains a crystal and a heap of sand remains a heap of sand – a union in the Teilhardian sense of the word produces a whole, which Teilhard called a 'complexity' (or *complexe*) which is defined through quantity *and* pattern. Not only "how much" is unified into a whole, but also "how" the union is realised qualifies the evolved being. The example of chemical isomeres (e.g. ethanol versus dimethyl ether) makes quite clear what is meant. In pheromones they clearly have a different meaning; for their informational value for the receiving member of a species is obviously lost with isomeric changes. The same applies to cannabis and other drugs.

It becomes clear that elements have in higher complex forms such as living beings, not only their material and structural value but they become carriers of information. Their integration into the living whole then occurs more for the information the element carries for the organism than for the material element in itself. The living being is not only a whole that unites elements through information but one that selects, e.g. from the outside world, what is to be integrated and what is not. It should be noted that the notion of information plays an important role in understanding the ongoing process of union, but we cannot treat that point here in detail.

One further point we must keep in mind, and which Teilhard insisted on quite clearly, is that union does not fuse the elements into a melting pot; rather it respects the elements and enhances their reality. Union differentiates, as Teilhard stated very often, giving to the pre-existing elements new possibilities of a participatory existence. In this view, a carbon atom in a brain-cell is not only a C atom – though the chemist might still identify it as such – but it somehow participates in human thinking. It has become somehow something more than a simple C atom thanks to its integration into a unified complexity.

The concept of union as the basic process of creative evolution has been generalized by Teilhard into the metaphysical realm by stating that any growth of being can be identified with a greater union. Or to quote Teilhard (XI, 208, n. 1)

plus esse = plus a pluribus uniri (passive formula)
plus esse = plus plura unire (active formula)

2. Evolution becomes meaningful in Man

The reading of evolution as a process of pure chance corrected by selection has its own difficulties and is by no means satisfactory. Teilhard was always amused by his friend G. G. Simpson's neo-Darwinist point of view, and they sparred quite frequently about it. It seems that Teilhard was immune to that kind of irrational scientific dogmatism which wants everything to be explained by the past and refuses to consider the outcome of a process as significant for the understanding of the process. Probably Teilhard was far too much sensitized through his longterm experience with Catholic dogmatism to fall into the pitfall of scientistic dogmatism. The fundamental difference in Teilhard's reading of the process of evolution as compared to the neo-

Darwinist reading is the Teilhardian hypothesis that the human being is the key to the understanding of the universe. In the most explicit way Teilhard stated this hypothesis in his *The Phenomenon of Man*: "Pre-eminent signification of Man in Nature and organic Nature of Mankind: two hypotheses which one might try to refute from the start" (I, 23) Teilhard considers these hypotheses as absolutely necessary if one is to understand the process of evolution.

It is a fact that in mankind the evolutionary process has developed the capacity to think in a reflective way; and if it is true that the whole human being has evolved out of the evolutionary past then man is part of the process of evolution and this process continues in man. This process is in itself essentially a qualifying process, bringing into being new qualities of existence. As Teilhard has shown quite convincingly, this qualifying process reached its highest degree in man who is the only being in our experience which is able to consciously act and react to the process of evolution. At least on Earth, after the invention of life and the change of the atmosphere through the invention of photosynthesis, no other single step in evolution has changed the surface of the Earth in a more complete way than the appearance of mankind.

Naturally, if we make quantitative judgements the only measure of evolutionary importance, then nothing but the all pervading protons with alpha-particles coming second would count. Even these, which make up for more than 99% of all matter, are quantitatively nothing as compared to the one part in a billion of the Big Bang energy they represent. If quantity in the universe is correlated with importance and value, then everything that has evolved is just a negligible quantity. This 'quantitative dogmatism' leads us directly to the myth in which mankind is just, together with all life, a mildew on a grain of dust lost in infinite space. Teilhard insists correctly on the fact that man can think this universe, and that evolution or nature start to think themselves in mankind. This universe is certainly not of any great interest because of its quantitative immensity, but because of the qualitative evolution that took place and continues to do so. To understand the qualitative aspect of the universe Teilhard decided it best to start from man who is the only being able to appreciate qualities, to ask for their meaning, and to experience them not only by an outside inspection but also by introspection through reflection.

Through introspection we know about our psychic reality: we experience the human unity, the "eu-centrical" unity (VII, 104 et passim) as a psyche, not as a bodily centered unity though there is certainly a bodily infrastructure on which the psyche builds and acts. The inside of reality is in Teilhard's interpretation the real unifying force, which appears in man as consciousness, as psyche, as mind, as soul – the names that can be used for the reality are certainly manifold

– and Teilhard holds that this reality so obviously present in man's inner experience can be followed backwards through the history of evolution. At first it appears only somewhat reduced in animals that are close to us in evolution – in chimpanzees, who use a symbolic language comparable to that of the deaf; in dogs, who are playful companions of the humans; in birds who are quite good learners, even creative learners, etc. The further we go backwards in evolutionary levels the fainter become the barely discernable traces of the inner reality. Once we have crossed the border-region of life, we might with Teilhard postulate something like a unity giving inner reality of the beings, but we cannot make it visible anymore.

The whole process of evolution is thus seen in Teilhard's view from a new angle. The material process, though not denied, loses its principal place of interest. Since the most important, and even materially the most efficient, outcome of the evolutionary process is the human mind, it becomes much more interesting to understand how the psyche evolved than to understand the evolution of bodily structures. The latter are certainly a necessary condition for man's emergence, but the interesting point in man's emergence is the fact that man is a thinking, reflecting being. If mankind represented just another species to be classified by the data of its anatomy, the human beings would have no special interest. They certainly would not think neither about their past nor about their future. There would be no science and no religion. It is Teilhard's central argument that any understanding of evolution that is to avoid the pitfall of scientistic reductionism must consider the evolutionary process as a whole as it emerges in man in a most definite way into the realm of spirituality.

Evolution in the view of Teilhard ceases thus definitely to be a materialistical phenomenon to be explained by materialistic laws of nature. In the Teilhardian view matter is itself charged, in an infinitesimal way, with spirit. It is described as having "spiritual potency" (XIII, 81 ssq.).

The Teilhardian view of evolution thus goes far beyond what is normally considered in evolutionary theories. Naturally, Teilhard who worked most of his life on the frontiers of palaeontology,[5] had no diffculty in integrating the facts of science into his vision, but he was able also to integrate those facts to which scientistic dogmatism refuses the right of citizenship because they belong in the realm of the human mind and spirit. A sound scientific assessment of Teilhard's view still needs to be formulated: it will have to show its capacity to integrate the whole of evolutionary reality, including mankind, into its vision. For the time being, Teilhard's view is one of the most appropriate. This would need to be shown in detail, in a more complete and extensive way than can be done within the limits of a short text.

References

1. Simpson, George, G. (1953), *Life of the Past*, Yale Univ. Press, see especially chapter 10: Theories of Evolution.
2. Cf. e.g. the article: "Abstammungslehre" in: Der Grosse Brockhaus, Tome 1, 1928, where many different theories are exposed as competing theories, not as a historical review.
3. Crusafont-Pairò, Miguel, B. Melendez, E. Aguirre (1974), *La Evolucion*, B. A. C., Madrid.
4. For more details see e.g.: Silk, Joseph (1980), *The Big Bang*, Freeman & Co, San Francisco; Weinberg, Steven (1977), *The first three Minutes*, Basic Books, New York, Reeves, Hubert (1981), *Patience dans l'Azur*, Ed. du Seuil, Paris.
5. See Pierre Teilhard de Chardin, *L'Oeuvre Scientifique*, 11 volumes edited by Nicole and Karl Schmitz-Moormann, Olten-Freiburg 1971.

The quotations from Teilhard are quoted by giving the volume and the pages of the French Edition of the *Oeuvres de Teilhard de Chardin*, 13 volumes, Editions du Seuil, Paris 1955-1976.

Process-Theology and Evolution

David A. Pailin

If theology is to present itself in the secular world of post-Enlightenment culture as a credible way of understanding the ultimate character of reality, it must among other things show that it has a way of apprehending the creativity of God which is both theologically and scientifically acceptable. As a contribution to this task I have been invited to consider whether process thought, particularly as developed by Whitehead and Hartshorne,[1] can be regarded as a promising foundation for a theistic understanding of biological evolution. The question, then, is this: 'Does process thought provide resources (though not necessarily all the basic conceptual resources) for an understanding of the character of evolution which is at once biologically tenable, metaphysically significant, theistically important and rationally credible?' As such it asks about an understanding which is to be assessed by its competence in satisfying four criteria: first, it must fit what current biological investigations are warrantably claiming to be the nature of genetic processes and evolutionary developments; secondly, it must make sense of those processes and developments in terms of an understanding of the ultimate and universal character of reality – and in terms of an understanding which shows that reality is fundamentally meaningful and its expressions valuable; thirdly, it must show that the nature of evolution can be plausibly regarded at some significant level as an expression of divine purposing, a response to divine activity and a contribution to divine satisfaction; and finally, the story of biological evolution which is developed to meet these demands must not be so far-fetched that rational reflection is likely to deem it ingenious but not ingenuous, clever but not credible.

This is a huge demand. In what follows I do not pretend to attempt to develop such a story. What I intend to do is to restrict myself to exploring some of the points at which process thought may be considered to have something to contribute to the construction of such a story – and to raise some questions which may be asked about those possible contributions. Underlying the approach to the issue of evolution and God adopted both in this paper and in process theology generally is the conviction that, as Charles Birch puts it, 'the object of creation in some way incorporates the ever present creativity of God, without becoming identified with it.'² This means both that the created order only persists because of the continual activity of God³ and that God is not merely a spectator of the world but 'participates in the life and being of his creatures.'⁴ From this it follows, according to Birch, that 'the sacred and the secular, the natural and the divine, are not uniquely separate divisions of reality.' Hence it is at least legitimate to hope for a synthesis of the insights of the natural sciences (and the rest of current culture) and of religious faith in a single, coherent, all-embracing understanding. Such an incorporation of evolutionary views into 'a more complete picture of reality'⁶ is, in the judgement of Birch and others, likely to be advanced if we approach the issue in terms of process thought. On what grounds may this conviction be regarded as justified?

It should not be overlooked that the Whiteheadian and Hartshornean developments of process thought are part – while arguably the most fruitful part so far – of a wider tradition in modern understanding. This wider tradition may be regarded as including such thinkers as Hegel, Marx, Peirce, James, Dewey, Bergson, Alexander, Lloyd Morgan, Smuts and Teilhard de Chardin. Theologically, though, the more interesting developments have come from those who have been influenced by Whitehead and Hartshorne. They include William Temple, Lionel Thornton and Daniel Day Williams, and such contemporary writers as Schubert Ogden, John Cobb, Lewis Ford and David Griffin. Furthermore, although Whitehead and Hartshorne are often – and not unreasonably – regarded as the joint founders of contemporary process theology, it should not be forgotten that Hartshorne is an independent thinker who had arrived at many of his basic ideas before he came into contact with Whitehead. There are both differences of approach and different conceptual structures in their developments of their thought which need to be recognized. While, for example, Whitehead sees metaphysical discovery as involving 'imaginative generalization' from 'particular observation' and as tested by further observation of its 'applicability',⁷ Hartshorne prefers the more rationalist approach of identifying the apparent conceptual possibilities and then showing *a priori* that only one of them is not ruled out by some intrinsic fault.⁸ While the 'primordial' and 'consequent natures' of 'God' have a foundational role in Whitehead's metaphysical understanding and while Whitehead has some stimulating insights into thought about God, Hartshorne's work is much more consciously theistic and has produced important novel insights into the concept of God. In this respect it is a source of confusion to attempt to treat what Whitehead says about the primordial and consequent natures of God as being parallel to what Hartshorne states about the existence and actuality of the dipolar reality of God. These distinctions express different ways of perceiving the divine.

In spite of these reservation, however, it is possible to outline the basic principles of process thought as developed in the works of Whitehead and Hartshorne. Among those that are particularly relevant to the question of a theistic understanding of biological evolution are the following:

First, to be actual is to be in a process and so a constituent of a series of becomings into being. Not only organic or living beings change: all observable objects are in process. This is not simply a generalization from what physicists report about the structure of matter and from our self-awareness of our own being. It is a consequence of the fact that to 'be' is to be related and to be responsive to other beings. An actual entity comes to be as it constitutes itself as a particular focus and interpretation of forces. This self-constitution (or 'decision') is a synthesis achieved by having internal relations both to the data of the past (including its own immediate past) and to the possibilities open to it.[9] What is unchanging is either what has been actual and is now past (and so has ceased to be a present focus and synthesizing interpretation of forces) or what is an abstraction from the actual.

Secondly, to be actual is to be in some temporal order. An actual entity is a momentary response to the past which provides a datum to contribute to the future.

Thirdly, to be actual is to be related. Whitehead, for example, speaks of the error of regarding 'simple location' as the 'primary way in which things are involved in space-time.' Instead it should be recognized that, 'in a certain sense, everything is everywhere at all times.' Each 'spatio-temporal standpoint mirrors the world'[10] and is incorporated into every other spatio-temporal standpoint that is to come to be. As Hartshorne puts it, reality is a social process.

Fourthly, the key notions for understanding the basic characteristics of actuality are those of 'actual occasions' (or 'actual entities'), 'prehension', 'concrescence' and 'nexus'. By 'actual occasions' or 'actual entities' Whitehead refers to 'the final real things of which the world is made up. There is no going behind actual entities to find anything more real.' As 'the final facts' these actual occasions 'are drops of experience, complex and interdependent.'[11] What is truly real, that is, is a momentary event whose actuality then perishes and which is thereupon succeeded by another such event. What we observe as enduring objects – from electrons and atoms to cells and galaxies – are composed of sequences of aggregates, societies or groups of such events.[12]

A 'prehension' is an act of grasping 'the general characteristics of an actual entity.' Accordingly a prehension is 'referent to an external world, and in this sense will be said to have a "vector character."' It reproduces all the characteristics of the actual occasion which it grasps and accordingly 'involves emotion, and purpose, and valuation, and causation.'[13] In coming to be actual, an actual occasion embraces two forms of prehensions: physical prehensions, which are its grasp of previous actual occasions, particularly its immediate predecessor, and conceptual (or mental) prehensions which are its grasp of the possibilities open for it to become. Positive prehensions, as kinds of experiencing, are termed 'feelings.'[14] Accordingly Birch and Cobb speak of 'living organisms' as 'subjects experiencing their world' and state that 'it is quite appropriate to say that cells "feel" their environment' although their 'feelings' are to be recognized to be 'rudimentary in comparison with human feelings, and entirely lacking in consciousness.'[15]

'Concrescence' refers to the coming to be of an actual occasion. Having prehended physically its situation and conceptually its possibilities, it determines what it is to be by a synthesis of these prehensions. Whitehead speaks of this self-determination as a 'decision' but he is careful to make it clear that the 'decision' whereby an actual occasion separates what is to be given as its subjective form[16] from what is not given 'does not imply conscious judgement' in every – or even in the vast majority – of cases. The term 'decision' is used in this respect 'in its root sense of a "cutting off"'[17] and refers to the limitation which fixes the precise character of the particular actual occasion. All actual occasions are thus creative as the determinate product of a unique synthesis of prehensions. On becoming actual, however, an actual occasion perishes, to become a datum for future actual occasions and to be succeeded by the concrescence of another.

'Nexus' (singular 'nexus') refer to particular facts of togetherness among actual entities. These 'facts of togetherness' are 'real, individual, and particular' in the same way that actual occasions are.[18] Consequently 'the ultimate facts of immediate actual experience are actual entities, prehensions, and nexus.' Everything else is 'derivative abstraction.' Failure to recognize this leads to the error of misplaced concreteness when an abstraction is regarded as referring to what is in itself actual. Ivor Leclerc points out that composites *per se*, as nexus, may be such that one should reject the view that acting pertains only their ultimate constituents. As nexus composites may be seen as 'abiding entities' which integrate their constituents in 'a single, higher-level entity, which *per se* as an integral whole acts relationally with respect to such entities.' An atom, composed of subatomic particles, may be regarded as 'an instance of such a composite entity' whose agency is not wholly derivative from that of its constituents and 'biological organisms' as 'still higher-level composites.'[19] One important implication of this view of nexus is that the loci of creativity may be seen as occurring at different levels – at those of the atom, the cell, the organism and the person. At the same time, while the unified occasions of the higher level nexus influence the parts which constitute them, they are held to do so without violating the autonomy which properly belongs to these parts. A cell is consequently to be seen as a nexus which has its own internal laws, which influences (and responds to) the subordinate actual occasions of which it is composed, and which participates in and responds to the activity of the larger organism to which it belongs.[20]

Fifthly, the process of reality is thus the successive coming to be of units of actuality – actual occasions or 'drops of experience' - which are constituted by the way in which each concrescing occasion prehends (and so massively or 'genetically' inherits) the character of its immediate predecessor; physically prehends all other actual occasions, graded according to degrees of importance for it; conceptually (or mentally) prehends the possibilities open to it, again graded according to their 'importance' ; and then makes a 'decision' to be this particular actual occasion in response to and synthesizing these prehensions.

Sixthly, the structure of all actual occasions is basically the same in all cases. This means that reality is to be seen as having a genuine unity of inter-connectedness. Whitehead puts it that

the process, or concrescence, of any one actual entity involves the other actual entities among its components. In this way the obvious solidarity of the world receives its explanation.[21]

Furthermore, since all actual occasions involve prehensions of and a response to the situation in which they come to be, each actual occasion is ultimately determined by its internal relations[22] and so has a 'subjective form.'[23] This is its creative act of self-definition. An event is said to be 'alive' if it has a power of novelty in its self-definition which means that it need not respond to its immediate predecessor by merely repeating it in a way that conforms more or less precisely to the changes in the environment occurring as that predecessor came to concrescence. In any case, as Birch puts it, 'to be is to act.' An individual creature is not 'constituted by divine action or decisions alone' for it must make 'its own creaturely decisions' in determining its actuality.[24]

Seventhly, God's role in the process of reality is essential but not wholly determinative. God is the power of creativity required by each concrescing actual occasion in three ways. In the first place God ensures the continuation of being. Although Whitehead writes in *Process and Reality* that the 'ultimate is termed "creativity"' and that 'God is its primordial, non-temporal accident,' this remark is to be interpreted in the light of his previous statement that 'in all philosophic theory there is an ultimate which is actual in virtue of its accidents.'[25] In other words, Whitehead is not maintaining that something called 'creativity' produced God but that what God *actually* is is the product of God's essential creativity. It is God, then, on whom all finally depend for their existence and who ensures that on perishing concrete actual occasions are succeeded by the concrescence of novel actual occasions. Secondly, God is the reality in which all concrescing occasions prehend the divine valuation of their predecessor and of all other past actual occasions for, on coming to concrescence and therefore perishing, each actual occasion is valued by God as part of the divine response to the world. This prehension is a prehension of what Whitehead calls the 'consequent nature' of God.[26] Thirdly, God is the reality in which all concrescing occasions conceptually prehend the possibilities open to them. As the possible or future is necessarily what is not yet actual, it can be prehended only as it is envisaged in the reality of what Whitehead describes as 'the primordial nature of God.'[27] This is in accordance with Whitehead's ontological principle which he summarizes as 'no actual entity, then no reason.'[28]

According, then, to Whitehead's understanding of the process of reality, God gives substance and direction to the process of actualization but so far as that process involves the realization of novel forms, it is not the product of divine coercion. As the urge and object of desire, the divine is said to 'lure' or 'persuade' the concrescing occasions. In the end, though, each concrescing occasion determines its own actuality in relation to its prehensions of past actual occasions, the valuation of them in God's consequent nature, and the possibilities for itself prehended in God's primordial nature.[30] While, therefore, God is the necessary ground of and source of possibilities for all actual coming-to-be, the relation of God to the world is not a pantheism where God determines all and is all but a panentheism in which all is in God – and God is in all – but each actual entity has its own, limited, power of self-determination.

Evolutionary ideas may be seen as one of three background influences which set the programme for the development of process thought. The other two are the awareness of history and the primary intuition of being a self as being that which changes through successive states. In this respect process thought can be regarded in part as an attempt to make metaphysical sense of the processive character of reality perceived in these three aspects of human understanding. As a result it is generally comfortable with evolutionary theories – though this is not to say very much! Process thinkers are, after all, self-conscious members of the modern age.

Although, as George Lucas has recently argued,[31] evolutionary theories do not seem to have played a significantly formative role in Whitehead's thought, Whitehead himself remarks in *Modes of Thought* that 'today the doctrine of evolution reigns' - while going on to point out that this doctrine need not be conceived as necessarily implying 'evolution upwards.'[32] Earlier, in *Science and the Modern World*, he had spoken of nature as 'exemplifying a philosophy of the evolution of organisms' which pointed to 'a wider evolution ... within which nature is but a limited mode.'[33]

Hartshorne has more to say about evolution but it is on the whole general as well as approving. He states that he has 'never consciously not been an evolutionist.'[34] His view of evolution, however, is not limited to biological processes. In an early work, *Beyond Humanism*, he argues that evolutionary notions are applicable to the inorganic as well as to the organic – and indeed to the cosmos as such.[35] More recently, in *Omnipotence and Other Theological Mistakes*, he affirms the 'evolutionary theory' that 'offspring vary from their parents and from one another partly by chance.' The 'fairly definite direction' of evolution is because 'natural selection weeds out many nonadaptive chance variations, so that from very simple beginnings is woven a very complex "web of life."' Forming the evolutionary process, though, is 'a basic set of physical laws setting limits to the reign of chance' and 'governing the behaviour of the basic elements.' These laws constitute 'a basic physical order' within which the chances of evolutionary developments can occur but which is not explicable by reference to evolution. According to Hartshorne this basic order is to be understood as 'divinely decided.'[36] Furthermore, although 'Darwin was a believer in causal determinism,' we should now recognize that 'his theory works even better on a nondeterministic basis' such as is provided by quantum theory.[37] God – or 'providence' - is thus to be seen as 'limiting' the scope of chance in the constituents of the physical world. As a result 'the nature of the elementary constituents of the physical world' is one of '*order in disorder*'[38] – the order being a providential limitation which makes evolutionary developments possible. 'The only positive explanation of order,' though, is through postulating 'the existence of an orderer.'[39] Hence Hartshorne asserts that evolution is only fully intelligible by reference to God. At the same time he is concerned to point out that while God has supreme freedom, the divine is not alone in being free. Creatures have varying degrees of freedom and accordingly God deals with a creation (or nature) that has within it 'a pervasive element of chance.' Evolution occurs partly as a result of the exercise of freedom, partly as the result of the chance interactions of contingent events (as when a particular particle happens to hit a particular nucleotide in a DNA molecule and alters the pattern of that molecule in a situation where the original states of the particle and of the molecule were independently determined), and partly as a result of the ways in which the effects of learned patterns of behaviour on physically inherited structures influence natural selection.[40]

These remarks, however, are very general and it is time to consider in more specific ways how the basic understanding of process thought may contribute to our perception of the relationship between evolution and God.

In the first place, as has already been indicated, process thought understands God to be intimately involved in each momentary occasion of actuality. Since evolutionary changes are composed of sequences – long sequences – of such occasions, God is intrinsically considered to be involved in any evolutionary process. The divine is the source of the prehensions both of the divine valuation of the past or perished actual occasions which constitute each concrescing occasion's environment and of the possibilities, including the initial subjective aim,[41] for that particular concrescent. As Ian Barbour thus puts it, the 'order' of reality is a product of 'God's structuring of possibilities' as well as of each occasion's 'conformation to its past', while 'novelty' arises from 'God's offering of alternative possibilities' as well as from each occasion's 'self-creation.'[42] God is thus held to be an essential agent in all that occurs. On the other hand, God's agency is not the sole influence on what happens and, while affecting each occasion, is not readily detectable.

Secondly, process thought understands creativity to be characteristic of all actual occasions. Each one establishes its own unique synthesis of its own subjective form out of its prehensions of the past and of the relevant contents (graded according to importance) of the consequent and primordial natures of God. Hence each actual occasion may be held to be to a minute extent evolutionary. What we describe as evolution is the pattern abstracted from what happens in the becomings of vast numbers of genetically linked actual occasions as creative syntheses.

Thirdly, process thought maintains that the evolutionary developments – as with all changes – are not deterministic. Although each concrescing occasion is limited by its own past and by its circumambient background as to what it may become, its synthesis is the result of that actual occasion's own determination in relation to the facts and possibilities before it. One consequence of this is that, contrary to Einstein's conviction that 'God does not play dice', it must be recognized that God takes chances. As creator God 'makes things make themselves'[43] and respects their limited autonomy in doing so. Thus, in Lewis Ford's phrase, 'God proposes and the world disposes.'[44] While, therefore, God may urge creatures towards greater complexity and further expressions of value, evolutionary advance achieves those goals through the decisions of the creatures and not by means of the exercise of irresistible might. Having determined the cosmic constants which limit the possibilities open to natural processes, God's power is exercised in the world as a tender love which patiently operates through the attractiveness of the 'conceptual harmonization' which it presents to the world. God, in other words, seeks to 'save' the world by 'leading it by his vision of truth, beauty, and goodness.'[45]

Fourthly, natural evil may be understood to occur as the result of the self-determinations of different actual occasions producing, through undesigned and unintended combinations, disharmonies and conflicts. Such evil does not occur because of the ill-will of certain agents but because the world is such that the furtherance of one goal (for example, the future of the genes of a particular insect or a virus) is incompatible with that of another goal (for example, the wholeness of a certain fruit or the health of my body). Furthermore, since the divine influence on events is one of persuasion rather than of control, God may seek to lure sequences of actual occasions into aesthetically creative patterns of activity but is unable to prevent conflict being possible if these are to be 'decision-making creatures.'[46] The upshot of the divine creation of creatures (as contrasted with the 'emanation' of divine self-expression and with 'making' what is wholly determined by the maker) is that

nature appears to be a huge experiment, and in that experiment, as in all experiments, there is room for accidents to happen. It bears little resemblance to a contrivance, designed and constructed by some sort of infallible cosmic engineer, into which a spanner was later thrown to gum up the works. We know it to have been evolved through painful stages over eons of time by a trial-and-error process.[47]

Natural evil may thus be understood, according to process thought, by reference to the self-determination of the creatures and as indicating the freedom-giving character of divine creativity. At the same time this understanding makes it very uncertain how far the divine can be held, as creator, responsible for the actual state of the creation and, accordingly, the extent to which the attribute of creativity can be given significant material content when used of God.

Fifthly, the role of God is not to be seen wholly in terms of a passive presenter of what has been and what may be – as actual but passive consequent and primordial natures for each concrescing occasion to prehend. Process theology also envisages God as seeking to influence the course or direction of evolutionary (and every other) development by 'lure' or 'persuasion.' The question that arises at this point is the definiteness of such luring or persuading. Is it to be held to be in a general direction or in each case as indicating a particular goal for that particular concrescing occasion? The answer to this question is important for appreciating how process thought envisages the specificity of the divine aim in the influencing evolutionary change. Unfortunately it is not easy to establish a precise answer to the question. Some comments in expositions of process theology imply that the presentation to each concrescent of an initial subjective aim and divine persuasion to actualize it is to be seen as particular and detailed. Other comments suggest that the divine activity in each instance is less specific in its material goal.

Whitehead, for instance, sees the relationship as one in which God provides the urge to creativity and the possible goals for each concrescing entity so that each 'originality in the temporal world is conditioned, though not determined, by an initial subjective aim supplied by the ground of all order and of all originality.'[48] What he says later, however, indicates that the precise character of a particular subjective form is regarded as being left to the concrescing occasion: Whitehead writes that 'each temporal entity ... derives from God its basic conceptual aim, relevant to its actual world, yet with indeterminations awaiting its own decisions.'[49] Thus while 'God's all-embracing conceptual valuations' condition the creative moves from the previous 'actual world to the correlate novel concrescence,' such transitions involve self-determinations which are always 'imaginative' in 'origin' and subject to the autonomy of the concrescing occasion.[50] In *God and the World* Cobb develops this view to hold that the divine activity in creation is to be seen as an urge or lure towards greater complexification[51] – what I might describe as a localized alternative to the general tendency of the second law of thermodynamics. Thus he writes of God's agency as 'the call forward'[52] which is found throughout life and seeks to draw each entity 'beyond the mere repetition of past purposes and past feelings' to 'finer and richer actualizations' in novel states.[53] Evolution is the emergence over billions of years of individuals with higher and higher degrees of ordering. From the chaos where low-grade actual occasions happened at random through stages of increasing conformation to predecessors, the process of evolution has eventually produced individuals with capacities for rich syntheses of novel experiences.[54] Lewis Ford describes this process as one in which the divine is continuously in dialogue with the creation, seeking in the creatures spontaneous responses to 'the new initiatives God is constantly introducing.'[55]

What seems to be indicated by such remarks as these is that God acts in two ways in influencing the process of evolution. On the one hand God acts fundamentally in establishing what we regard as the valid laws of nature.[56] These 'laws' both ensure that there is a universe at all and provide the structures within which evolutionary changes may occur. On the other hand God acts within these structures by luring or persuading concrescent occasions in the direction of greater aesthetic enrichment. How, though, does process thought envisage the manner of such 'luring' or 'persuasion'? This brings us to a sixth – and to me the most bothersome – possible contribution of process thought to the understanding of evolution.

Sixthly, the understanding of reality found in process thought not only uses but seems to depend for its credibility to a large extent upon a psychical (or panpsychic) view of the constituents of reality. Whitehead seeks to avoid a mind-matter dualism not by reducing one of the pair to being a form of the other but by regarding both mind and matter as abstractions from the essentially bipolar ('physical and mental') nature of each actuality.[57] According to his position each occasion is a subject which 'feels' its environment and responds to it. The difference between the inorganic and the organic is not that the former has no internal relations and the latter has internal relations but that the latter can take into account greater ranges and complexities of data and produce more novel syntheses of them than the former. At the same time the way in which a 'subject' 'feels' and 'decides' about the data grasped by it is normally rudimentary and unconscious.[58] It is only in the comparatively rare higher-grade occasions that consciousness and, even more rarely, self-consciousness is present.

According to various process theologians this way of understanding reality means that there is no real problem about envisaging the emergence of life and of mind from the inorganic. Ultimately, however tenuously and rudimentarily, all actual occasions have a structure which is characteristic of life and mind. By saying that each concrescing occasion 'prehends' or 'takes account of' its environment and 'determines' its own synthesis of its prehensions, one attributes to it 'feelings' and 'decisions' as a 'subject' to some degree. The problem in that case is not to discern how mental activity emerged in the evolutionary process, since that activity is present in some form throughout reality, but how consciousness and, even more, self-consciousness arise from the rudimentary forms of mental activity characteristic of lower-grade actual occasions. Furthermore, the psychical (or panpsychic) view of reality not only provides a basis for understanding the presence of mind in reality but also makes sense of a notion of final causation in evolution since it sees in each entity a subjective side which responds to lures and selects the goal for its own self-satisfaction.

The psychical view of reality is sometimes defended on the grounds that our understanding should start with ourselves and then move on to the more obscure and puzzling realms of cells, atoms, electrons and bosons, seeing the latter beings by analogy with the former rather than trying to understand the former in terms of our indirect and tentative attempts to construct models of the latter which are independent of our primary self-awareness of our own mode of being. Hartshorne thus states that 'all our best thought is anthropomorphic in the sense that we must take our own reality as [a] sample of reality in general – the sample we most surely and adequately know.' It is only by generalizing from our experience that we can understand other things, even in physics.[59] If, though, this is the nature of understanding, there is no good reason to deny that patterns of 'feelings' are, at least analogically, attributable to all actual occasions and that their self-determinations, as syntheses reached by 'decisions', are 'mental' acts.

Before, though we consider some of the problems which arise when we consider the view of evolution suggested by process theology, let us note four claims which it is apparently advancing. First, it holds that life is found in the choice of novelty and in the quest for aesthetic enrichment. Secondly, it suggests that God acts in the processes of natural evolution as a localized lure exerting an opposite pull to the move towards increasing entropy. Thirdly, change occurs in an enduring object through the decisions of the actual occasions which constitute its route of inheritance. So far as each individual actual occasion is concerned change does not occur by chance but is an expression of a subjective aim, albeit generally at an unconscious level. Chance supervenes as a result of the undetermined interaction of two or more actual occasions – as when a particle following its route of inheritance accidently strikes a nucleotide in a DNA chain which is following its own independent (or, rather, to be strictly accurate in this social universe, its own practically independent) route of inheritance. Fourthly, God as creator is necessarily limited in the influence that can be exerted over individual decisions. To create is to produce that which has its own (if limited) autonomy and to respect its self-determinations.

The story told by process theology about evolution may seem to have a number of attractive features, especially so long as it stays at the level of generalities. Lewis Ford gives a typical expression of such understanding when he writes that

Process theism .... sees the future as organically growing out of its past. All such actualization depends upon the vicissitudes of creaturely response ... God's general, everlasting purpose is everywhere one and the same: the elicitation of the maximum richness of existence in every situation. Yet because creaturely response varies, the achievement of this good is highly uneven and follows many different routes. In biological evolution many other lines were tried – amphibians, reptiles, marsupials – before mammals emerged, and of the mammals only certain primates were responsive to the call to become human. Among men the response to God varied considerably ...[60]

For Ford divine providence is in this way to be held to be 'manifest in creation' as acting by persuasion.[61] The resulting story may then claim to be biologically tenable, metaphysically significant, theistically important and rationally credible as a way of uniting belief in God as creator with what recent studies have indicated to be the character of biological evolution. When, however, we move from such general remarks to ask what must presumably follow concerning the particular events of the story which give rise to biological change, problems begin to arise. What in general appears plausible turns out to be less so when we examine what it implies in detail about God and evolution.

A minor – though nevertheless real – difficulty is that the influence of God by 'lure' or 'persuasion' on evolution seems so ineffective over vast spaces and ages that it becomes questionable if any significant notion of creative activity can be attributed to God. Birch and Cobb, for example, speak of 'Life' (their term for 'the central religious symbol' - i.e. God[62]) as being an 'enormously powerful' 'cosmic principle that works for higher order in the midst of entropy' but they also have to admit that this 'Life' has 'little effect' in 'vast areas of the universe' and is able to evoke 'spectacular transformations' (such as we find on this planet) 'only when very special conditions exist.'[63] What they here admit seems indisputable but it does raise serious doubts about whether this 'cosmic principle', whether it be dubbed 'Life' or 'God', can in any significant way be described as a purposive and agential creator who is actively involved in and to some important extent materially responsible for influencing what has evolved. Does reference to 'God', in other words, add anything significant to the claim that by chance some changes very rarely but occasionally occur in the cosmos as biological studies suggest? Barbour responds to the scepticism implied in such a question by holding that 'chance' alone is not a satisfactory explanation: reference to 'law' is also needed to find a credible explanation of the emergence of certain complex and relatively stable configurations of particles, atoms and molecules. The 'dice' determining the chances of combination and interaction are thus to be seen as 'loaded.'[64] Nevertheless, even if we acknowledge this 'loading' and the constraints recognized by reference to 'natural laws', it is far from clear that the limitations on pure chance which they imply are materially significant enough to warrant being described as expressing the purposive activity of a divine creator.

The major difficulty with the detailed implications of the view of evolution and God suggested by process theology, though, arises when we consider how God is supposed to influence – by 'lure' or 'persuasion' – the changes involved in evolutionary developments. Here we are dealing with both the initial appearance of and then subsequent developments in the information patterns provided by the nucleotides constituting the DNA and RNA macromolecules. The problem facing any attempt to find significant and creative activity by God in evolution is indicated by Barbour's reminder that at the 'lower levels' of

182

reality 'physical patterns predominate over mental ones, law over freedom, and efficient causes over final causes.' The divine, furthermore, is only one of a complex of causes involved in the becoming of each occasion. As a result God's contribution to the appearance of novelty 'may be beyond detection.'[65] The question is, though, whether it is credible to consider that God purposively influences the emergence of specific patterns in the constituents of the DNA and RNA, even if that influencing be undetectable. Only if such influencing can be regarded as credible can God's creative activity be held to be more particular than a general determination that the fundamental order of nature includes both an urge to localized and stable complexifications and the possibility of (minute) change between an actual occasion and its successor.

One way in which some process thinkers have considered the conceivability of such particular divine influencing is through the psychical aspect of their understanding of reality. Ford, for example, does not limit God's creative activity to the 'cosmological function' of supplying an 'impetus toward greater complexification'. He also maintains that God 'serves as a lure for actualization, providing novel possibilities of achievement' that seek the 'modicum of spontaneous response' which is 'possible even on the atomic and molecular levels'. Thus while atoms and molecules are predominantly 'traditional in their habits,' divine persuasion, as 'the urge to maximize the possibilities' present in a situation, may evoke at this level of reality 'the actualization of some evolutionary advance.'[66] Is such a conception of the divine activity credible?

It seems clear that the conception depends upon the tenability of the psychical view of reality. As Barbour argues, however, we must be careful not to read too much into the metaphorical terms used by Whitehead: 'events in a cell have only an incipient mental aspect whose contribution is negligible in practice.' Both their way of inheriting their past and their response to their environment can at best be held to reflect only 'an exceedingly attenuated form of aim or purpose.'[67] When, though, the psychicalism is so severely limited that the mentality is practically negligible, it provides only a very problematic basis for explaining the divine influence on evolutionary developments. In the first place it is important to remember that when Whitehead speaks of an actual occasion 'deciding' its subjective form, the term 'is used in its root sense of a "cutting off."'[68] It does not imply that an actual occasion – say an atom or a molecule or a nucleotide – determines what form it shall adopt after conscious, let alone self-conscious, deliberation. On the other hand, when the factor of consciousness or of introspective awareness and choice is removed from decision-making, it is not clear how the 'decision' of an actual occasion's self-determination would differ from a synthetic resolution of the forces of its prehensions, modified by a modicum of randomness, which happened automatically. It seems, that is, that when process thought uses notions like that of 'decision' to explain changes involved in evolutionary development, it may be trading on the meaning of notions which find their paradigm usage in terms of self-conscious mental activity. If this be so we are left with considerable (and perhaps insoluble) puzzles about what may be meant when the notions are applied to non-conscious levels of reality. The Swansons forcefully state this difficulty when they ask 'What could it mean to say that an amino acid [perhaps we should say 'this particular molecule of amino acid'] .... has subjectivity?..... Does it really make sense to say that an electron entertains abstract possibilities and decides among them?'[69]

Secondly – and following on from this objection – it may be questioned whether it makes sense to talk of God seeking to 'lure' or 'persuade' an atom or a molecule or a nucleotide to adopt some change in its structure or in its relationships when consciousness is not meaningfully predicable of such entities. Such notions, and the complementary ones of 'responding to' and 'freely embracing'[70] a novel aim presented as a divine lure, seem to lose their significance when applied to non-conscious entities. If there is no consciousness, the divine 'lure' or 'persuasion' becomes in effect another factor among the many whose resultant, with perhaps a degree of randomness, determines what occurs. At the level of the constituents of the DNA molecule, changes in whose structure and relationships produce evolutionary developments, it thus does not seem possible to talk meaningfully of 'lures' or 'persuasions' which 'attract' the relevant series of actual occasions to choose to synthesize their prehensions in ways that result, even if only extremely rarely, in free decisions for novelty. If, though, the divine 'lure' or 'persuasion' is reduced to being another factor among the many whose unwitting and unwilled resultant 'decides' what comes to be, God cannot be excused from responsibility for what occurs. No 'freedom' is being safeguarded in the case of non-conscious entities if the divine chooses not to control what happens. The relative weakness of divine influence on this model merely indicates a failure to act effectively. It does not absolve the divine from responsibility for what results if a stronger 'lure' would have been an overwhelmingly potent factor in producing a different result. The fact that the divine apparently does not so act may, though, be taken as evidence that the model for understanding divine activity is at fault rather than that God is unnecessarily ineffective.

Thirdly, if we accept that a genetic change occurs when a nucleotide changes its place or is replaced by another in a DNA molecule and, in Whiteheadian terms, that a nucleotide is a nexus which may be treated as an enduring object, as a series of actual occasions, it is questionable whether it is credible to apply to the becomings of a nucleotide what can be said of God's influence on the becomings of a human person. Cobb, for example, says of human existence that God

entertains a purpose for the new occasion, differing from that entertained by the previous human experience. He seeks to lure the new occasion beyond the mere repetition of past purposes and past feelings .... to finer and richer actualizations ....[71]

Granted that at the lower levels of reality the divine will is almost wholly for accurate repetition, nevertheless if God is to be creatively significant in influencing specific evolutionary changes, God must presumably be considered (by analogy with what is said of the divine lure for human beings) as occasionally seeking to influence nucleotides to change places or to drop out of a DNA chain or to insert themselves into one. Furthermore the character and incidence of observed changes suggests that the divine creative activity in this regard is either extremely rare or, as seems more arguable, massively ineffective. The evidence is that vastly more abortive changes occur than potentially fruitful ones, and that of the latter many genetic variants are basically stored until, if ever, suitable conditions arise for their development. Leaving aside, then, the hierarchical issue of whether the divine may also have to be conceived as seeking to influence directly the atoms of a nucleotide and, in turn maybe, its particles[72] in order to evoke changes in the nexus that is a nucleotide, the story of specific divine creative lures for nucleotides as the manner of intentional guidance for evolutionary change seems too ineffective and too wasteful[73] to be theologically acceptable as an understanding of significant divine activity. The resulting picture of God bears more resemblance to a pathetic park-keeper feebly whistling at a barking, scrabbling, fighting, rampaging horde of dogs to get them to come to heel or to a yachtsman fussily trying to push aside an ore-carrier than to the intentional agency of the proper object of worship.

Is there, though, any alternative in process thought to the picture of God's creative activity as a series of specific lures which seek to evoke changes in DNA molecules? There is – and interestingly it is a position that finds expression in a number of works on process theology. It is the view that at the level of the DNA particular evolutionary changes happen by chance as DNA molecules are very occasionally accidentally altered in ways that turn out to be fruitful (or, at least, not self-destructive). Hartshorne, for example, suggests that while some 'chance variations' are due to the accidental combination of the genes of the parents, other larger ones – 'mutations' - result 'from chance encounters between particles (such as cosmic rays) and the genes[74] while Birch considers that evolutionary developments can be understood as the product of 'random mutations'. When the length of the genetic series and the effects of selection are taken into account, what may at first seem 'improbable' becomes 'probable.'[75] More recently Birch and Cobb have put it that 'once in a few million or a few billion times the replication of the multiplying cells is not exact' and 'by chance' this mistake in the copying of the DNA may very occasionally 'spell out a message that confers characteristics that enhance the chance for survival and reproduction.'[76]

If, however, specific evolutionary changes occur by chance and not as a result of the lures of particular divine aims, is there any content left for claims about divine creativity? There is, but its reference is much more general than that implied by traditional religious understanding of God as creator. God's creative activity is to be seen as a universal influence on the order of nature which evokes in it a certain tendency towards complexification and novelty. In other words, God as creator is to be conceived as one who establishes that the structure of reality is such that it combines stability with a certain degree of openness to novelty and that its actual constituents are drawn towards the formation of increasingly complex patterns. Within this structure, though, God is not to be regarded as seeking to guide the evolutionary processes to produce any particular forms. What actually evolves depends on the chance interactions of the constituents of reality within the framework given by the cosmic constants. Having, though, established that the process has a tendency towards complexification, the divine may well be considered not only to enjoy the value of whatever emerges but also to know[77] that the moves toward the more complex will eventually in some way and in some form produce high-order nexus that are self-conscious, free and capable of contributing to the divine experience corresponding degrees of aesthetic enrichment.

If this view of divine creativity is adopted, the doctrine of God as creator will not appeal to those security-minded believers who want to assert that everything is as it is because God has so planned it. On the other hand, the view that God as creator establishes the structure within which actual occasions are drawn into increasingly complex nexus by chance interactions within an overall order of natural laws and that God appreciates and preserves the value of all that thereby comes into being may be an understanding that is biologically tenable, metaphysically significant, theistically important and rationally credible. If it can be so judged, it provides an understanding which gives some material content to the notion of God as creator and to the world as a significant product of divine purposing and a significant object of divine enjoyment.

186

Notes

1. Alfred North Whitehead (1861-1947): English philosopher who initially worked on the foundations of mathematics (co-operating with Bertrand Russell in writing *Principia Mathematica*) and then on philosophy of science, first in Cambridge as a Fellow of Trinity College (1884-1910) and then in London University. In 1924 he accepted an invitation to Harvard. During the following years he developed a comprehensive metaphysical system which took account of modern scientific thought. His understanding is developed in such works as *Science and the Modern World* (1926), *Religion in the Making* (1926), *Process and Reality* (1929), *The Function of Reason* (1929), *Adventures of Ideas* (1933) and *Modes of Thought* (1938).

   Charles Hartshorne (1897-): American philosopher who encountered Whitehead's ideas when his own were already well developed and he was editing (with Paul Weiss) the works of Peirce. He taught at the University of Chicago (1928-1955), Emory University in Georgia (1955-1962) and at the University of Texas at Austin. His primary interest has been in philosophy of religion and, in particular, in the understanding of God. Among his major contributions to this field are *Beyond Humanism* (1937), *Man's Vision of God* (1941), *The Divine Relativity* (1948), *Reality as Social Process* (1953), *The Logic of Perfection* (1962), *A Natural Theology for Our Time* (1967) and *Creative Synthesis and Philosophic Method* (1970). When visited in March 1986 he was still active and had contracts to write three books!
2. Charles Birch, 'Creation and the Creator,' first published in the *Journal of Religion* 37, 2, (April 1957) and reprinted in I. G. Barbour (ed.) (1968), *Science and Religion: New Perspectives on the Dialogue*, London, SCM Press, p. 194.
3. cf. *ibid.*: 'If God's activity were withdrawn, the object of creation would no longer exist.'
4. *ibid.*
5. *ibid.*, p. 195.
6. *ibid.*, p. 200.
7. A. N. Whitehead (1978), *Process and Reality*, Corrected Edition edited by D. R. Griffin and D. W. Sherburne, New York: Free Press, p. 5.
8. cf. C. Hartshorne, 'Postscript', in Santiago Sia (1985), *God in Process Thought*, Dordrecht, Boston, Lancaster: Martinus Nijhoff, p. 119: 'The technical basis of my metaphysics is ... exhaust the conceptual options, judge each option by rational rules of conceptual coherence.'
9. cf. Whitehead, *Process and Reality*, pp. 23, 42f.
10. A. N. Whitehead (1926) *Science and the Modern World*, Cambridge University Press, p. 114.
11. Whitehead, *Process and Reality*, p. 18.
12. cf. Charles Birch and John B. Cobb (1981), *The Liberation of Life*, Cambridge University Press, p. 86: 'an atom is not a substantial entity but a multiplicity of events interconnected with each other and with other events in a describable pattern. A mouse is a far more extensive society of events, electronic, cellular and organismic, interconnected in far more complex patterns.'
13. Whitehead, *Process and Reality*, p. 19.
14. *ibid.*, p. 23; cf. pp. 40f.
15. Birch and Cobb, *Liberation of Life*, p. 134.
16. cf. Whitehead, *Process and Reality*, pp. 85f.

17. *ibid.*, p. 43.
18. *ibid.*, p. 20.
19. Ivor Leclerc, 'Some Main Philosophical Issues Involved in Contemporary Scientific Thought', in John B. Cobb and David R. Griffin (eds.) (1977), *Mind in Nature*, Washington: University Press of America, p. 104.
20. cf. Whitehead, *Science and the Modern World*, p. 81; Ian G. Barbour (1966), *Issues in Science and Religion*, London: SCM Press, p. 451.
21. Whitehead, *Process and Reality*, p. 7.
22. cf. *ibid.*, p. 59.
23. cf. *ibid.*, pp. 85f.
24. Birch, 'Creation and the Creator', p. 204.
25. Whitehead, *Process and Reality*, p. 7.
26. cf. *ibid.*, p. 345.
27. cf. *ibid.*, pp. 343f.
28. cf. *ibid.*, p. 19.
29. cf. *ibid.*, pp. 343f.
30. cf. Birch, 'Creation and the Creator', p. 204; Birch and Cobb, *The Liberation of Life*, pp. 191, 195.
31. cf. George R. Lucas, 'Evolutionist Theories and Whitehead's Philosophy', *Process Studies* 14, 4: Winter 1985, pp. 287-300.
32. A. N. Whitehead (1938), *Modes of Thought*, Cambridge University Press, p. 153.
33. Whitehead, *Science and the Modern World*, p. 115.
34. Charles Hartshorne, 'How I Got That Way' in John B. Cobb and Franklin I. Gamwell (1984), *Existence and Actuality*, Chicago University Press, p. xii.
35. cf. Charles Hartshorne (1975), *Beyond Humanism*, Gloucester, Mass: Peter Smith, pp. 139.
36. Charles Hartshorne (1984) *Omnipotence and Other Theological Mistakes*, Albany: State University of New York, p. 67; cf. pp. 68f; cf. 'Postscript', in Sia, op.cit., p. 113; Whitehead, *Process and Reality*, p. 283.
37. Hartshorne, *Omnipotence and Other Theological Mistakes*, p. 69.
38. *ibid.*
39. *ibid.*, p. 71.
40. cf. *ibid.*, pp. 84f.
41. cf. Whitehead, *Process and Reality*, pp. 108, 244.
42. Barbour, *Issues in Science and Religion*, p. 447.
43. Hartshorne, *Omnipotence and Other Theological Mistakes*, p. 73 – he is here quoting a phrase of Charles Kingsley.
44. Lewis S. Ford (1978), *The Lure of God*, Philadelphia; Fortress Press, p. 21.
45. Whitehead, *Process and Reality*, p. 346; cf. pp. 343ff; cf. also Hartshorne, *Omnipotence and Other Theological Mistakes, passim* and especially pp. 16-26 on the concept of divine power.
46. Hartshorne, *Omnipotence and Other Theological Mistakes*, p. 70; cf. A. N. Whitehead (1926), *Religion in the Making*, Cambridge University Press, p. 60; John B. Cobb and David R. Griffin (1977), *Process Theology: An Introductory Exposition*, Belfast: Christian Journal, p. 70.
47. Birch, 'Creation and the Creator', p. 203.
48. Whitehead, *Process and Reality*, p. 108; cf. p. 244.
49. *ibid.*, p. 224; cf. p. 244.
50. *ibid.*, pp. 244f.

51. John B. Cobb (1969), *God and the World*, Philadelphia: Westminster Press, pp. 64, 67.
52. *ibid.*, p. 52.
53. *ibid.*, p. 82; cf. pp. 64, 67, 91f.
54. cf. Cobb and Griffin, *Process Theology*, pp. 54ff.
55. Ford, *Lure of God*, p. 21.
56. cf. Whitehead, *Process and Reality*, p. 108; A. N. Whitehead, *The Concept of Nature*, University of Michigan Press, Ann Arbor Books, 1957, pp. 25f.
58. cf. Cobb, *God and the World*, pp. 71ff; Birch and Cobb, *The Liberation of Life*, p. 134.
59. Hartshorne, 'Postscript', in Sia, op. cit., p. 116; cf. Birch, 'Creation and the Creator', pp. 197, 204.
60. Ford, *Lure of God*, pp. 24f.
61. *ibid.*, p. 23.
62. Birch and Cobb, *The Liberation of Life*, p. 195.
63. *ibid.*, p. 189.
64. Barbour, *Issues in Science and Religion*, p. 387.
65. *ibid.*, p. 450.
66. Ford, *Lure of God*, p. 59.
67. Barbour, *Issues in Science and Religion*, p. 451.
68. Whitehead, *Process and Reality*, p. 43.
69. D. L. Swanson and E. S. Swanson, review of Cobb and Griffin, *Mind in Nature*, in *Process Studies*, 8, 1: Spring 1978, p. 48.
70. cf. Ford, *Lure of God*, p. 59.
71. Cobb, *God and the World*, p. 82.
72. Alternatively, if influence on superiors brings about appropriate changes in inferiors, God may be held to lure the DNA molecule itself or perhaps even higher levels of nexus.
73. cf. Birch and Cobb, *The Liberation of Life*, p. 193: 'We may wonder whether Life could have adopted another strategy for evolution. Whatever abstract possibilities there may be, Life accepted the price of enormous waste.' Nevertheless they deny that the method of relying on 'random mishaps' to produce genetic changes is 'an extraordinarily inefficient method of creation' for the process seems 'to extract the maximum value out of this way of producing variation.' (*ibid.*, p. 47).
74. Hartshorne, *Omnipotence and Other Theological Mistakes*, p. 68.
75. Birch, 'Creation and the Creator', p. 212.
76. Birch and Cobb, *The Liberation of Life*, p. 46.
77. On the possibility of such knowledge being possible in relation to stochastic processes, cf. David J. Bartholomew (1938), *God of Chance*, London: SCM Press, 1984.

V.
Retrospect and Prospect

The Status of the Science-Religion Dialogue

Viggo Mortensen

I want to facilitate our judgements by offering you a classification of what has been said at the conference and in a wider context in the science-religion dialogue. In particular, I would like to mention two of my fellow countrymen.

Restriction

The great Danish philosopher Søren Kierkegaard had an extremely critical attitude towards natural science. He could be obliging and kind towards the individual natural scientist, as we see in his correspondence with his brother-in-law P. W. Lund. At about the same time when Darwin rounded Cape Horn with the good ship *Beagle*, P. W. Lund was also in South America. Contrary to Darwin, Lund definitely sought God's traces in the history of nature. As he did not find them, but instead saw the same variation evidenced by Darwin as evolution, he eventually ended up insane.

Towards natural science as such, however, Kierkegaard was ruthless.

It is no good trying to cope with natural science. One finds oneself standing there defenceless and is in no position to control. The researcher immediately begins to dissect with his details, now one has to reach Australia, now the moon, now a cave beneath the ground, now to hell up in the ass – chasing an intestinal worm; now it is time to use the telescope now the microscope; who the hell can stand that! (Pap. VII, 1 A, 200).

Of course nobody can stand that. That is why there is more in the daily newspaper on astrology than on astronomy. Kierkegaard's view is that natural science threatens to change life from being an existence of decisions and seriousness into a life of observations.

In our time, the natural science is especially dangerous. Physiology will eventually be so comprehensive that it swallows ethics as well. Sufficient traces of a new endeavour are already to be seen, efforts to treat ethics as physics, whereby all of ethics becomes illusion, and the ethical is to be treated statistically on average figures, or to be calculated as one calculates oscillations in natural laws. (Pap. VII, 1 A, 182).

Perhaps Kierkegaard here anticipated one of the basic problems of the modern world, namely the *expansion* of the scientific method into the fields of life aspects and world views. For a long time, at least the theologians hoped as a prolongation of Kierkegaard to be able to resist, to keep the sciences out of the field of existence *restrictively*. The question now remains if time has come to move beyond both restriction and expansion.

It is possible by means of catch words to describe the stages of development in the relationship between science and religion: from unity to conflict and condemnation to separation.

The state of separation was in many ways a natural reaction to the confrontation between religion and natural science that Darwin had created in the late 19th century. It became clear in the light of this last and most vehement confrontation that the old unity among the sciences was lost forever.

Often enough it has been emphasized that theology came out of this confrontation on the losing end. Even theologians felt this way, and so society saw it. Although theologians in answer to the challenge argued for separation, they seldom said that it was out of weakness that they gave up allowing their doctrines to have explanatory force in the empirical field. On the contrary it was often referred to as a strength, a strength gained through a shortening of the front, to use a military term.

The theological reconstruction which was necessary to adapt to the new situation lasted nearly a hundred years. By then, a position had been built up which is now almost classical; it is characterized in the American discussion as neo-orthodox. L. Gilkey describes it in the following way:

The inquiries of the physical sciences and those of theology are now seen to be asking fundamentally different kinds of questions, in totally different areas of thought and experience. Consequently the answers to these questions, the hypotheses of science, and the affirmations or doctrines of theology, cannot and do not conflict. Religious myth has finally become that for which it was most aptly fitted: a symbolic story expressing the religious answer to man's ultimate questions. (Gilkey 1970, p. 34).

Just as within cosmology there is a standard model for the birth of the universe, we also can talk about a standard model for the relation between theology and natural science: separation.

In the United States it has been necessary to officially systematize this separation under pressure from the influence of the boom of creationism. In 1972 the National Academy of Sciences stated it this way:

Religion and science are ... separate and mutually exclusive realms of human thought.

There are several answers to how these "separate and mutually exclusive realms of human thought" are to be further defined in relation to each other. One possibility is the creation of an ontological dualism. If such a division is made, one is always as a theologian on retreat against science, and one may be tempted to fall into the "God-of-the-gaps trap". At the same time, this view gives no basis for the demand for universalism implicit in Christian talk about creation and providence.

This kind of theology has been called

ad hoc manoeuvres to avoid confrontation with the sciences or to satisfy the demands of "modern man" (Austin 1976, p. 56f).

In that connection R. Bultmann and his demythologisation programme is often mentioned.

If there are difficulties in dividing the world into two classes, the two-kingdom-arguments are refined by talking about layers, dimensions, aspects and so on. The danger is that this becomes a purely metaphorical or abstract language which does not further a precise understanding. The thesis that I will defend is that this situation is not durable. One of the direct results of this conference is, I think, that we all agree upon this. Even John Durant, who seemed to talk most of separation, would not want it to be "schiedlich-friedlich". And Pastor Hans May talked about "The ecumenical movement of the sciences". The question is: How is it to come about?

That it has come to this state of affairs is the result of several strands both within theology and science, together with a number of other internal and external factors, such as those of a sociological nature.

One such strand is the development, within the philosophy of science, of the realisation, that even strictly natural scientific recognition is based on defined methodological presuppositions, presuppositions which cannot be purely justified within natural science. Science cannot and does not claim to be able to explain reality in all its dimensions. Even the causal explanatory model ignores certain phenomena, meaning that the results of natural science are relativized. They work with functional connections which can be used to provoke certain causal changes.

A second reason that the problem regarding relations between natural science and theology has changed is a pragmatic one: namely that the crises of modern civilisation are in part due to the technology built on the methods of natural science.

Therefore the dialogue between theology and natural science continues on a new basis revolving around the problems concerning arms production, environmental destruction, unlimited growth and the ecological crisis. So the discussion is no longer concentrated so much on the major, old, basic questions but takes its starting point in the actual problems, often of an ethical nature which require consideration and action.

One of the great problems confronting our dialogue is: should we resign ourselves to the ethical issues? There is no doubt in my mind that we would more easily come to an agreement in ethics and practice than in the epistomological issues. I would suggest, however, that we should not forget any of them.

The two languages
The situation of separation was able to develop so strongly because such different schools and 'isms' as scientism, positivism and existentialism could at least agree that theology and natural science belonged in two different fields. Each in their own way helped to cement the position of separation. The position is furthermore strengthened by linguistic arguments – usually the so-called theory of language games, which derives from the later Wittgenstein.

The point of developing religion into an independent, autonomous language game is that one avoids having to justify one's concepts. Religion is a practical way of life with its own independent language and its own logic. If you enter such a way of life, your norms are changed and reality looks different, and there are no criteria to help you when choosing a religious way of life.

The question is: is the immunity to falsification which is gained through this theory is not bought at too high a price, namely the isolation of the religious language game both from other intellectual disciplines and from other religious communities? (Cfr. I. Barbour 1974, p. 128).

Critics of the language theory in this field hold that it is not possible to avoid the demand for verification so easily. One cannot blame a modern agnostic like Kai Nielsen for demanding to be told if a certain sentence is true, or if, as he puts it, it "is in a coherent order just as it is". In his view, the notion that religion is a language game which can be valued only in a religious context, which he calls "Wittgensteinian fideism", changes religion into an unimportant phenomenon in the ordinary secular world.

An appealing way out of the dichotomy which the theory of language games suggests, is to seek in everyday language the common language out of which all the different language games have grown. This can be done because of the family likenesses existing between the different languages: they have roots in everyday language and make use of metaphors when a new meaning is to be created. The metaphor is a "desirable linguistic device used to express and suggest hypotheses for both scientists and theologians", (p. 157), so MacCormac says, and he thereby attempts to dissolve the traditional tensions between scientific and religious language by using the scientific term "hypothesis" about the assertions of faith and theology as well. This is also Pannenberg's view.

There are not two languages, a language of religion and a language of science, but one language, ordinary discourse, that is modified in like manner by both enterprises to form the metaphors of conveyance and root-metaphors. (Austin 1976, p. XVI).

I am very sympathetic towards this way of bridging the gulf between religion and science. The immediate result apparent from this insight into the language-philosophical and philosophy of science discussion is that the case for staying in the situation of separation appears strengthened. The contrast between natural science and theology becomes mainly methodological. Whereas scientists are clearly in favour of using methods, theologians are suspected of giving up any methods.

The result of the criticism of metaphysics within analytic language philosophy is, for instance, that metaphysical statements can have an emotive meaning at the most. The division between science and theology becomes identical to the distinction between objective and subjective.

Expansion

If we all agree that the state of separation is unsatisfactory, we must leave this position, although it is very difficult as this means leaving a secure place; but it has to be done, and in my view it can be done with confidence because:

The substantial content of theology, if it is not in perfect harmony with scientific knowledge, cannot be in sharp incongruity with it, and what we say about God must be congruent in some way with what we know about human experience and its objects through the sciences ... To affirm that there cannot be deep incongruity between theology and scientific knowledge, and that such knowledge can also be theologically construed, is to continue in a very old strand of the Christian tradition. (J. Gustafson 1981, p. 252).

This is not a solution to our problem, but a starting point for a research programme. To elaborate on this, I will briefly touch upon the opposite extreme of restriction, namely expansion, which is found both in a scientific and a religious form.

The scientifically expansionist attitude is characterized by the assumption that discoveries, methods or results within the scientific field can be applied outside this field as well, for instance as a foundation for certain value conceptions or sociopolitical values. Sociobiology gives the clearest example of a contemporary scientifically expansionistic attitude.

Dr. Durant talked about the crusading of sociobiology. But in Bresch's argument sociobiological theories were taken into account. So that could be a possible topic for a future conference: Scientific expansionist theories and their validity. As a consequent naturalistic position it is of the utmost interest for the science-religion dialogue.

I consider sociobiology to be an interesting phenomenon which may teach us a great deal, but it must also be criticized. Wilson himself overemphasizes the naturalistic point and becomes reductionist. When reducing the phenomena of morality and anthropology, the demand for a way of description other than the scientific, becomes more strongly felt, a demand shared by theology and philosophy and on which theology must insist – if it wishes to keep its integrity.

If we claim survival to be the highest ethical value, we ought to give people an understanding of where and how we are unique, because that is what is needed to survive.

If scientific expansion is taken to its conclusion, not much seems to be left. All human phenomena, including those of the highest spirituality, are explained by reference to their genetic determinants. To defend religion and theology against such a scientific expansion, it seems that the only possibility is to hold that evolution's way is God's way, and thus that natural selection is God. And in fact we find something like this in, for instance, Teilhard de Chardin and R. W. Burhoe, the founding editor of *Zygon*. The goal for Burhoe has three parts: 1) Through a revitalization of religion he will 2) create a synthesis between science and religion and thus 3) bridge the gap between science and values.

I find Burhoes expansionist ideas stimulating and provoking. But let me just give one remark. Burhoes ideas of revitalizing religion by integrating God into the sciences, could actually, against his intentions, lead to the abolishing of religion. When religion can be explained as a mere manifestation of brain functions, and God can be explained by genetics, then religion becomes nothing but words – words that we could just as well do without.

Other ways of relating religion and science will at least retain an element of the standard model, in that they all regard religion as having some sort of independence.

Integration

A new metaphysics?

The reaction against theological and philosophical restriction did not only appear as scientific or theological expansion. There has also been an attempt to go back to an earlier model of the relationship between theology and science: namely, to let metaphysics be the meeting point. But is not metaphysics dead? Dr. Durant mentioned this, and his analysis made me think that what we need most is a new metaphysics. Of those who have concerned themselves with metaphysics, the first name that must be mentioned is that of A. N. Whitehead. I find Whitehead's work fascinating, but must also consider whether what A. R. Peacocke says of his system is correct, namely that it "is no longer of

197

currency even in an intellectual and philosophical climate deeply influenced by science". Still, he believes that Whitehead's attempt stands as "the most systematic attempt to date to understand God's action in the world in relation to the scientific picture of that world" (Peacocke 1979, p. 140 and 141). Karl Schmitz-Moorman talked of uniting Theilhard and Whitehead. I would suggest that we pursue the direction given by Whitehead without being tied down by his metaphysical system. That is exactly what I think is the case with the Danish philosopher and theologian K. E. Løgstrup (1905-1981).

K. E. Løgstrup's Metaphysical Reflections

Outside Denmark Løgstrup is known almost exclusively for his ethical thinking, since only his main work on ethics "The Ethical Demand" has been translated. In the preface James Gustafson points out that Løgstrup gives "a philosophical and theological foundation for ethical programs which take into serious account the uniqueness and concreteness of the particular situations or circumstances of moral action. His "phenomenology" of moral experience ... portrays human existence in terms of the root relationship of trust between persons." (p. ix). Here, already, two elements are mentioned: the phenomenological method and those phenomena, such as trust, which are later called the sovereign manifestations of life. Løgstrup builds upon these two elements and they are fully elucidated in his later works, which consist of a metaphysics in four volumes: a philosophy of language, a philosophy of art, a philosophy of nature and history, and a philosophy of religion, all of which have the subtitle: "metaphysical reflections". Here already is a warning against understanding these works to be an attempt to revive older metaphysical systems that have already been discredited. Løgstrup seeks to identify features of human life that invite metaphysical reflection, and that are susceptible to religions interpretation.

Løgstrup's main opponent is in many ways nihilism. He settles with this opponent in more than just a theological way, as do, for example, the existentialist theologians by preaching the Gospel "senkrecht von Oben" as the only alternative to nihilism. Løgstrup shows that, in a fundamental way, nihilism can be shown to be philosophically wrong, for which again he has a theological reason, "for if the coming of God's kingdom into our life is not to be an esoteric event, then the planet where it has happened, and nature and history where God's kingdom has arisen, and the universe to which they belong, must all be God's. And it must be our fault if it is not evident that it is so." (Manuscript from the archive: Is there a theological anthropology?)

It might seem obvious that the fault lies with natural science, since it starts with a very different set of questions. But it is not so simple, as Løgstrup is aware. He indeed sees nihilism as a child of natural science in many ways, but he also sees that we live on natural science to a great extent. So there is a need for a more differentiated attitude.

As opposed to transcendental philosophy, which isolates the subject and places it on the edge of the universe ("a gypsy on the border of the universe" (Monod)) – Løgstrup is intent on developing an ontology where man is not separate from the universe, but is seen as a part of it and in unity with nature. As he says: We must try to understand the cosmos or the universe not so much as being our surroundings but rather as being our source.

Against the logical positivists, who methodically and ontologically reduce all phenomena to scientific terms, so that the phenomena become illusory, Løgstrup argues for an understanding of the phenomena, such as one can find in everyday language and in the immediate experience, where the phenomena are looked upon as full of meaning and significant. Besides the causal understanding there is also an analogous one.

That understanding is difficult for science to grasp, for the most characteristic thing to be said about it is, as Løgstrup sees it, that it originates out of a separation or a renunciation, or expressed differently, natural science has a reductionist approach to reality.

To begin with this is not a polemic but an intended objective description of what the natural science person does, when he or she is doing science. The methods of science being abstraction, generalization etc., the immediate experience is reduced, as one renounces knowledge of certain features of the phenomena. Of such renouncements Løgstrup mentions three in his philosophy of nature: the renouncement of sense perception, everyday language and reason.

1) That science renounces sense perception sounds at first a little peculiar, as we are talking about empirical science. But it must be seen in connection with Løgstrup's thorough analysis of sense perception, where the opponents are those who talk in favour of the subjectivity of the sense qualities, e.g. Russell's intra-cranialist-theory. The renunciation of natural science shows itself in the transformation of the experienced sense perception into a physically explicable causal course. "The world in its senseness is replaced by the world in its measurableness". (Løgstrup 1984, p. 117). Contrasting this Løgstrup emphasizes two points in his phenomenological analysis of sense perception: Sense perception's omnipresence and lack of distance from the perceived object.

Although, when you perceive something, you are physically in one place, you are actually in the sensation with what is perceived – your body's one-place-presence *versus* your sensation's omnipresence. In sensation there is no distance. Secondly he stresses that in sensation there is no manufacturing in the form of interpretation. The manufacturing comes with language. But in his phenomenology Løgstrup tries to describe sensation as an experienced phenomenon and through this to grasp the underlying structures of reality, which are not intelligible to science.

What, then, is perceived in the sensation? Løgstrup's answer may at first seem a little odd, "the universe". Or: in this sensation without distance the universe is present, which means that any perceiving person (and we all are) cannot make her- or himself free from the universe. Humankind has in fact cosmos as its source, which means that the sensation comes from the universe. Then it can be understood how Løgstrup also here progresses from the phenomenological analysis to a philosophical reconstruction of the Christian concept of creation. Thus Løgstrup argues that certain phenomena can only be fully understood from the universe, from cosmos, thus implying speculative philosophical statements about cosmos. The absolute contrast to a position like Løgstrup's would be a scientific naturalism that maintains that the unity of humankind with cosmos could be fully explained scientifically, an enterprise that he would judge as reductionistic.

2) Secondly, Løgstrup finds that everyday language is eliminated in natural science. "Everyday language is replaced by the number" (p. 117). What Løgstrup has in mind is the ability of everyday language to integrate human existence in the things and causes of the world. This trait of everyday language is eliminated as subjective in the scientific endeavour; instead the scientist uses mathematically disciplined language.

Løgstrup insists that in our sense perception we are in contact with real features of the universe. Likewise he insists that everyday language refers to genuine features of the historic and natural life of man. The way in which language is used shows a knowledge of the phenomena, a knowledge that is used exactly in the phenomenological philosophy to which, inspired by Husserl and Hans Lipps, he turns.

To illustrate what Løgstrup means by phenomenology one can point to the first paragraph in "The Ethical Demand", containing a phenomenological analysis of the phenomenon "trust". These phenomena are in Løgstrup's later writings called the sovereign or spontaneous lifeutterances (Danish: suveræne livsytringer; German: souveräne Daseinsaüsserungen). Ethics is thus, according to Løgstrup, based on these phenomena, which are not ethical themselves. As pre-cultural phenomena they carry the whole existence, and thus they offer a picture of how life really ought to be. So here the is-ought gap really has been bridged. The ethical demand arises out of our failure and disobedience, dogmatically expressed, our sin. The interdependence from which the demand arises is interpreted by means of the Judeo-Christian concept of creation.

3) That science also renounces or eliminates reason must not be taken as an insult to the scientists, as if they should be especially unreasonable. Such a statement points out that what natural science deals with are in themselves reasonless causal chains. But apart from that there are also phenomena in nature which can only be understood with humankind's historical reason. As an example of such phenomena Løgstrup mentions the self-organization in organic nature, which is due to an order he calls analogous. His opinion at this point reflects his work with the problem of universals. Against nominalism the singularity of the universal is maintained.

The relationship between the singular and the typical represents an order that is analogous, analogous also to the order of the universe. Usually we regard the causal understanding as being the only one. We use it in our everyday life and in science, where it is effective when it comes to controlling and managing things. Apart from that there is also an understanding that is analogous. The claim is that causal understanding is based on an understanding that is analogous. Out of the basic analogous order of the universe language also grows which then, in accordance with its source contains an analogous order and if we go to the domain of the living systems there is – apart from cause and effect – also self-regulation. This self-regulation is also a kind of analogous order, and an important move is made when it is claimed that the analogous character of our understanding and the self-regulation in living systems are phenomena that are open to a religious interpretation.

The analysis leads to some practical consequences concerning our behavior towards nature. The natural sciences' occupation with nature threatens to end in an abstract spirituality, where nature is reduced to a case of general laws and an area for using technology.

Complementarity?
Thus Løgstrup takes it for granted that science can give us a knowledge of reality, but at the same time that it is reductionistic in its approach to reality. That is why the phenomenological analysis and the metaphysical speculation that leads to the religious interpretation have to be maintained.

Considering this it would be an obvious thought to claim complementarity between the two (or more) approaches to reality.

Niels Bohr, who introduced the concept of complementarity to overcome the difficulty in measurement in quantum mechanics – that one is unable to discern sharply between the event and the spectator, between subject and object – could already use this concept of complementarity outside physics, both within the other sciences and to characterize general phenomena, i.e. the relationship between love and justice.

A general definition of the concept of complementarity would read: complementarity covers the relation that two sides of a cause both complement and mutually exclude one another. The complementary insights belong together, as they understand the same object, but they exclude each other, as they cannot occur at the same time. Thus complementarity also stands for the possibility to experience the same object as something different.

Bohr thought that he had not only solved a painful problem in physics but also that he had come across a basic feature in all human understanding. That is why he chose the religious yin – yan sign for his shield and the motto: Contraria sunt complementa.

Others have, in continuation of this, tried to use the concept to determine the relationship between religion and science. As typical spokesmen for this C. A. Coulson and D. M. MacKay could be mentioned. MacKay defines complementarity as a logical concept of relation. If it is said about two assertions that they are valid from specific different logical standpoints, but necessary for the full understanding of the phenomenon in question, they are complementary.

I am very attracted by the idea of using the concept of complementarity to relate science and religion to each other. It opens up for the point of view that the two approaches have a status of their own and can contribute with independent understanding, but they can also let each other alone, if the trait is urged that they exclude each other. Then the model of complementarity becomes an all too logical consequence of the restrictive standard model. The restriction becomes too obvious and the state of separation is cemented.

Although I cannot follow the synthetic endeavours of the expansionist models to the end, I find it possible to learn from them that there are more points of resemblance between the various approaches than previously thought of. In continuation of Løgstrup's metaphysical project we must move on to a position beyond both restriction and expansion. Reality cannot be divided into two areas, one scientifically and technically controlled, the other religiously interpreted. Reality is one. This one reality can be seen in different ways, but its unity has to manifest itself, also in the way we talk about it.

References

William H. Austin (1976): *The relevance of Natural Science to Theology*. London.

Ian Barbour (1974): *Myth, Models and Paradigms*. New York.

Ralph W. Burhoe (1981) *Toward a Scientific Theology*. Belfast.

Langdon Gilkey (1970): *Religion and the Scientific Future*. New York.

J. Gustafson (1981) *Theology and Ethics*. Oxford.

K. E. Løgstrup (1971) *The Ethical Demand*. Chicago.

K. E. Løgstrup: *Vidde og prægnans*. Metafysik I. København 1976.

K. E. Løgstrup: *Kunst og erkendelse*. Metafysik II. København 1983.

K. E. Løgstrup: *Ophav og omgivelse*. Metafysik III. København 1984.

K. E. Løgstrup: *Skabelse og tilintetgørelse*. Metafysik IV. København 1978.

Earl MacCormac (1976): *Metaphor and Myth in Science and Religion*. Durham, N.C.

A. R. Peacocke (1979): *Creation and the World of Science*. Oxford.

A. N. Whitehead (1926): *Science and the Modern World*. Cambridge.

E. O. Wilson (1975): *Sociobiology. The New Synthesis*. Cambridge, MA.

E. O. Wilson (1978): *On Human Nature*. Cambridge, MA.

Questions for the Continuing Dialogue between Science and Theology

Arthur Peacocke

Reflection on the foregoing contributions has, it seems to me, raised the following questions.

I The relation of science and theology

(i) How should science and theology be related? What degree of separation is appropriate – and in what respects?

(ii) Is it necessary to have an agreed metaphysics in order appropriately to relate science and theology?

If we do not have an agreed philosophy of science and an agreed philosophy of religion, can we say what "God creates" means? That is, without such agreed philosophies of science and of religion, is anything left of the doctrine of creation?

(iii) Should science provide a direct resource for theological concepts and *vice versa*?

II The future

(i) Can any predictions be made about the future from evolutionary biology?

(ii) Can any predictions be made about the future from cosmological evolution?

(iii) How does theological eschatology relate to 'cosmological eschatology', that is, to reasonable extrapolations from current scientific knowledge?

(iv) Should theology have a view of *future* human evolution, for example, into new forms of intelligent life (cf. Freeman Dyson)?

III Providence

(i) 'Chance' seems to play a role in biological evolution – so is God 'dice-playing'?

(ii) What is God 'up to', i.e. what is God aiming at in the whole cosmic process? Can we discern, or even deduce this? Is 'love' an appropriate designation for God's purposes?

(iii) What is God responsible for in the created order?

IV Evolution and ethics

(i) If pain, suffering and death are intended by God to promote the evolutionary process, why should we bother to mitigate or diminish them? Whence *our* concern for others who are not our kin?

(ii) Evolution involves pain, suffering and death – are these to be regarded as parts of the natural process and so of God's way of creating? *OR* Are they to be regarded as an aspect of 'sin' and so to disappear in the 'new heaven and new earth'?

(iii) Is there a natural, evolutionary explanation of the emergence of values?

(iv) Do natural objects have 'rights'? That is, should they be objects of *moral* concern to us?

V Doctrinal

(i) What is the placing of *human* existence
- in evolution?
- in the cosmos?
- in the purpose of God in the light of the wide scope of cosmological evolution?

(ii) Should we regard redemption as redemption *from* a past state of a humanity which has fallen from a state of perfection? *Or* is it redemption *to* a completion and fulfilment displayed paradigmatically in Jesus the Christ?

(iii) Does the concept of God as creator need to undergo radical revision in the light of biological and cosmic evolution?

(iv) Is the created world in a state of 'sin'?

(v) Do we need a revised Christology since Jesus Christ *qua* human being is himself an evolved creature in the universe?

(vi) Should such a revision (v) affect how we view human sanctification by the grace of God?

(vii) How does God relate to an evolving cosmos –
- immanence?
- pan-en-theism?
- as partial cause (*cf.* process theology)?
- as 'Spirit'?
- as '*Logos*'?

Address at Morning Prayer

Hans May

"Get it into your heads what's happening today! We are just in the process of leaving the Stone Age!"

Mr. Bresch reminded us yesterday morning, with this quotation from Teilhard de Chardin, that we, the human race, are standing on the treshold, are in the process of transition, either to something new or to disaster. It would appear to be our pattern of behaviour up to now that carries the seeds of disaster within it. The combination of fear and aggression in human behaviour patterns has in the past been important for human survival. In view of the arsenal of weaponry we possess today it has become a deadly threat. That is how I understood Mr. Bresch. The logic of evolution demands a change in our patterns of behaviour. " Get it into your heads what's happening today! We are just in the process of leaving the Stone Age!"

But how can we bring about this change in our patterns of behaviour? How can we make the new man, the man who is capable of surviving in the future, appear on the earth? Sometimes, as I ponder this question, I sit down here in the chapel and gaze at the Cross, and this morning I would like to invite you to join me and gaze at it too. As I do so, I always find myself experiencing three things.

The first is the experience of joy. I gaze at Christ and I hear his words: "Ye have heard that it hath been said, 'an eye for an eye and a tooth for a tooth'. But I say unto you that ye resist not evil. But whosoever shall smite thee on thy right cheek, turn to him the other also... and whosoever shall compel thee to go a mile, go with him twain. Ye have heard that it hath been said, 'Thou shalt love thy neighbour and hate thine enemy'. But I say unto you: Love your enemies and pray for them which persecute you, that ye may be the children of your Father which is in Heaven.

Blessed are the meek: for they shall inherit the earth.

Blessed are they which do hunger and thirst after righteousness: for they shall be filled.

Blessed are the peacemakers: for they shall be called the children of God."

And as I hear this voice, I know: here speaks the new man, the one who alone is able to survive in the future, who has crossed the threshold out of the Stone Age. And I look upon him – and rejoice.

The second feeling I experience is one of deep grief. They killed him, and he speaks to me from the cross. And it was no mere chance that they killed him. They did know what they did.

For he told them the truth about themselves.

He proclaimed a new righteousness, and practised it.

He preached and lived love for one's neighbour as the only commandment governing relationships between man and man. And because that burst the bounds of their patterns of behaviour, they killed him. He gave divine wisdom a human form – and they rejected him.

He brought light into the world, and the world did not understand it.

"Get it into your heads what's happening today! We are just in the process of leaving the Stone Age". But the men of the Stone Age wanted to stay in the Stone Age, just as we have remained in the Stone Age. The stone on our altar makes this plain. It is a stone from the concentration camp at Auschwitz. We brought it here and set it up as an admonition and a reminder that we are stone-age men. And we placed it on the altar because there is a connection with the One who has crossed the threshold out of the Stone Age. They wanted to remain in the Stone Age, and so we have remained in the Stone Age to this very day. That is why they crucified him, that is why we crucified him in Auschwitz. And I look upon him – and grieve.

The third feeling I experience is that of a hope that comes entirely from God and is directed entirely towards Him. Christ loved the stone-age men, even those who killed him. He gave his life as a surety of the love of God. He could have evaded the task of standing surety in this way, in order to save himself. He did not. He has remained our surety for the new world. He hangs on the cross with arms outstretched and invites us to put our trust in love. Because he lived that love himself, I am able to believe that love is possible.

Will we too perhaps, one day, yet be transformed by the love of God, as He was transformed by it?

Will we too perhaps, one day, yet dare to follow Him, and putting our trust in Him, change our patterns of behaviour?

Will God perhaps one day yet lead us too over the threshold out of the Stone Age?

"For we have got it into our heads what has happened here! He, the Crucified, has left the Stone Age!"

List of Contributors

Svend Andersen (b. 1948). Senior Lecturer/Associate Professor at the Institute of Ethics and Philosophy of Religion (Theological Faculty), University of Aarhus. (DK-8000).

Carsten Bresch (b. 1921). Professor of Genetics at the University of Freiburg (D-7800). Head of "Zentrallaboratorium für Mutagenitätsprüfung der Deutschen Forschungsgemeinschaft".

Sigurd Daecke (b. 1932). Professor of Systematic Theology at the Rheinisch-Westfälische Technische Hochschule Aachen. (D-5100).

John Durant (b. 1950). Staff Tutor in Biological Sciences in the Department for External Studies at the University of Oxford. (GB-OX1 2JA)

Philip Hefner (b. 1932). Professor of Systematic Theology at the Lutheran School of Theology, Chicago. (USA-IL 60615-5199).

Jürgen Hübner (b. 1932). Professor of Systematic Theology at the University of Heidelberg. Senior Research Fellow at the Protestant Institute for Interdisciplinary Research, Heidelberg. (D-6900).

Bernd-Olaf Küppers (b. 1944). Senior Research Fellow at the Max-Planck-Institut of Biophysical Chemistry, Göttingen. From 1979 till 1984 Lecturer of Philosophy at the University of Göttingen. (D-3400).

Wolfgang Lipp (b. 1941). Professor of Sociology at the University of Würzburg. (D-8700).

Per Lønning (b. 1928). Professor of the History of Christian Thought at the University of Oslo. From 1981 till 1987 Research Professor at the Institute for Ecumenical Research, Strasbourg. From 1987 Bishop of Bergen. (N-5000).

Gerrit Manenschijn (b. 1931). Associate Professor at the Department of Ethics (Faculty of Theology), Free University of Amsterdam. (NL-1007).

Hans May (b. 1931). From 1957 till 1962 minister of the Lutheran Church. Since 1978 Director of the Evangelische Akademie Loccum. (D-3055).

Viggo Mortensen (b. 1943). Senior Lecturer/Associate Professor at the Institute of Ethics and Philosophy of Religion (Theological Faculty), University of Aarhus. (DK-8000).

David A. Pailin (b. 1936). Senior Lecturer and Head of Department of Philosophy of Religion, University of Manchester. (GB-MI3 9PL).

Karl Schmitz-Moormann (b. 1928). Professor of Philosophical Anthropology and Ethics at the Fachhochschule Dortmund. (D-4600).

Arthur R. Peacocke (b. 1924). Director of the Ian Ramsey Centre, St Cross College, Oxford. (GB-OX1 3LZ)

Diether Sperlich (b. 1929). Professor of Population Genetics at the Institute of Biology, University of Tübingen. (D-7400).

Gerhard Vollmer (b. 1943). Professor at the Department of Philosophy (Zentrum für Philosophie und Grundlagen der Wissenschaft), University of Giessen. (D-6300).

Index of Authors

214